Insights into Flipped Classrooms

This book is aimed at those interested in the flipped learning model as well as language teachers who are considering or are already incorporating flipped learning in their classes. The book is broken down into four main parts. First, I will look at a description of flipped learning, with a clear definition of what flipped learning is and what it is not. Part II of the book focuses on flipped learning, specifically in language education, covering research and pedagogical implications related to the four language skills and various teaching methods, such as task-based language teaching and content-based language teaching. The third part of the book is aimed primarily at researchers, both those with experience and those who are just starting out. It includes a series of vignettes of studies that investigated the effects of flipped learning as well as suggestions on how these studies could be replicated and lead to further research. The book concludes with an overview of the main points discussed within and a suggestion of how the flipped learning model could be structured into your language classes.

Adrian Leis is an associate professor at Miyagi University of Education with more than 20 years' experience teaching English in Japan. He obtained his Ph.D. from Tohoku University with a focus on flipped learning and linguistic output in the Japanese EFL environment. He has published more than sixty academic articles and is the editor of several academic journals.

Language Teaching Insights Series
Series Editors: David Nunan & Glenn Stockwell

Burston & Arispe: *Mobile-Assisted Language Learning and Advanced-level Second Language Acquisition*

Eginli: *Insights into Emotional Well-Being of Language Teachers*

Farrell: *Insights into Professional Development in Language Teaching*

Horwitz: *Becoming a Language Teacher (2nd ed.)*

Jitpaisarnwattana & Reinders: *Insights into Language MOOCs*

Khezrlou: *Insights into Task-Based Language Teaching*

Lai: *Insights into Autonomy and Technology in Language Teaching*

Leis: *Insights into Flipped Classrooms*

Mohebbi (Ed.): *Insights into Teaching and Learning Writing*

Son: *Insights into Digital Literacy and Language Teaching*

Tanaka-Ellis: *Insights into Teaching and Learning with Technology*

More information about titles in this series can be found at
https://www.castledown.com/academic-books/book-series/language-teaching-insights/

Insights into Flipped Classrooms

Adrian Leis
Miyagi University of Education

Castledown
Melbourne – London – Tokyo – New York

For Mum & Dad

*Although you may be gone,
you still guide me every day.*

4th Floor, Silverstream House, 45 Fitzroy Street Fitzrovia, London W1T 6EB, United Kingdom
Level 9, 440 Collins Street, Melbourne, Victoria 3000, Australia
2nd Floor Daiya Building, 2-2-15 Hamamatsu-cho, Minato-ku, Tokyo 105-0013, Japan
447 Broadway, 2nd Floor #393, New York NY, 10013, United States

First published 2023 by Castledown Publishers, London

Information on this title:
www.castledown.com/academic-books/view-title/?reference=9781914291104

DOI: 10.29140/9781914291104

Insights into Flipped Classrooms

© Adrian Leis, 2023

All rights reserved. This publication is copyright. Subject to statutory exception and to the provisions of relevant collective licencing agreements, no reproduction, transmission, or storage of any part of this publication by any means, electronic, mechanical, photocopying, recording or otherwise may take place without prior written permission from the author.

Typeset by Castledown Design, Melbourne
ISBN: 978-1-914291-10-4 (Paperback)
ISBN: 978-1-914291-08-1 (Digital)

Castledown Publishers takes no responsibility for the accuracy of URLs for external or third-party internet websites referred to in this publication. No responsibility is taken for the accuracy or appropriateness of information found in any of these websites.

Contents

List of figures ... ix
List of tables ... x
Acknowledgements ... xi
About this book ... xiii

PART I   FLIPPED LEARNING   1

Flipped learning: A definition ... 3
Before, during, and after class ... 8
The analogue age and digital age of flipped learning ... 11
The pros and cons of flipping your classroom ... 14
What isn't flipped? ... 20
Using closed captions ... 22
What if students don't watch the videos? ... 26

PART II   FLIPPED LEARNING IN SLA   31

Introduction ... 33
Speaking ... 34
Writing ... 46
Listening ... 57
Reading ... 65
Grammar ... 75
The possibles ... 83
   Task-based language teaching ... 84
   Content-based language teaching ... 87
   Young learners ... 91
   Assessment ... 96
   Synchronous Online Flipped Learning Approach® ... 99

PART III   VIGNETTES   103

Introduction ... 105
Vignette 1: *Mohammad Amiryousefi* ... 109
Vignette 2: *Mei-Rong Alice Chen and Gwo-Jen Hwang* ... 111
Vignette 3: *Alessandra Imperio* ... 115
Vignette 4: *Michael Yi-Chao Jiang, Morris Siu-Yung Jong, Wilfred Wing-Fat Lau, Ching-Sing Chai, and Na Wu* ... 117
Vignette 5: *Adrian Leis, Simon Cooke, and Akihiko Andrew Tohei* ... 120

Vignette 6: *Jeffrey Mehring #1* 122
Vignette 7: *Jeffrey Mehring #2* 123
Vignette 8: *Suphatha Rachayon and Kittitouch Soontornwipast* 125
Vignette 9: *Martha Ramírez* 128
Vignette 10: *Rebecca Lee Su Ping, Elena Verezub, Ida Fatimawati bt Adi Badiozama, and Wang Su Chen* 130
Vignette 11: *Mark Feng Teng* 132
Vignette 12: *Adrianne Verla Uchida* 135

PART IV CONCLUSION 139

The Golden Pavilion and PETS 141
   Presentation through pre-class materials 142
   Evaluation and encouragement 143
   Tasks and teamwork 143
   Strengthening and strategizing 144

Glossary 147
References 161
Index 193

List of figures

1.1	Overview of the revised Bloom's Taxonomy	9
2.1	Summary of the pedagogical implications for flipping a speaking class	45
2.2	The English essay hamburger	56
2.3	Summary of the pedagogical implications for flipping a writing class	57
2.4	Summary of the pedagogical implications for flipping a listening class	65
2.5	Summary of the pedagogical implications for flipping a reading class	74
2.6	Summary of the pedagogical implications for flipping a grammar class	83
2.7	Summary of the pedagogical implications for flipping a TBLT class	87
2.8	Summary of the pedagogical implications for flipping a CBLT class	90
2.9	Summary of the pedagogical implications for flipping a class for younger learners	95
2.10	Summary of the pedagogical implications for flipping assessment	99
4.1	The blurred Kinkakuji	141
4.2	The flipped clear Kinkakuji	142

List of tables

1.1   An overview of the basic structure of a traditional class and a flipped class   5

Acknowledgements

First and foremost, I would like to express my gratitude to Glenn Stockwell and David Nunan for giving me the opportunity to share my thoughts and ideas related to education and flipped learning through this book.

Many thanks also go to the following people for the cooperation, support, and feedback on various parts of the book: Mohammad Amiryousefi, Léonard Téwindé Bamogo, Michael Burri, Ching-Sing Chai, Mei-Rong Alice Chen, Simon Cooke, Edo Forsythe, John Gray, Alison Hasegawa, Ai Hirai, Gwo-Jen Hwang, Alessandra Imperio, Michael Yi-Chao Jiang, Morris Siu-Yung Jong, Wilfred Wing-Fat Lau, Helaine W. Marshall, Jeff Mehring, Mitsuhiro Morita, Naotsugu Nakashima, Suphatha Rachayon, Martha Ramírez Rodríguez, Kittitouch Soontornwipast, Rebecca Lee Su Ping, Wataru Suzuki, Kiyoshi Takahashi, Tetsushi Takemori, Mark Feng Teng, Akihiko Tohei, Adrianne Verla Uchida, Azusa Wada, Junichi Wada, Chizuko K. Wallestad, Matthew Wilson, and Na Wu.

Last, but not least, I would like to show my appreciation to Blake Tanner and all the staff at Castledown for their endless patience and support throughout the process of publishing this book. I have learned so much while working with this wonderful team.

Adrian Leis

About this book

Back in the early twenty-tens, I was having a chat at a party with my good mate Aki Tohei. We were talking about education and our classes—as teachers tend to do when having a few drinks—when I mentioned a challenge that I was facing in my English composition class. I had two deaf and hard-of-hearing (DHH) students in the class, and I was trying to figure out ways to get them involved in the lesson with the other students as equally as possible. I had tried various ways, including wearing a Bluetooth microphone (you know, the kind you used to wear on your ear so you could talk on the phone while driving) and connecting it to a computer in front of the DHH students so whatever I was saying in the class would appear on the computer screen in front of them via speech-to-text software. The results were not good. When I checked to see how well the microphone and computer had been able to catch what I had been saying, what I saw on the screen was shocking, to say the least. My mother would have washed my mouth out with soap if she had read the colorful language mixed in with the mumble-jumble that the DHH students were trying to decipher. Needless to say, I had to come up with some new ideas, and I had to come up with them fast. So, it was over these drinks with Aki that he told me about the increasingly popular teaching model at the time: flipped learning. Unlike many brilliant ideas that appear at a party, this one actually stuck. And since then, flipped learning has been the focus of many of my classes, research projects, and even my Ph.D. It is also thanks to him that you are reading this book right now. Thanks, Aki!

This book is aimed at pedagogy students interested in flipped learning as well as language teachers who are considering incorporating (or have already incorporated) flipped learning in their classes. I will introduce various techniques to use in classes taught under the flipped learning model as well as discuss numerous examples of flipped learning research. So, if you are interested in conducting some studies related to flipped learning, there is something in here for you as well.

The book is broken down into four main parts. First, I will look at a description of flipped learning, with a clear definition of what flipped learning is and what it is not. I will give a brief overview of the history of flipped learning and the major role that **Web 2.0** played in increasing its popularity. Part 1 will also include some discussions related to the research of flipped learning in subjects not necessarily closely linked with English language education. To finish up the first part of the book, I will give a few suggestions about what to do before the class, during the class, and after the class when using flipped learning in your course.

Part II of the book focuses on flipped learning specifically in language education. I will cover research and pedagogical implications related to the four language skills (i.e., speaking, writing, listening, and reading) as well as grammar instruction, and consider how flipped learning can work together with various methods recently gaining attention in language teaching research, such as content-based language teaching (**CBLT**), content and language integrated learning (**CLIL**), and task-based language teaching (**TBLT**).

The third part of the book is aimed especially at researchers, both those with experience and those who are just starting out. Part III will start with discussions about how to design flipped learning research projects. This will be followed by summaries of a number of studies that investigated the effects of flipped learning as well as suggestions on how these studies could be replicated and lead to further research.

The final section of the book will round everything up in a brief way, revisiting the main points of flipped learning and what has been discovered through research conducted in second language acquisition. By that stage of the book, I imagine you will have a pretty good understanding of what flipped learning is all about and I hope you will be ready to take on the challenge of implementing flipped learning into your own classroom and perhaps doing a little research in the field as well, if you have not done so already.

Finally, I should talk about the kind of language that will be used in this book. As you may have noticed already, I am using a pretty relaxed register. This is the way I teach my classes. It is the way I give presentations at academic conferences. Also, as those who know me well enough will hopefully agree, it reflects my laid-back nature and "Australianness." Therefore, in this book I aim to create an atmosphere that feels like we are sitting down at a café and casually talking about ways to teach our students more effectively. That being said, we will be covering quite a few academic topics in the book, so there may be some terminologies appearing from time to time that are not the kinds of words that you might use in daily conversations or when chatting with friends over a few drinks. Therefore, for ease of understanding, I have added a glossary at the back of the book. So, if you would like to confirm the meaning of any words that you see in bold, like **this**, just flip through to the back of the book and check them out there. Okay, are you ready? Let's get into it!

PART I

FLIPPED LEARNING

Flipped learning: A definition

My mother was an unbelievable person, and I miss her very much. Despite raising five children, she did an immeasurable amount of charity work in the community, was always interested in and involved in her children's education, and cooked incredible meals (lamb roast and beef stroganoff were my favorites). She was always supportive of whatever her kids decided to do in life, and it is no exaggeration to say that she is the reason I have become the person I am today. Even though she was not a teacher, she taught me so much about leadership and education. I have many, many memories of her kindness and the love she showed to those around her.

Now, not every memory I have with my mother is entirely full of happiness. Like any child-parent relationship, there were some tough times, too. I may not have understood it at the time, but there was always something to learn in the way she raised me. For example, I remember one day close to 40 years ago, when I was in elementary school, cleaning my shoes to get ready for school the following week. I had shined one of the shoes so much that I felt I could have used it as a mirror. The other was still dirty from walking in mud, kicking rocks while walking home from school, and doing whatever else young boys get up to in their shoes. Seeking praise from Mum, I took both of my shoes to the dining room, where she was working on some tax returns or some kind of adult stuff that did not seem important to me. "Guess which one I cleaned, Mum!" I innocently said. The reply was not what I had been expecting, as she snapped, "Adrian, I don't have time for guessing games!" As I pouted and went outside to finish off cleaning my shoes, I realized then that adults always seem to be busy and made a vow that when I grew up, I would make sure that I was not one of those busy people[1].

Yet here we are. Busy as ever. And although it is not limited to the teaching profession, it seems that we especially get busier and busier every year. A lot of this busyness appears to come from non-classroom-related matters, which inevitably results in us being unable to spend as much time with our students as we should. So begins the search for ways to use our limited classroom time more efficiently. If we want to accomplish the main objective of education—which, as James Keefe (2007) suggests, is for students to learn—we need to consider ways to reduce the time in which students are simply sitting back passively listening to the teacher ramble on about some topic that they are not always interested in. We need to increase the amount of time in which students are taking control of their learning, discussing ways to solve problems, and be-

---

[1] Don't worry. Mum soon put her "adult work" to the side to tell me what a great boy I was. She even guessed the right shoe!

ing creative with the language and topic of their studies.

With advancements in technology, and as we will see especially with the creative prospects that came with **Web 2.0**, the door was opened to a plethora of possibilities that teachers could access for their classrooms. On the topic of technology, and obviously we are going to talk about technology quite a bit throughout this book, I might add here that although I can see that technology and the applications available for smart devices are fantastic for students, regardless of what they are studying, I really believe that the most significant advantages of advancements in technology are for the teacher. Suppose, for example, we can save ourselves two or three hours of marking time each week by having students do quizzes online instead of on paper. In that case, we can create extra time to spend preparing classes, creating new materials, providing individual coaching to our students, or—just as important—relaxing with family and friends. So, with **Web 2.0**, teachers are now able to give students opportunities to collaborate with other students anywhere on the planet who have access to the Internet, build websites and blogs that can be shared openly or with a select group of individuals, or create and watch short movies through video-sharing websites. And this is just the beginning! But it is this final prospect, the ability for teachers and students to create and share videos online, that brought about a burst of immense popularity in what is now known as flipped learning. However, this concept had, in fact, already been around for years beforehand.

Let's get back to the initial question of this section: What is flipped learning? The definition given by the Flipped Learning Network (2014a, p. 1) presents flipped learning as

> a pedagogical approach in which direct instruction moves from the group learning space to the individual learning space, and the resulting group space is transformed into a dynamic, interactive learning environment where the educator guides students as they apply concepts and engage creatively in the subject matter.

In a nutshell, a flipped classroom is a learning environment that utilizes a type of **blended learning** to allow students to access the explanations that would typically be given by the teacher during the class time *before* the lesson. Then, in the face-to-face classroom sessions, students can spend more time holding discussions and doing tasks that would usually be given as homework under the direct guidance and supervision of the teacher. Finally, after the lesson is over, students are able to go back and check their teachers' class notes and explanations to reconfirm the content of the lesson anytime they need to. Table 1.1 illustrates an example of the structure of the flipped classroom in comparison to a traditional non-flipped classroom, as may be seen in an English as a foreign language (**EFL**) course.

Table 1.1 *An overview of the basic structure of a traditional class and a flipped class*

	Traditional Classroom	Flipped Classroom
Before the class	• Students prepare by reading the textbook and studying vocabulary.	• Students watch explanation videos, read the textbook, and prepare for discussions.
During the class	• Students listen to the teacher explain the target grammar structure and content of the textbook. • Students practice the target language. • Students actively participate in tasks and discussions based on topics given by the teacher during the class. • The teacher summarizes the main points of the lesson.	• Students are given a quiz regarding the content of the textbook and videos. • The teacher explains any misunderstandings based on the results of the quiz. • Students actively participate in tasks and discussions based on topics given by the teacher in the pre-class videos. • The teacher summarizes the main points of the lesson.
After the class	• Students review the class and do practice exercises based on notes taken during class.	• Students review the class while re-watching the class explanation videos and advice received from peers and the teacher during class.

As can be understood by looking at Table 1.1, flipped learning brings many advantages to the table. Before the class, the videos help students understand the content of the lesson more thoroughly. Thus, they have basically understood the content of the class before it begins. As a result, students will often come to class ready to participate with more confidence. During the class, the teacher has more opportunities to **scaffold** students in their learning. Because there is no longer a need to spend the majority of class time explaining the content of the textbook, teachers are able to use class time more efficiently: More effort can be expended implementing peer coaching into their lessons as well as working individually with students on overcoming their weaknesses and solidifying their strengths. These strengths and weaknesses can be easily discovered by using short online quizzes at the beginning of the lesson. Then, when students are reviewing after the class, they still have access to the explanations given via video by the teachers and can concentrate their review on the contents of the discussions and tasks completed in class.

Flipped learning vs. the flipped classroom

Flipped learning has increased in popularity over the past few years, and along with this popularity, there has also been an increase in the number of terms related to flipped learning. The two main terms you will find are flipped learning and the flipped classroom. The difference between them may seem subtle, and in everyday conversation I personally see no particular problem with using them to mean the same thing. However, in academic terms, it is good to know the difference.

The Flipped Learning Network is a website run by some of the pioneers of flipped learning. Its website (flippedlearning.org) aims to work as a "hub where educators around the world can share and access resources, tips, tools, and more" (Flipped Learning Network, 2014b, Who We Are, first paragraph). On the website, a clear distinction is made between a flipped classroom and flipped learning, with a flipped classroom being defined as an environment like the one I described above. For the learning taking place in a flipped classroom to be characterized as flipped learning, teachers need to ensure that the principles behind the four pillars (F-L-I-P™) are incorporated into the learning process (Flipped Learning Network, 2014a).

The first principle of "F" describes the class as being a *flexible environment* for learning. Teachers should encourage independent learning, as students are free to choose where and when they wish to study. Teachers also need to be flexible with assessment, realizing that some students may take longer to master the content of the lesson than others.

Second—the "L" aspect of flipped learning—the teacher is aware of the *learning culture*. In traditional classrooms, the teacher would often take charge, creating a "chalk and talk" kind of environment. In flipped learning, the student is at the center. Face-to-face class sessions are dedicated to giving students opportunities to further their understanding of the topics through, for example, discussions or debates. The teacher acts as a supervisor, giving hints and **scaffolding** when necessary to bring out more meaningful learning.

The third concept (i.e., "I") refers to the *intentional content* in flipped learning. While monitoring students' progress, teachers may need to make subtle changes to materials used in the learning process. They should also be prepared to give suggestions regarding other information they can share with students that might enhance their learning. In addition, materials may need to be adapted to meet students' ages, proficiency levels, subject content, and learning styles.

Finally, the "P" of F-L-I-P™, teachers need to be *professional educators*. Like any career, teaching is a life-long learning process. We cannot get stuck into the same habits we have been using for the past 20 years. As educators, we are responsible for reflecting on our teaching and considering what has been successful and what has not. Being involved in professional development, attending and giving presentations at conferences, and even casually discussing teaching techniques with colleagues while having a coffee can often lead to higher quality teaching.

The concepts behind the four pillars of F-L-I-P™ give those implementing flipped learning into their classrooms something to fall back to when reflecting on their teaching. It is good to come back to these from time to time and check whether you have been continuing on the expectations of fellow members of the flipped learning community or have fallen into a bit of a rut. The Flipped Learning Network has kindly made a printable PDF of the four pillars of F-L-I-P™ available for anyone to use as part of their journey into the flipped learning world. I suggest you check it out.

Flipped mastery learning

A third common term which has appeared over the past few years is *flipped mastery learning*. While flipped mastery learning follows the same concepts of flipped learning as mentioned above, it puts a lot of emphasis on making sure students have understood the content of one area to a satisfactory level before moving onto the next. The idea of flipped mastery was born from Cara Johnson's concerns that her students were not fully understanding and learning the content in a flipped learning environment (Johnson, 2018). The principal guideline behind flipped mastery learning is: "Don't let the students move on in their learning until they have proven mastery of the current learning" (Johnson, 2018, p. xii).

Flipped mastery learning requires teachers to understand that their students will learn at different speeds, thus make adjustments to their syllabuses to allow for faster and slower learners. As it will most likely result in students working on different content at different stages of the course, it will require support and understanding from students, parents, colleagues, and administrators, as well as flexibility from the teachers themselves regarding the way face-to-face sessions are run and assessment is conducted. To my knowledge, there has not been a lot of research conducted with flipped mastery learning in foreign language education, to date. But without doubt, it offers a broad range of possibilities (see Johnson, 2018, for more on flipped learning mastery).

Is it a fancy word for scaffolding?

In everyday terms, **scaffolding** refers to the temporary construction around a building that is used to support it as it is being built or remodeled. In education, it is a little more complex. There are a number of definitions of scaffolding, ranging from Donato (1994), who interpreted it as a "situation where a knowledgeable participant can create supportive conditions in which the novice can participate, and extend his or her current skills and knowledge to higher levels of competence" (p. 40) to Schumm (2006), who explained it as "providing support for students in their language, and then gradually diminishing the support as students become more independent" (p. 530). In addition to these clarifications, Verity (2005) suggested that scaffolding was "the cognitive support given to a novice learner to reduce the cognitive load of the task" (p. 4).

Regardless of which definition of scaffolding you like the most, I think we can all agree that in simple terms, scaffolding is the situation in which teachers are supporting their students to reach their potential. Scaffolding is often used in discussions related to the Zone of Proximal Development (**ZPD**) (Vygotsky, 1962, 1987; Vygotsky & Cole, 1978), and that scaffolding from the teacher is used to support students within their ZPD as they strive for higher levels of understanding. In language learning, like the scaffolding around a house that is removed once the building is strong enough to support itself, the scaffolding from a teacher is reduced once the student is comfortable using language that had earlier been a little difficult (e.g., Nassaji & Cumming, 2000; Nassaji & Swain, 2000). That being said, however, it is important to remember in the scaffolding process that "students should not be spoon-fed with too many hints" (Baleghizadeh *et al.*, 2011, p. 51) and they "should not be deprived of free exploration while performing a task" (Baleghizadeh *et al.*, 2011, p. 51).

So, from this perspective, flipped learning certainly is a way of scaffolding students in their learning. Flipped learning provides support for the students through the pre-class videos, then enables more teacher-student contact time during the face-to-face class sessions, to give direct feedback when necessary. So, to answer the question of whether flipped learning is a fancy word for scaffolding or not, I will say "no," because scaffolding is a much broader term and goes much deeper than the ideology of flipped learning. But, flipped learning certainly follows the definitions of scaffolding given earlier to a certain degree and is one clear way of providing the support students need, while still giving them the opportunities to think about and understand the content better by themselves.

Before, during, and after class

Perhaps one of the most famous guides used among educationalists when thinking about human cognition and learning is Bloom's taxonomy (Bloom, 1956). The taxonomy includes six classifications (i.e., knowledge, comprehension, application, analysis, synthesis, and evaluation), ordered from simple to abstract, to provide "a framework for classifying statements of what we expect or intend students to learn as a result of instruction" (Krathwohl, 2002, p. 212). A revised version of Bloom's Taxonomy (Anderson & Krathwohl, 2001), as illustrated in Figure 1.1, provided the guidelines in verb form (rather than in the original noun form), showing that teachers want students to remember and understand the content, to apply and analyze that knowledge, before evaluating what they have learned and finally creating new or original work.

Bloom's Taxonomy and its updated version are often referred to when looking at the structure of education and how classes are conducted. According to the original concepts of mastering a topic laid out by Bloom (1956), the bottom three levels of the taxonomy (i.e., remembering, understanding, and applying) are typically conducted in the classroom under the direct guidance of teachers. Then, the upper three levels (i.e., analyzing, evaluating, and creating) are given to students to do in their own

Part I: Flipped Learning

Figure 1.1 *Overview of the revised Bloom's Taxonomy*

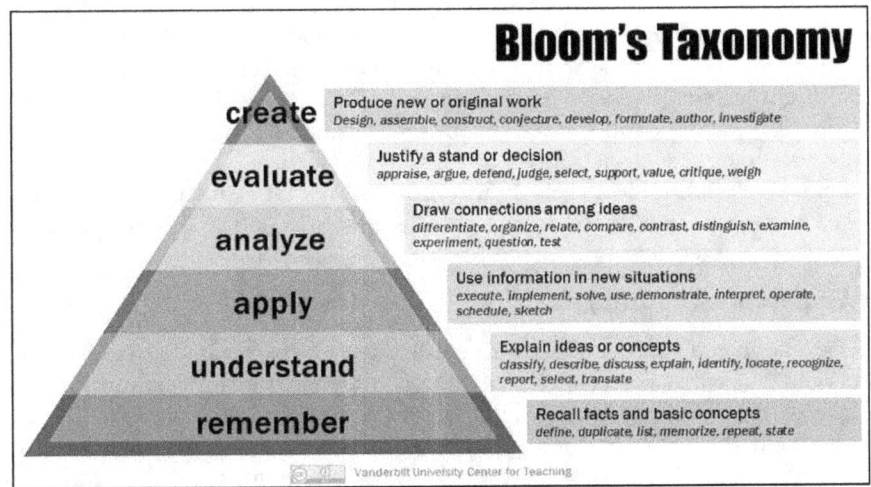

Note. This figure is reprinted from the Vanderbilt University Center for Teaching website: https://cft.vanderbilt.edu/guides-sub-pages/blooms-taxonomy/

time. The structure used in flipped learning, however, slightly differs. While keeping the concepts of the four pillars of FLIP summarized by the Flipped Learning Network (2014a) in mind, let's take a brief look at what we can expect before, during, and after our face-to-face class sessions when we are involved in flipped learning. Because I will introduce a little more concretely what teachers in numerous EFL and ESL teaching contexts with various learning objectives have been doing in Parts II and III of this book, I will keep the descriptions below quite simple and straightforward.

What happens before class?

In traditional classes, the majority of the teachers' and students' time is spent focusing on the remembering and understanding levels of Bloom's Taxonomy, which leaves little to no time to allow students to apply what they have learned (Bergmann & Sams, 2014). Therefore, to create an environment in which students have opportunities for application and analysis of the content they have learned, "teacher-created videos are best used as content-delivery tools in the bottom two tiers of Bloom's taxonomy: Remembering and Understanding" (Bergmann & Sams, 2014, p. 30). This is probably the first significant change that occurs when flipping your class: What had previously been done in the classroom in front of your students is now done outside of the classroom, in your students' homes, at the school library, or perhaps the local café.

As we will see later in this book, there are several options when it comes to the way of providing the lectures and explanations usually given during class. Throughout this book, it will be apparent that supplying students with videos of explanations of the class content (given by the teachers themselves or in some other way) via video-sharing websites and learner management systems (**LMS**) is, without doubt, the most common choice for teachers. Nederveld and Berge (2014) list a series of options for teachers and trainers to present content to students for out-of-class viewings, such as video lectures, audio lectures, sharing resources, quizzes, collaboration tasks, and collections of student reflections. Teachers can also share topics for discussions, debates, and speaking tasks conducted during the face-to-face class sessions.

What happens during class?

Because in the flipped classroom students are already familiar (well, they should be) with the class content before they enter the classroom, these face-to-face sessions can be dedicated to having students apply and analyze what they have learned (i.e., the third and fourth stages of Bloom's Taxonomy). When it comes time for the lesson to start, the students should already be familiar with and have understood the content of the lesson, so we expect that they will enter the face-to-face class sessions with confidence to take on the tasks they are about to be given as they apply and analyze the information they received beforehand (Leis, 2022a).

However, it is possible that some students are yet to become familiarized with flipped learning or are unwilling to take responsibility and watch the required videos or do other necessary pre-class tasks (Blau & Shamir-Inbal, 2017; Johnson *et al.*, 2014; Talbert, 2015). Therefore, to confirm students' understanding of the materials distributed to them prior to class—and, as I have mentioned in my own study (Leis, 2022a) and will be mentioned again later in this book, if students prefer to just read the materials without watching the videos, that's fine—it might be beneficial for students' learning and helpful for teachers when they are monitoring during students' activities if some kind of assessment is given to students at the beginning of the class. In an **EFL** environment, this might be done through a simple quiz or short roleplay at the beginning of the class.

Once the teachers have been able to gauge how much the students have comprehended from the pre-class materials, the remainder of the class time can be spent having students apply the skills they have acquired before class. In a speaking class, for example, this might be done through roleplays or presentations. Listening classes might focus on particular strategies passed from the teacher to the students. Whatever the language skill that is being focused on in the class, it is essential for teachers to continuously monitor the students' activities and use scaffolding strategies where necessary.

What happens after class?

Finally, we have the "create" and "evaluate" steps of Bloom's Taxonomy (1956). After face-to-face sessions in the flipped learning model, students can be encouraged to reflect on what they have learned through the teacher's explanations and interactions with others in the classroom. Students may go back and re-watch the videos from before the class, but this time with a new perspective based on what they learned through the applications and analyses that were conducted during the class (SEE Team, 2019).

Teachers may also set their students assignments in which they present (either orally or through written form) their evaluations of the lesson content and design or create original ideas or solutions, for example, related to concepts that have been covered before and during class (Mabrey III & Liu, 2013). Such projects can help students develop portfolios of their work through the course, giving both teachers and the students themselves clear illustrations of their progress throughout the course (Estes *et al.*, 2014).

My final comment here, and this is not limited to flipped learning contexts, is that students should be encouraged to reflect on their study habits. Was the environment and time in which they prepared for class beneficial or a hindrance to their understanding of the content? Were they active during class in the sense that they were willing to apply the knowledge they had gained without being overly concerned with the possibility of errors? What did they learn from other students during the face-to-face sessions? How did their peers use the newly gained knowledge in various ways? Reflecting on study habits and what they learned before and during class mirrors the principles of **metacognitive strategies** (e.g., activities one might undergo to control study habits) and can lead to better progress in your chosen field in the future (e.g., Efklides, 2006).

The analogue age and digital age of flipped learning

The analogue age of flipped learning: Before 2012

There is no clear record regarding the birth of flipped learning, and the idea of helping students prepare to participate more actively in class has probably been around since the dawn of time. However, some academics suggest the flipped classroom concept originated from the work of Lage *et al.* (2000) with their suggestions of the *inverted classroom*. This approach to teaching, coined *classroom flip* by Baker (2000), has enabled teachers and students to take learning beyond the time limits and physical limits of the classroom, setting the tone for educators in the early decades of the twenty-first century.

One of the earliest references to a flipped classroom that I have found was presented by physics teacher Eric Mazur. Even though a distinct terminology was not given to describe this teaching structure at the time, Mazur (1997) and later Crouch and Mazur (2001) described classes in which the students requested to be given lecture notes before the actual lectures so they could take more meaningful and accurate notes. After some time, however, the students mentioned that Professor Mazur was simply reading from the notes, which was not an especially interesting way of conducting the class. (What a shock that must have been for him!)

So, in response, Professor Mazur decided to distribute the lecture notes a week before class, then hold mini quizzes at the beginning of the class to measure just how much the students had understood the content of those lecture notes (and to check whether they had actually read the notes, I imagine). After that, the focus of the class was on the misunderstandings and questions the students had related to the content and discussions surrounding various topics each week. Because students had already read the lecture notes beforehand, the majority of the designated class time could be spent concentrating on debates and interactions among students under the direct supervision of the teacher, who was also in the classroom, of course. The teacher acted as a guide and open for consultation from the students whenever needed. The capacity to take the focus of class time away from the teacher and place it on the students and their ideas is the very essence of the flipped classroom.

From that time, this structure gained interest among many instructors in a wide range of fields, and more evidence appeared from scientific research and academic articles related to the benefits of giving students opportunities to view lecture materials before the class. The majority of papers related to flipped learning were seen in the sciences and mathematics. Although these studies were all describing pretty much the same structure to teaching (i.e., the students study the class content beforehand and the main lecture is spent practicing and discussing the content), they went under different names. Some examples include Jeremy Strayer (2007), who used both "classroom flip" and "flip classroom" in his Ph.D. dissertation related to tutoring mathematics; Moravec *et al.* (2010), who reported on their "Learn before Lecture" or LBL procedure in biology classes with first-year university students; and Freeman *et al.* (2007), who discussed the advantages of a "Peer-instruction technique" for increasing active learning in biology classes.

In the analogue age of flipped learning, the number of studies related to flipping language learning was minimal. Some studies recognized the benefits it may bring for students whose first languages were not English (e.g., Freeman *et al.*, 2007), but papers related purely to language learning, as far as I could see, was limited to that of Ashby (2011), who used vodcasts (i.e., creating video files and uploading them to a website) as part of her phonology classes at a university in the United Kingdom. In her study, Ashby observed improvements in her students' performances and their positive attitudes towards learning in a flipped classroom (e.g., students often discussed lecture content with peers before attending the class). Based on the results of her study and the reported success of flipping an English Language Arts course at a high school in the U.S. (Clintondale High School, 2010), Ashby recommended that more language-related classes should be flipped in order to optimize the students' learning experiences. As we will see throughout this book, Ashby's recommendations were undoubtedly justified.

The digital age of flipped learning: 2012 and beyond

The digital age of flipped learning, which makes use of the creative benefits of **Web 2.0**, is often formulated from the advice of Jonathon Bergmann and Aaron Sams (2012). Although Bergmann and Sams had been mentioned in regards to the flipped learning model prior to 2012 (e.g., Ashby, 2011, cites Bergmann and Sams, 2010, in her article and mentions that they began flipping their classes in 2007), it was really the 2012 book *Flip Your Classroom: Reach Every Student in Every Class Every Day* that changed the way learning was structured for millions around the globe.

Since then, flipped learning, which now focused on providing students with guided preparation for class by using vodcasts in a similar way described in Ashby's (2011) study, has been used by instructors and studied by researchers on a global scale. Teachers were able to create their own original videos and distribute them to students via video-sharing websites such as YouTube, upload them to their own blogs, or share links with students to information on the Internet that was related to the topics that were being studied in class. One of the most prominent examples of a website often used for flipped classrooms is the series of instructional videos made available online by Khan Academy. By sharing content with students to view at their leisure, a new light can be shone on education as it emphasizes that all people learn and concentrate in different ways, at different places, and at different times (Khan, 2012).

The popularity of the flipped learning model escalated after the suggestions of how to successfully bring flipped learning into classrooms presented by Bergmann and Sams (2012). Like during the analogue age, much of the early research was still focused on the fields of science and mathematics. Following up his 2007 Ph.D. dissertation on the flipped classroom model, Strayer (2012), for example, reported on how he used the flipped learning model as part of his statistics classes, suggesting that the students in the flipped classroom generally had positive outlooks on this teaching model. Other examples reporting the benefits of flipped learning included Johnson's (2013) master's thesis based on flipped learning in mathematics and Schindelka *et al.* (2013) in epidemiology classes.

To spread the success of the flipped learning model, the Flipped Learning Network was established in 2012 and provided a salient definition of flipped learning to illustrate that conducting flipped learning is not simply about providing students with lesson content before the class (as was described earlier); it includes the face-to-face class sessions where students should be given more freedom, encouraging learner **agency** and autonomy. As a result, the work of the Flipped Learning Network branched out to numerous fields, with a huge amount of success being reported in hundreds of research papers worldwide (e.g., Moraros *et al.*, 2015, with post-graduate epidemiology students in Canada; Seery, 2013, in university chemistry lectures in the United Kingdom; Grant, 2013, with music majors in Australia; Østerlie, 2018, in physical education classes with adolescents in Norway; Hirata and Hirata, 2020, in computer programming courses with Japanese university students; and Roach, 2014, in economics with university students in the United States).

A common theme that can be seen in research related to flipped learning, regardless of the field being focused on, is that it allows for more active learning as students become involved in deeper discussions and participate in more meaningful practice in the face-to-face sessions than they tend to in traditional classrooms. Flipped learning is also reported to lead to higher self-confidence and lower **anxiety**; students already have a general understanding of the lesson content as they walk into the classroom, feeling ready to take on challenges they are about to face. For these reasons, it makes sense to use flipped learning in language teaching. That is the purpose of this book: to give insights into the principles of flipped learning and introduce examples of successfully executed flipped learning in English as a foreign language (**EFL**) and English as a second language (**ESL**) contexts. Through the topics discussed within, I hope that I can give you some suggestions to help you carry out flipped learning in your classroom with stellar results.

The pros and cons of flipping your classroom

A few years ago, I gave a presentation at an academic conference which had the title, "The pros and pros of flipped learning." In the presentation, I summarized three different research projects that I had done and how through using flipped learning I saw my students expend more effort in their studies and their writing proficiency skyrocket. Being my usual presentation style, I think I also talked a bit about wine in the presentation, too. And all of this in 20 minutes! I do have to be honest, though: Not everything about flipped learning is as wonderful as first appears. Sometimes it gets tough. So, in this section, in addition to discussing a few of the reasons why I feel flipped learning is successful, I'm also going to run through a few problems and hiccups you might face along the way as you incorporate flipped learning into your class. First, let's have a look at some of the reasons why flipped learning seems to be successful.

Flexibility

The thing about regular classes is that they are set in prepared classrooms and at specified times. There's not much we can do about that. However, when we make the content of the class available online—which students can watch on their smartphones, tablets, laptop computers, or whatever they want to use—we give the students the flexibility to choose when and where they want to watch the videos. If the students prefer to go to the beach to watch the class videos, that's fine. If the students want to watch the video in the final minutes before the class starts, that's fine; it's not ideal, but that's the decision that the students make.

In addition to this freedom of when and where to watch the videos, the students are also given the opportunity to choose how to watch the videos. If they would prefer to watch the videos without closed captions (we'll get into closed captions later), they can turn them off. If the students need to re-watch part of the videoed explanation to clarify something they didn't understand, they can do this easily, too. Because students are watching the class content in their own time, they can make the choice of when, where, and how to watch the videos. Such options are not always available for students in traditional classrooms where often the teaching style needs to be one-size-fits-all.

Increased confidence

Following on from the previous point, because students have been given opportunities to understand the content more thoroughly, either by having the closed captions there to help them catch what the teacher was saying more easily or re-watching the more difficult explanations given in the videos, their understanding increases, resulting in their approaching the lesson with more confidence. This is especially true for students whose English proficiency is not quite up to the standard of others in the classroom (Leis, 2022a).

Both self-confidence and **anxiety** have received considerable attention in the second language acquisition (**SLA**) literature. Studies have shown that the more self-confidence students have in their language ability, the more willing they are to communicate in the target language (Aoyama & Takahashi, 2020; MacIntyre *et al.*, 1998). Consequently, as students' willingness to communicate increases, evidence points to increases in their language ability (Yashima, 2009; Yashima *et al.*, 2004). Thus, if we are looking to help students come to the classroom with a little more self-confidence, especially those who were previously anxious about actively participating in the class due to a self-perceived lack of language ability, then the flipped learning model is certainly the way to go.

Increased learner agency

In my opinion, often the biggest problem with teachers is that we love to teach. Many of us seem to feel that we need to stand at the front of the classroom giving facts and knowledge that we decide the students must know. However, the origins of education—and I mean going back to when universities were first established in countries such as Morocco, Egypt, the United Kingdom, and India—education was not about simply listening to the teacher telling students what to do. Education was more about scholars sitting in circles and discussing ways to improve the standards of living. Although I understand that the teacher has a responsibility to guide students in their studies, of course, more opportunities need to be given to students to take charge of their learning. This is where the construct of **agency** is especially important.

The concept of **agency** is a complex matter. As Sarah Mercer explains, agency is "not only concerned with what is observable but it also involves non-visible behaviours, beliefs, thoughts and feeling" (Mercer, 2012, p. 43). Because the flipped learning model reduces the amount of time the teacher is explaining the content of the class, there are more opportunities for the lesson to be focused on the students. We've established that fact numerous times in this book already. Many classes following the flipped learning model in the past have used the class time to have students do practice exercises under the teacher's supervision. This is fine, of course, and follows the original ideas behind flipped learning. However, as Martin Seligman—perhaps the first name one thinks of when hearing the terminology learner agency—asserts, the construct of agency is moving away from the focus being on the individual (i.e., I, me, my opinion, my ideas) to partnerships and collaboration (i.e., we, us, our opinion/s, our ideas) in the modern era (Seligman & Seligman, 2019). Flipped learning allows us the freedom to do this in our classes, encouraging students to work together on various issues related to the content of the textbook.

As a final note on group work, I think it is also critical to consider the role of leadership within the group. Often, the students with higher self-confidence or the more extroverted students will either be chosen as group leaders or will volunteer themselves to take the reins. As we have seen, though, communication and collaboration are critical parts of education and promoting learner agency in all our students. Therefore, as Johnstone (2012) suggests, when using group work in the classroom, it may be a valuable habit to regularly rotate leadership roles, ensuring the less confident and more introverted students are also given opportunities to be in control of the group.

Focus on weaknesses

A final point I will look at here is related to the students' weaknesses. Even if the students watch the videos again and again, and they use the closed captions to help increase their understanding of the content, there are still going to be places that they just might not get. This is why the quiz conducted at the beginning of class is an essential part of flipped learning. It is through these quizzes that teachers are able to establish whether or not students have understood all of the concepts introduced in the videoed explanations. Based on the results of the quizzes, teachers can grasp which points students have understood perfectly, therefore do not need to be covered in the lesson any further, and which points students have misunderstood, if any, and need a little additional explanation before moving on to group work and discussions.

For this to work, however, it is essential for teachers to carefully consider how they are going to conduct the quizzes at the beginning of the class. Using pen and paper is not going to work as it takes too long for the teacher to distribute the quizzes, have them returned, and confirm which **items** were easy and which were not. This is where our students' smartphones[2] and online testing applications become indispensable additions to our classroom materials. The use of mobile devices for language education is not a necessarily new discussion, and previous studies have shown how the advantages of using them in language learning (e.g., Leis, Tohei, & Cooke, 2015; Levy, 2009; Morgana & Kukulska-Hulme, 2021; Stockwell, 2016). It can be risky to give suggestions about which online applications to use for quizzes, because it seems that the number of such applications is increasing on a daily basis. In the past, I have used the testing functions of Google Forms, Flubaroo, and Kahoot, all of which worked perfectly for what I needed. Whatever you choose to download and use, make sure it is easy to use, provides quick feedback, and allows you to quickly see your students' strengths as well as their weaknesses and why they were weak in those areas. Choosing the right quiz software or application can help you get your students fixing up their own errors early in the class and put the focus on creative and collaboration work: the main objectives of flipped learning.

Now as much as we'd all like to finish it there, there are, of course, weaknesses—or limitations if you prefer—with flipped learning. In fact, I probably could have started this section by looking at the cons, because by discussing the problems with a certain way of teaching we are able to discover ways to make it even better. So, without further ado, let's have a look at a couple of problems you might come across when you are implementing flipped learning into your class.

---

[2] One argument against using smartphones in the classroom is that students may not own one. I understand that this may be a possibility. However, society is changing so quickly that smartphones, tablets, phablets, and other mobile devices that can access the Internet are now fundamental items. In the past, owning a smartphone brought you many advantages to your everyday life. Now, not owning a smartphone brings many disadvantages to your everyday life. That being said, I understand that these devices are not cheap. Therefore, I urge academic institutions to provide their students with access to such devices, at the very least to be used at school, to assist them in their learning experiences.

Making videos is tough work!

For me, this was probably the biggest challenge I faced when making the videos for my students. It goes without saying, but the amount of time it takes you to prepare the videos really does depend on the quality of video you are aiming for. It is perfectly fine, of course, for you to stand in front of a chalkboard with the camera recording and give the same kind of instruction that you would in the classroom. However, this way does have its risks when we consider the temptations that students are faced with when studying online. (I'll get to those temptations in a minute.)

If we want to make higher quality videos—and we don't need to be making Hollywood blockbuster level videos here—it is going to take a little extra time. When we think about planning the video, creating the slides, preparing a script (it's easier to add the closed captions to your video later if you have a script prepared), recording your voice to go with the slides, and putting everything together into a movie, it can take a few hours to create a 10-minute explanation video[3]. In the university classes that I flip, I generally prepare between 12 and 15 videos per semester. That time adds up very quickly.

To overcome the time burden, I strongly recommend collaboration work with friends and colleagues who are using the same textbook; students don't seem to be overly concerned about who made the videos (Leis & Brown, 2018), as long as the content is engaging.

My storage has all gone!

A second challenge that many teachers probably face when incorporating flipped learning into their classrooms is that their computers' storage will soon fill up. If you are using high quality recording for your videos, it is going to use a lot of space on your computer, especially when you are making numerous videos for your courses.

The solution here is not too difficult. Investing in a removable hard disk will allow you to save all of the materials without overloading your

---

[3] Just because you are making videos for your students to watch outside of class time, it doesn't mean that you can go on and on in your explanations. Like in the classroom, we need to be keeping our explanations concise. The attention spans of human beings seem to be declining. In the past, listening to a speaker tell hours-long stories was seen as entertainment; sitting and listening for a few hours was part of life. Now, we appear to lose interest within minutes, perhaps even seconds, if the television program isn't upbeat and keeping us focused through pre-recorded laughter tracks in comedies and prepared villains in reality programs. Therefore, according to surveys, keeping videos to less than 10 minutes is recommended (Talking Tree Creative, 2020). Cockrum suggests "one minute per grade level as a maximum time" (2014, p. 115); if a student is in her 11th year of school, then an 11-minute video will be ideal. Furthermore, a strong start is essential. To keep your audience involved in the video, the first 30 seconds is vital. It is at this time when around one-third of viewers will have switched off if you have not engaged them in the content (Pedersen, 2015). Although teachers are not entertainers, we do need to consider ways to keep our classes entertaining. Keep your videoed explanations short, sharp, and interesting to watch.

main computer, which often results in it slowing down or, in the worst-case scenario, crashing.

The students prefer the other way

Despite all of the benefits of flipped learning that we have looked at so far in this book, there are, of course, some students who will prefer the traditional way. As I have mentioned a few times already, it is possible that students want to challenge themselves without the **scaffolding** that the videos provide (Leis, 2022a). Some students might prefer the traditional way of learning and would prefer you to just teach the lesson normally.

Communication with your students is going to be essential if you find yourself in this situation. Having conversations with your students about the purposes of time spent in the classroom, various ways that humans learn, and what is expected of the teachers and students throughout the course is vital to make your flipped course successful (Talbert, 2016).

Too many temptations

Although there are various ways of distributing the videoed explanations to your students, video sharing websites such as YouTube and Vimeo are probably going to be your most common platforms. The advantages of using such platforms are that first, unless you are using a paid account it is going to be free, and second, unless you make your video private, you can share the content easily with a wider audience.

The problem is, however, that your video is not the only video on these sites. The algorithms of Internet sites are so advanced that your students will be faced with the temptations of more attractive and professionally created videos at their fingertips. Have you ever had such an experience like this? You sit down to do some work on your computer one evening and think to yourself, "I'll just have a quick look at one or two videos on the Internet to get myself warmed up to work." One after one, interesting and funny videos are served to you on a platter, and before you know it, it is two o'clock in the morning and you are watching videos about how to make ice cream. I know I have!

This happens to almost all of us and it's nothing to be ashamed of. Videos on the Internet are **intrinsically motivating**. They are fun and time goes by quickly when we are watching them. So, we need to take hints from these videos that are successful on video sharing websites. This doesn't mean that we need to go crazy and act like some the world's most famous YouTubers, but we can aim for videos that are a little more professional and use slides that will be more inspiring for your audience. The book *Presentation Zen* (Reynolds, 2011) and its associated website https://www.presentationzen.com/ are rich with tips for improving your presentation skills and design of your slides.

What if there is no internet?

The final con I am going to cover here is the dilemma of not having Internet access. A lack of Internet access might be due to 1) students living in remote areas, 2) they've used up their data quota for the month, or 3) their parents have turned off Internet access due to the student not following screen time rules at home.

If you find yourself in one of the situations mentioned above, it certainly makes flipping your course a little tougher. But there are still various options for you and your students. One of the easiest ways is to download your videos onto USB sticks for your students to watch on their computers. Flipped learning guru, Jon Bergmann, described a course in which an English teacher in Argentina added audio to PDFs, which were then distributed to the students via Bluetooth (Bergmann, 2018). If your school has Internet access, another option would be to allow students to view the videos in the library or a classroom specified for viewing such videos. Just like any aspect of teaching, when it comes to problems with Internet access, we need to be there to help our students overcome any hiccups they face in their learning.

So, there you have it. There are still numerous obstacles that we need to overcome when we are flip our classes. But I think the benefits certainly outweigh the hindrances. Through collaboration, clear communication with our students, and being professional when creating the materials for our students, these problems can be swept aside with ease.

What isn't flipped?

I remember attending a particular conference a few years ago, and there was a presentation with flipped learning in the title. Naturally, being the topic that I was interested in, I highlighted it as a must. The presenter was extremely professional and gave a very concise summary of her study. But there was one big problem: What she was describing was not flipped learning.

In the study, she talked about how she had had her students prepare and record self-introductions on their smartphones at home. The students then had to email their videos to the teacher, who was the one making the presentation at this conference. Okay. Reasonable start: she was having the students do some work at home rather than doing it in the classroom. That's not exactly the idea of flipped learning, but it is undoubtedly on the way, and it was too early to make final judgments at that stage. The presenter then explained how she conducted a survey in which students were asked to describe their experiences creating the videos at home and their opinions about whether or not they would like to do similar activities in future classes. Then that was it.

Hang on. Where is the flipped component? I raised my hand during question time to ask, "How did you use the videos that the students had made at home during class time?" The answer was, "I didn't." Okay. Now we have a problem. This isn't flipped. It is just giving the students extra homework, which they probably weren't too happy about.

One of the critical elements of flipped learning is to have a clear-cut connection between what students are doing outside of school and what is happening inside the classroom. We are not giving the students extra work to do when we bring a flipped factor into our classes; we are guiding the students in their preparations for class so they will be able to understand the content of the face-to-face sessions more deeply, so the main focus of the lesson itself will be the students and their ideas, and so we will be able to concentrate on strengthening and clarifying the students' weaknesses and misunderstandings while reinforcing their strengths. Of course, what the presenter had students do for homework is fine, and, as we will see in the remainder of this section, I recognize the contribution smartphones make in language learning. Having students use their smartphones is, without doubt, a fantastic way to improve their language skills, and there is a plethora of studies that discuss the potential and benefits of using smartphones in language classes (see, for example, Godwin-Jones, 2017; Jones *et al.*, 2017; Leis, Tohei, & Cooke, 2015). However, if we want to call what the presenter was describing a part of flipped learning, we need to make a couple of changes.

The good news is that all hope is not lost. There is still much potential in what the presenter had done to incorporate a flipped component into her classroom. What could she have done with the student-created videos in her regular class time? For starters, I think she could have looked at the content of each video. In the study she referred to in her presentation, the videos were self-introductions. Such videos would be immensely valuable at the beginning of a course to better help students get to know each other. Having students share videos of themselves with others, then including activities and tasks in the classroom based on the content of those videos, could help reduce the **anxiety** some students may feel when speaking in front of a group of peers, especially those you are meeting for the first time. The activities and tasks might include, for example, information-gap exercises, **cloze tests**, or writing short biographies. In comparison to giving self-introductions in the classroom in front of your peers, having students create videos outside of class time would also allow for editing and re-recording, when necessary, as well as open up opportunities for students to be creative in the videos they produce about themselves. This would give teachers insight into who the students are, their language proficiency, and their personalities.

Furthermore, when having students stand in front of the entire class to introduce themselves, a classroom atmosphere may emerge in which just one student is being focused upon. Although focusing on individual students might be advantageous at specific moments during the class time, to increase and maintain all students' concentration throughout the entire lesson, it is often more constructive to use techniques that keep all of our students busy and involved in the lesson at all times. For example, by having students create self-introductory videos and watch each other's recordings outside of class time, then centering tasks and activities conducted during the lesson on the contents of those videos, we are more likely to create a classroom environment in which every student feels heavily involved in the learning process every minute of the entire lesson.

When having students create videos for a flipped classroom environment, there is also the potential of including an aspect of peer coaching. For example, the teacher could have students—in either individual projects or collaborative projects—become experts in particular areas of what is being studied in the textbook that semester and have the students give mini-lectures in place of the teacher. Of course, the teacher would need to inspect these videos carefully beforehand to ensure the content is accurate. Still, suppose the students are explaining class content via videos that they have created themselves, and the lessons in the classroom are focused on activities and tasks that the teacher has prepared, we can see a huge number of opportunities to increase the amount of practice and production of the language. Now, we have excellent potential for a fantastic, flipped classroom. The idea of having students create the videos to be used in part for the flipped classroom reflects the principles of **project-based learning**: a way of teaching that has long been viewed as successful in education in general and has gained attention from EFL instructors in particular in recent years (Becket & Slater, 2018; Poonpon, 2017).

There is much to learn from the presentation I attended; the ideas were fantastic. However, I also feel that before we get overly excited about the whole concept of flipped learning, we need to sit back a little and consider whether what we are doing with our students is actually flipped or not. Keep the connections between what is happening outside and inside the classroom strong, and you'll be well on the way to a great flipped learning environment.

Using closed captions

As I mentioned in the preface of this book, one of the reasons I initially got interested in flipped learning was in an attempt to help two students who would struggle both understanding and interacting in regular classes due to their being hard of hearing. Although the university I was teaching at had organized note-takers—students who would sit in on the class and take notes for **deaf and hard-of-hearing** students—it was still not an ideal way to understand the content to the same degree as other students. I found that, at times, the deaf and hard-of-hearing students would fall behind the other students during the class because they were confirming with their note-takers about what I had been explaining in the lesson. Of course, there were issues when the note-takers themselves had to confirm what I had said, so from time to time, this would result in moments of silence in the classroom; while some students had finished their tasks, others were taking a little longer due to a delayed start. As a teacher who likes to keep all students busy all the time during the class, I had to come up with something suitable and come up with it fast. That is when flipped learning came to the rescue.

As I began using flipped learning in that class, I started to notice that not only were the deaf and hard-of-hearing students understanding the lesson content and participating more actively and confidently, but it was having a similar effect on the other students as well. I could see two main reasons for the positiveness during class once flipped learning had been activated: 1) the ability to watch and re-watch the videos explaining the textbook content at the students' leisure outside of the classroom, and 2) the availability of closed captions on these videos. The points about flipped classroom videos allowing for more flexibility with students' learning strategies and encouraging more learner agency have been covered already in this book. These points are not limited to students learning languages in EFL environments but any subject in any context. However, I think having the option of viewing closed captions can bring about numerous benefits for all language students, regardless of their language proficiency and whether they are deaf and hard-of-hearing or not. There are various ways of displaying closed captions on a screen that have been experimented with over the past few decades. Some of these ways are effective, and others are not so. Let's have a look at how we might input closed captions into our videos and an important point to consider when having the closed captions displayed on the screen.

Unless you have excellent typing skills, inputting words into a computer can be very time-consuming. With recent advances in speech recognition software (Deng & Li, 2013; Oh & Song, 2021), inputting text into a computer is becoming easier. In fact, the accuracy of such technology is improving to such a degree that sending texts, writing emails, and even putting parts of this book together can be done without touching the keyboard. Speech recognition has also been discussed as an excellent tool for language learning (Levy, 2009). However, no matter how advanced the technology may become or how high the accuracy might be, there are always going to be misunderstandings and inaccuracies, and further improvements are certainly called for (Miner *et al.*, 2020). Although these mistakes might be forgivable in videos designed for classes with native speakers, in EFL classes where students are looking to their teachers for examples of "perfect" English grammar spoken in "perfect" English pronunciation[4], errors, mistakes, and slips of the tongue can often be fatal,

---

[4] I put "perfect" in quotation marks here to show that I am being a little sarcastic. There is, of course, no single perfect English pronunciation.

especially when, like all written discourse, the closed captions are on the screen to stay.

Another vital point when it comes to using closed captions in videos for flipped learning in EFL environments is the way the closed captions appear on the screen. One way of adding captions to a video and is often seen in English proficiency tests for **deaf and hard-of-hearing** students is to have the words hurriedly scroll across the computer or television screen, kind of like the way the results of horse races are shown on the sports channel. Another way is to allow our computer software to automatically produce the closed captions for us. This is the easy way, of course, but mistakes are inevitable if we choose this way, and often the places where the sentences are cut appear to be pretty random. If you have ever seen a movie with closed captions, you might have noticed that this is not the way they are presented. They are carefully thought out, making the content easy to understand for anyone requiring them. To provide our students, regardless of how well they can hear, with authentic models of how spoken English can sound, it is essential for teachers to consider the use of **intonation phrases** in the closed captions. Although there is an abundance of research related to intonation phrases in the field of phonology (see, for example, Pickering, 2017), the amount of literature pertaining to this vital aspect of spoken English in the production of closed captions is very thin.

In phonology, intonation phrases are described as sense units, breath groups, intonation units, thought groups, and tone groups (Brazil, 2010; Levis & Pickering, 2004). Put very simply, intonation phrases are the chunks of language between our pauses as we speak. These chunks of speech may occur naturally as we talk or may appear as prefabricated language chunks, that is, "as a series of several words that are typically used together in a fixed expression" (Burri *et al.*, 2019, p. 4). When preparing closed captions for videos to be used in flipped learning, my suggestion is to animate the captions by computer to appear and disappear at the exact timing and speed of natural speech, that, is in intonation phrases. It is a lot of work, I admit. But I can say with confidence that using intonation phrases as a basis for writing your closed captions will result in better listening comprehension, understanding of the content, and eventually better-spoken language among your students. It's a much better reflection of how we speak. Here's a little more evidence.

The fact that intonation phrases are critical when presenting information orally has been shown in much previous research, not just in the English language. One famous example—well, famous at least among phoneticians in Japan—is a study looking at the importance of intonation phrases conducted by Miyoko Sugito in 1999. Sugito made a 70-second recording of a television broadcaster reading a piece of news and digitally removed all pauses from one copy of the recording. She then had 20 random people listen to the news report twice, once without the pauses removed and once with the pauses removed. Listeners reacted by saying that although they had no problems comprehending the news report with pauses, they had no idea what was being said once the pauses were removed. It became too fast. Sugito stressed, and this is important, that adding pauses in language allows humans to reintegrate information in their short-term memory and consequently process it into their long-term memory (Sugito, 1999). Therefore, unless pauses are used in speech, the listener doesn't have enough time to comprehend what they have heard. The same should be true for closed captions. Without the pauses in written text appearing on the screen, it will be too cognitively demanding for our students to understand what is going on.

In addition to increasing the ease of understanding for students and reflecting authentic English, there is one more reason that I will mention here: anxiety. Anxiety has been researched an enormous amount in the past. I am sure most of us are aware of the importance of helping lower our students' **affective filters** (Krashen, 1982; Krashen & Terrell, 1983) and making them feel more comfortable speaking without being concerned with grammatical inaccuracies. In a similar way, anxiety has received much attention in second language acquisition, with much of the research being centered around the work of Elaine Horwitz, Peter MacIntyre, and Tammy Gregersen. (For more on anxiety in second language acquisition, see, for example, the seminal paper by Horwitz *et al.* (1986), and works such as MacIntyre (2017), Gregersen (2003), and Dewaele and MacIntyre (2019).

As part of my Ph.D. research, I looked at how closed captions could be produced and what effects those methods had on students' levels of anxiety (Leis, 2016). I conducted an experimental study comparing two ways of displaying closed captions on the screen: a scrolling method and in intonation phrases. I wanted to see which way resulted in lower anxiety for students, particularly those who would be relying on the closed captions the most: deaf and hard-of-hearing students. The participants, who had varying levels of hearing, chose six passages at random, which were displayed on a screen in either the scrolling method or in intonation phrases. To measure the students' levels of anxiety, they wore heartrate monitors—the kind that runners often use to measure their heartbeats as they run—to see if there were any dips (i.e., feeling more relaxed) or spikes (i.e., feeling more anxious) in their heartbeats as the two closed captions styles were shown on the screen[5]. Through the heartrate patterns and interviews held with students after viewing all six passages, the results were obvious: Using closed captions in a scrolling method was clearly more anxiety-inducing than using intonation phrases. Furthermore, the closed captions displayed in intonation phrases were easier to

---

[5] A similar way of measuring anxiety through measuring the participants' heart rates was conducted by Gregersen *et al.* (2014) and MacIntyre and Serroul (2015).

understand, and students felt much more comfortable.

So, how long should these intonation phrases be? Well, to a certain degree, it is up to the speaker. However, Tench (1996) explains that intonation phrases generally last between one and two seconds in usual speech. Therefore, depending on how long you speak, you might make one or many more intonation phrases. Another way of measuring the length of intonation phrases, besides how many seconds they last, is to look at the number of accented words. John Wells (2006) explains that an intonation phrase typically contains only one or two stressed words. However, it is possible for one intonation phrase to have up to five! It should also be noted that intonation phrases usually have grammatically coherent structures and often depend on punctuation (Burri *et al.*, 2019).

I don't want to get too much into intonation phrases now, because I will start to go off track. But if you are interested in looking more into this fascinating part of spoken language, the work of John Wells is probably a great place to start. I hope you can see the importance of not only using closed captions in our flipped classroom videos but that the way we display these closed captions go a long to providing more comprehendible content and authentic models of language. To get the maximum benefits, however, these closed captions shouldn't be just appearing on the screen randomly; as producers of our own mini movies, we need to be carefully considering ideas from the field of phonology to get hints about how these closed captions will appear on our students' screens.

What if students don't watch the videos?

I have had quite a few opportunities to give workshops and presentations about flipped learning. Almost every time I give a talk about flipped learning, one of the questions that is asked is, "How can we make sure our students have watched the videos that we have prepared for them?" My attitude to this has changed a bit over the past few years.

Initially, I had the same concerns; even though I had put in the effort to make the explanations in the videos as straightforward as possible, it seemed that some of the students weren't even watching the videos. It was pretty disappointing, to say the least! Now, of course, I started the lessons each time with a short quiz about the content of the videos and the textbook, as you do if you are following the typical structure of a flipped classroom. So, to further encourage ("pressure" might be a better word) the students to watch the videos, I started adding little Easter eggs (small unexpected bonuses) or short comments unrelated to the textbook to each of the videos to make them both a little more entertaining, but also—and perhaps more importantly to me at the time—to ensure the students would watch those videos. Then, in the quiz at the start of each lesson, I would include an **item** or two related to that Easter egg or short story.

To give an example, in one video, I was discussing anxiety in language learning and how to create a classroom environment in which students are more willing to lower their **affective filters**. I added a picture of a kangaroo relaxing under a tree between two slides in the middle of the video. In my explanation, I commented, "Look at this fella. Doesn't he look relaxed? This is how we want our students feeling in our classrooms, right?" Then, in the quiz conducted at the beginning of the class, one of the items asked, "Which of the following animals appeared in this week's video?" Students had to choose from four different animals, and if they chose the wrong animal, it was an obvious sign that they hadn't watched the video.

One of the problems with the above example is that once students catch on to what the teacher is doing, they might just skip through the videos to find the photo featured that week. To prevent students from doing this, another strategy is to make a comment about a picture, or something more closely related to the textbook to confirm whether or not students are actually listening and not simply staring at the screen with the words going in one ear and out the other. For example, you might have a picture of a bulldog on the screen, but in your commentary of the video, say something like, "Look at this bulldog. Isn't she beautiful!? You know, bulldogs were always my favorite kind of dog when I was younger, but now I am a huge fan of staffies[6]!" Then, in your quiz for that week, you could ask something like, "What is Adrian's favorite kind of dog?" Once again, I think you would need to make these quiz items multiple choice because the purpose of these questions is to encourage students to watch the videos about the class content; you shouldn't be too worried if they can spell kangaroo or Staffordshire bull terrier or not.

However, as I mentioned earlier in this section, my thoughts on the question of how to make sure our students are watching the videos have changed in recent years. We all study and learn in different ways, right? Just because I feel that flipped learning is a fantastic way to improve my students' understanding of the textbook content, it doesn't necessarily mean that my students will agree. In a recent study, I investigated students' attitudes to flipped learning (Leis, 2022a). In that study, I had university students—some of whom were in classes that were being flipped and others who were in classes that were not—write study diaries each week reflecting on how they prepared for classes. Both of the courses that were being taught focused on language pedagogy. For those in the flipped classroom, I asked where and when they had watched the videos. Then, I conducted some interviews with students from each group. In the interviews we talked about their study habits and how they prepared

---

[6] Staffy is the nickname for Staffordshire bull terrier. I have a Staffy now—Jake is a very, very cool dog!

for my pedagogy classes. One of the most critical questions in the interview was related to the videos I had prepared for the classes. To the students who were studying in the flipped classroom, I asked how valuable the videos were for their studying and how much more confidence they had in class having watched those videos. To the students in the non-flipped class, I asked if they thought their understanding of the textbook's content would have been better if I had provided them with videos and if they thought they would approach the face-to-face classes and discussions in those sessions with more confidence having watched those videos.

What I found, primarily through the interviews, is that in both groups—the flipped class and the non-flipped class—the students who had higher linguistic self-confidence[7] (i.e., the students who felt confident in their language ability) remarked that they thought that the videos were not necessary. They wanted to test their own English ability by going through the textbook first without any help from the teacher. In the end, they really only used the videos to confirm the discussion topics for that week. On the other hand, the students with medium and low linguistic self-confidence showed a strong preference for having the videos there to watch, either before reading the textbook or while reading the textbook.

So, where does that leave us with the original question about ensuring students are watching the videos? My feelings now are that we don't need to worry too much about whether the students are actually watching the videos or not. This might sound like I am counter arguing myself on the importance of flipped learning, but let me explain.

I still believe that flipped learning is fantastic to bring to the classroom, of course. However, I think the videos that we make available for our students do not need to be mandatory viewing. A more important question might be about how we can ensure the students are actually reading the textbook and not simply relying on our videoed explanations. We can summarize the main points in the videos and push the students to read sections of the textbook more closely as part of those videos. We can also share the discussion topics that will be covered in class and give a few hints about how to prepare for those discussions in the videos. I now think that we don't need to add kangaroos and dogs to our videos just to persuade our students to watch videos they might not necessarily need. And those discussion topics can be shared with students through

---

[7] How to measure linguistic self-confidence can be kind of tricky. In this study, I gave the students the option of writing their diaries and conducting the interviews in their first language (**L1**) or the **target language**. If students wrote their diaries entirely in English and preferred to have the interviews in English, I determined their linguistic self-confidence as being high. If the diary entries and interviews were a mix of Japanese and English, I marked their confidence as medium. In the case where the diaries and the interviews were in Japanese (even though I was asking the questions in the interviews in English), their linguistic confidence was put down as being low.

some kind of **LMS** or given to students at the beginning of the course as part of the syllabus. If the students want to watch our videos, that's great! If the students would prefer to challenge themselves and read the textbook alone, that's just as good. The videos are still there in case they get a little stuck along the way. Like all aspects of teaching, I think that we need to be flexible in what we do in the classroom to meet our students' needs and learning styles.

PART II

FLIPPED LEARNING IN SLA

Introduction

Okay, so now we are going to have a closer look at studies in second language acquisition that have investigated flipped learning and their results based on the four skills of language (i.e., speaking, writing, listening, and reading), as well as grammar instruction, and a few other ways it has been implemented into the modern EFL classroom.

The number of studies focusing on flipped learning in language education is increasing day by day. Hardly a morning goes by that I am not sent a notification about new research related to flipped learning that has recently been published. There are also many books dedicated to ideas and strategies for language teachers to flip their classrooms (see, for example, Brinks Lockwood, 2014). Some studies were difficult to put into one section, such as the paper by Lee and Wallace (2018), who compared changes in the English writing, speaking, and overall grades of Korean university students studying in flipped or non-flipped classrooms, concluding that the confidence of students in the flipped classroom increased throughout the course.

When looking at research to include in Part II, I tried to keep an open mind and cover a wide range of regions and ages of students to give an indication of in what areas flipped learning appears to be successful. There have been some fantastic articles published in recent years giving analyses of flipped learning research in **SLA** that I can highly recommend in addition to the more focused ones that I cover in Part II. Forsythe (2017a), for example, gives an excellent overview of the success of using computer and mobile technologies in EFL and how this success clearly justifies the flipped learning model to be implemented in foreign language education. This is a point that will be covered many times in the chapters ahead. Forsythe (2017b) goes further to also provide suggestions related to how to implement recent developments in technology into flipped classrooms. This second article by Forsythe is also essential reading to go with Part II of this book. As we will see in several studies covered in Part II (and Part III), recent research regarding flipped learning has been going beyond simply comparing a flipped classroom and a non-flipped classroom to comparing two flipped classrooms with one having an added component related to the latest technology, such as **gamification**, online applications, and speech recognition software. Finally, Vitta and Al-Hoorie (2020) provide a thorough meta-analysis of the ever-increasing number of papers related to flipped learning in SLA, giving a comprehensive description of the success of flipped learning from various perspectives. Although I recommend all three of these papers, any one of them will give you great insights into flipped learning in language education over the past decade as well as future directions.

When reading through this section, there is no need to go in the order in which I put the skills. First, go to the language skill that interests you most, the one you will most likely be teaching (or perhaps already do), or whichever you are interested in researching. Of course, if you are happy with how I put the order together, that's fine, too.

In each section of Part II, I have started with a story. This is something that I do whenever I give presentations at academic conferences. Initially, you might be wondering why I am talking about my daughter or my days playing cricket when I was younger. But the stories are all in there for a reason, partly to create a segue into the main topic of the chapter and partly to create a connection between what we are talking about in the chapter and our everyday lives. I often use the same strategies in my classes at university as well. For example, I have a motivation lesson in which I talk about my son playing basketball at the beginning. The story creates the segue into the lesson that I want, but at the same time, I am hoping that when the course has finished and someday in the future the students are watching basketball on television, their memories will be triggered back to the message I had for them in that class.

Each section of Part II will be broken down into four main parts:

1) the opening story and introduction;
2) an overview of previous research related to that skill in second language acquisition;
3) a thorough discussion of research related to that skill in flipped learning circles; and
4) suggestions for pedagogical implications for teaching that skill.

The final section of Part II—The possibles—covers five other areas, each one a little more briefly than the five main ones.

There is just one final thing I need to mention before we move on, so please bear with me for a moment longer. It is important to remember that technology is changing rapidly. An application that has gone viral today might be seen as ancient history tomorrow. So, when we look at techniques that involve the use of technology, including those in the flipped classroom, we need to be flexible and not fall for the trap of simply using what is trendy. Be open-minded and consider how that technology will be beneficial for students from a theoretical framework as well as in practice.

Speaking

I have a daughter. She is wonderful. I like to say that she's a bit of a daddy's girl, but I'm not sure exactly how much she would agree. When she was in kindergarten, we would wait together for the school bus to take her away with the other kids for the day. While waiting, we would play games like "step on each other's foot," "bottom spanking," and "Adrian

Janken[8]." They are all great memories of my daughter, who is now all grown up (but just as cute!). One day, when the kindergarten teacher arrived, she said to my daughter, "You are the spitting image of your father," to which my daughter, to my shock, burst out into tears. When we asked what was wrong, she replied, "I don't look like daddy! I don't have a beard!!"

That is what is so wonderful about children. They are willing to try out silly games like "step on each other's foot," as well as being innocent enough not to be concerned about saying things that adults might find funny or a bit strange. Their imagination opens endless opportunities. Unfortunately, as the late Sir Ken Robinson argues in his TED Talk, "Do schools kill creativity?" (Robinson, 2006), it seems that as children get older, this willingness to be a bit silly seems to disappear. Whether that is due to the influence of schools or not is a debate for another day. Nevertheless, spontaneity and the willingness to make a few mistakes are critical in conversational speaking. As language teachers, we need to help students prepare to successfully hold conversations off the top of their heads. We need to help them prepare, but at the same time be cautious of being overly prepared to the extent that our students are simply memorizing pre-written scripts. In this chapter, we'll look at how the skill of speaking has been investigated in second language acquisition and how flipped learning has played a part in improving students' speaking skills.

Speaking research in SLA

When one thinks about learning a second or foreign language, speaking is most likely the skill in which they want to become highly proficient. But when it comes to speaking a foreign language, it is much more than simply opening your mouth and letting the words fall out. For example, clear pronunciation and enunciation are, of course, vital; you are not going to be able to convey your message if nobody can understand you. We also need to think about what kind of verbal discourse it is that we are performing: Is it interactive, including conversations between two or more people, or non-interactive, such as giving a speech or leaving a message on someone's answering machine (Harmer, 2007)? First, we'll take a very quick glance at SLA research related to speaking from these

---

[8] *Janken* is the Japanese word for the Rock Paper Scissor game. It is very popular in Japan and is used almost all of the time to decide who will go first in activities both inside and outside of the classroom. Adrian *Janken* is a variety of *janken* that I invented that requires you to use both hands. You cannot produce the same item with both hands (e.g., rock on both hands is not allowed). So, a combination of rock and paper is permitted. The winner of Adrian *Janken* is the person who wins based on the item that is not shown. So, in a game where Person A has his left hand as rock and his right hand as paper, he has not shown scissors. Person B has her left hand as scissors and her right hand as paper, so she has not shown rock. Person B's rock will defeat Person A's scissors (i.e., the *janken* items not revealed), so Person B is the winner. Adrian *Janken* makes the usual mundane *janken* just a little more cognitively demanding and encourages a little creativity, as students need to see what they cannot see.

three angles. Then, we look at some previous research in the flipped classroom world associated with teaching the skill of speaking.

Pronunciation

One area of SLA that concerns many students is their pronunciation: Even if I am speaking with grammatically perfect English, will I be able to make myself understood? Will I be ridiculed because of my strange accent? With English being recognized as a **Lingua Franca** and the respect more linguists show for the varieties of **World Englishes** (Jenkins, 2006), there is a trend among language teachers and researchers to move away from encouraging students to aspire for the same pronunciation as a native speaker and aim for intelligible and comprehensible speech that will not affect their communication (Murphey, 2014; Saito, 2011a). Numerous techniques have been suggested to assist language students in achieving comprehensible pronunciation, such as the effects of explicit instruction (Saito, 2007; 2011b; Zhang & Yuan, 2020), the use of automatic speech recognition technology (Hsu, 2016), and even the use of virtual reality (Alemi & Khatoony, 2020).

Another area looking at language students' speech intelligibility has been the focus on the rhythm of speech. The rhythm of language is related to whether syllables are stressed or unstressed, the length of syllables (i.e., long or short), pitch (i.e., high or low) of combinations of these variables as words and sentences are spoken (Crystal, 2008). The rhythm of language is generally described as **syllable-timed**, which uses a consonant-vowel syllable structure without reduction of stressed vowels, or **stress-timed**, which has a consonant-vowel-consonant syllable structure. It is commonly accepted that almost every native English speaker tends to speak with a stress-timed rhythm. Kirkpatrick (2007), however, explains that syllable-timed rhythm does occur in exceptional circumstances in British English, for example, when people are using baby talk or showing irritation or sarcasm. Fernandez and Cairns (2011) also suggest that some languages (e.g., Brazilian-Portuguese) have been demonstrated to have properties of both stress-timed rhythm and syllable-timed rhythm languages. Therefore, as Dauer (1983), Roach (1982), and Yavas (1998) explain, the difference between stress-timed rhythm and syllable-timed rhythm is not absolute but gradual: No language is perfectly syllable-timed or perfectly stress-timed. That is, all languages display both sorts of timing. It should be noted that a third rhythm of language—**mora-timed** rhythm—has also been identified to account for the Japanese language (Ladefoged, 1982; Ladefoged & Johnson, 2015).

As a result of transfer, many students whose **L1** is a syllable-timed language or **mora-timed** language often speak English with a syllable-timed rhythm instead of a stress-timed rhythm. Whereas some researchers have argued that this does not affect the intelligibility of speech (e.g., Jenkins, 2000), others have suggested that it does (e.g., Nishihara & Leis, 2014).

Thus, although the pronunciation of individual sounds within words at the morpheme level does not appear to affect how comprehensible one's English is, the rhythm of one's utterances seems to do so. Evidently, a bit more research is required before we can reach any clear conclusions about this matter.

Interactive

When it comes to discussions related to interaction in the foreign language, one of the first debates that arises is the point of which is more crucial in oral communication: fluency or accuracy? The 1940s and 1950s saw a massive spike in the popularity of the **Audiolingual Method**, a method of teaching that emphasized the importance of practicing through short, snappy drills that quickly helped students become able to speak set phrases accurately and with good pronunciation (e.g., Practor & Celce-Murcia, 1979). Although this method enjoyed some immediate success, it also had its critics as students were unable to be flexible in their use of the language. This is illustrated in a popular joke among language teachers at the height of the **Audiolingual Method**'s popularity:

Friend: Well, how did your trip to Germany go? You're such a good German student, you must have had a great time talking to Germans!
German Student: Well, actually it was kind of tough. [*Pause.*] I knew my lines, but the Germans didn't know theirs! (Horwitz, 2020, p.110)

As language educators and students realized that errors do not have to be avoided in language learning, a shift was seen to a more communicative focus. As explained by Brown and Lee (2015, pp. 31–32), the characteristics of communicative language teaching include considering all components of communication, the relations between the form of language and how it is used, the balance of fluency and accuracy, and teachers' responsibilities in giving corrective feedback, authenticity, giving students the freedom to study in their own styles, the teacher taking the role of facilitator rather than being a dictator, and increasing students' sense of agency in the learning process. For more on the communicative focus of teaching English, in addition to the works cited above, see Harmer (2007), Larsen-Freeman and Anderson (2011), Lightbrown and Spada (2013), Littlewood (2010), and Ur (2012).

Non-interactive

In comparison to interactive and communicative speaking, non-interactive speaking and monologues, such as public speaking and memorized scripts in drama, have not received much attention in the field of SLA. Much research focused on public speaking has investigated the anxiety felt by students (e.g., Kalra & Siribud, 2020; Yaikhong & Usaha, 2012), while others have looked at the effects of techniques, such as learning from **TED Talks** (Li *et al.*, 2016), **Pecha Kucha** (e.g., Mabuan, 2017; Rokhaniyah, 2019), and hints from the globally recognized public speaking and leadership training organization, Toastmasters International (e.g., Yu-Chih, 2008). The use of video technology on smartphones has also been suggested as a technique to improve students' public speaking skills (e.g., Leis, Tohei, & Cooke, 2015), but the area of non-interactive speech is undoubtedly one that requires much more attention in future investigations.

Previous research of flipped learning and speaking

Anxiety, whether it is based on concerns about grammatical accuracy, misunderstandings, or simply being worried about getting your message across successfully or not, appears to be high among students learning English. This might be true more so when it comes to speaking than for the other language skills of listening, reading, and writing (Yaikhong & Usaha, 2012). Where this anxiety comes from (e.g., being worried about lack of vocabulary, low fluency, or intelligible pronunciation or rhythm) is a topic for another day. But it would be hard to argue against the fact that speaking in a second language in front of others—it doesn't matter if it is with one person, two people, ten people, or 10,000 people—is a pretty daunting experience for many of our students. What is more, speaking is arguably the most difficult of the language skills to master (Zhang, 2009). With high anxiety more often than not leading to low speaking proficiency (Dewaele & MacIntyre, 2014; MacIntyre, 2007; MacIntyre & Gregersen, 2012), educators are given the enormous task of making their students feel more comfortable and confident in their verbal encounters. Flipped learning may provide one of the answers.

In a paper by Chen and Hwang[9] (2020), the researchers investigated how using flipped learning in a speaking course would effectively lower their students' English-speaking anxiety and create a more comfortable learning atmosphere in which students would be willing to verbally communicate more. In Chen and Hwang's study, a comparison between two classes was conducted. Both groups used flipped learning, but one of the groups had the added feature of **concept mapping** (Novak, 1990, 2002) included. The element of concept mapping was included as it has for long been shown in various studies as effective for increasing students' organizational and note-take skills in language education (e.g., Buran & Filyukov, 2015; Hsu, 2019; Hwang *et al.*, 2019; Liu, 2014; Moreira & Moreira, 2011; Nunan, 1999). The results of the study showed that although the students who were studying under a typical flipped classroom still showed remarkable progress in their speaking skills over the eight-week **intervention** period, the students who had the concept-mapping techniques added to their face-to-face class time made even more pro-

---

[9] A vignette for the Chen and Hwang (2020) study can also be found in Part III of this book.

gress. Improvements were reported in students' speaking proficiency, anxiety surrounding speaking, listening scores, and critical thinking awareness. These results indicate that what teachers do in the face-to-face classroom time is just as important as what happens before the class. Let's look at another example.

Hung (2018) reported on a study investigating how the English-speaking anxiety of 48 second-year Taiwanese university students was affected by the addition of **gamification** to the flipped learning model. The students were divided into two groups, both of which followed the usual procedure of a flipped classroom: students watched videos as part of their preparation for the face-to-face class (in this study, videos from TED Talks were used), the actual face-to-face session was used for group work, and feedback on students' progress was provided by the teacher. The difference between the two groups in Hung's (2018) study was that students in the conventional flipped classroom held discussions and completed worksheets in small groups during the face-to-face session. On the other hand, students in the Experiment Group still followed a similar learning structure but were engaged in gamed-based learning activities during the face-to-face classes. These students played games designed by the teacher that used game boards printed on large sheets of laminated paper and small cards with a number of QR codes that led students to various opportunities to win or lose the game in addition to questions based on the content of videos that the students had watched before the class.

To measure students' anxiety levels, Hung (2018) used the Foreign Language Classroom Anxiety Scale (Horwitz *et al.*, 1986), which had students describe their English-speaking anxiety on a **Likert scale** from one to five at both the beginning and the end of the study. Furthermore, to get feedback on their feelings about the materials used in the classes, the students were given 12 items adapted from an Instructional Materials Motivation Survey (Keller, 2010). Finally, interviews were conducted with the students to obtain further information regarding their anxiety and motivation towards speaking English.

The surveys and interviews in Hung's (2018) study clearly showed that at the end of the period, the students who experienced playing games during the face-to-face sessions were less anxious and more highly motivated to speak English than the students who had not played the content-based games. The students mentioned in their interviews how the board games were fun and that the teacher's designs were attractive. Also, because there was a game atmosphere, unlike taking a test or completing a quiz, students "would not lose face even if I lost the game or performed poorly, because it was just a game" (Hung, 2018, p. 304). From a motivational perspective, this comment from one of the students in Hung's study especially stands out, as researchers of the self-worth theory look to encourage students to reduce a feeling competition and comparisons among students in class (Covington, 1992, 1998; Leis, 2021a, 2021b, 2022b; Leis et al., 2022).

While Hung (2018) showed that adding gamification to the face-to-face class time brought about a more significant reduction in students' linguistic anxiety, other studies have looked at the use of digital technology as part of the class preparation process. Michael Yi-Chao Jiang and his colleagues[10] (2021), for example, incorporated automated speech recognition technology into a flipped classroom to investigate its effectiveness in improving students' pronunciation. Recognizing that many teachers who flip their classes limit the technologies used to simple videos, Jiang et al. (2021) set out to use "cutting-edge technologies that could help establish an immersive learning environment" (p. 110). It was thought that by integrating such technology into flipped learning, students would be more prepared for their face-to-face classes. In addition, the burden of providing individual feedback in large classes could be lightened for teachers. At the same time, students' speaking proficiency and the complexity of what they say would also increase.

In their study, Jiang and his colleagues chose automated speech recognition (ASR) software (also known as automatic speech recognition) for half of the students to use in their pre-class self-learning time. Previous research has shown ASR software to be beneficial for students in EFL contexts (e.g., Evers & Chen, 2020; Franco et al., 2010). In general, students had positive views of using such technology to assist with their pronunciation (Dillon & Wells, 2021). The students in Jiang et al.'s (2021) study were randomly divided into two groups: one being taught in a flipped learning environment and the other being taught under the flipped learning model while also having students use ASR technology. The ASR software gave feedback to the students in the form of a transcript, which allowed students to clearly notice any errors in their speaking and pronunciation. Based on the results of four speaking tests conducted throughout the research period, it was discovered that by using the ASR technology, the students were able to see significant improvements in the complexity of the speech and large reductions in the anxiety they felt surrounding speaking in English. The authors concluded that while flipped learning was indeed successful in making the students feel more comfortable speaking English and improving the quality of their English, the addition of ASR technology saw even greater benefits for the learners, from both linguistic and affective perspectives (Jiang et al., 2021).

Helping students prepare for speaking exercises by adding other techniques, such as **concept mapping** and ASR technology, appears to have successfully lowered students' anxiety to speak. This, in turn, raised their speaking proficiency. So how about when we look more directly at the

---

[10] A vignette for the Jiang et al. (2021) study can also be found in Part III of this book.

effects of flipped learning on speaking skills, such as pronunciation and overall speaking ability?

The study by Abdullah and his colleagues (2019) is as good a place to start as anywhere, so let's go from there. In the study, the authors used a mixed-method design to measure changes in the speaking proficiency of 27 undergraduate university students as a result of studying in a flipped classroom. As preparation for classes, students were required to watch short videos (i.e., 5–10 minutes) in which the teacher of the course gave summaries of the content of the textbook in a typical flipped classroom style. Face-to-face class time was then dedicated to allowing students to practice speaking interactions with their classmates under the direct supervision of the teacher. Students' levels of speaking proficiency were compared in a **pre-test-post-test design** and measured using individual presentation assessment forms under the criteria of confidence, body language, grammatical accuracy, fluency, and organization, with each having a maximum score of five. The results of a **paired-samples** t-test indicated significant improvements ($p < 0.05$) in the students' oral proficiency as the average scores improved from 12.28 to 15.51.

Although this study did not include a control group, the **quantitative** and **qualitative** results clearly indicated the positive effects of flipped learning on the students' spoken skills. The authors divided 12 of the participants into groups of four members according to the proficiency scores in the pre-tests. In group interviews, the students shared their experiences and opinions of flipped learning for improving their English-speaking proficiency. The responses from the students, regardless of their proficiency, were overwhelmingly positive, with expressions about how their confidence had increased, "We become more confident because there are many chances to speak and participate" (p. 139), which was salient "especially for those students who feel shy or unconfident when it comes to speaking or sharing their opinions with their peers" (p. 140). Students also commented on how the face-to-face class time was able to be focused on the students and that the role of the teacher was "to guide us, observe, guide and give us comments" (p. 140). Abdullah *et al.*'s (2019) study shows how flipped learning can bring about clear improvements in speaking skills. This study, however, still focused mainly on students' presentation skills rather than interactions, and the lack of a control group in the design could be seen as a weakness.

The gains in speaking performance have been seen in various other studies conducted in numerous contexts in which the flipped learning model was compared to a control group. For example, Quyen and Loi's (2018) study with 60 undergraduates (aged 19–21) showed significantly improved performances ($p = 0.02$) among the flipped classroom students, who watched videos of sample conversations and explanations of target grammar structures before class, in comparison to those studying in a traditional English communication class. The students' speaking skills in Quyen and Loi's (2018) study were judged based on how well students could hold a conversation in English and answer prepared questions. Proficiency scores were based on students' pronunciation, grammatical accuracy, use of vocabulary, content, and fluency, using a scale adapted from Weir (1990).

The effects of studying in a flipped classroom have been researched in numerous studies conducted with students of different ages and in different contexts. Regardless of the age and cultural background of the students, positive effects have been observed in, for example, first-year students majoring in English education at a university in Turkey (Köroglu, & Çakir, 2017), adult EFL learners (average age = 33) in Turkey (Yeşilçınar, 2019), absolute beginners of Mandarin Chinese (Wang et al., 2018) living in China, undergraduate EFL students in Taiwan (Wu et al., 2017), hospitality students aged 19–24 in Malaysia (Singh et al., 2018), first- and third-year university students in Japan (Obari & Lambacher, 2015), seventh-grade students (aged 12–13) in Jordan (Aburezeq, 2020), and first-year non-EFL major university students in Thailand (Li & Suwanthep, 2017).

All of these studies were conducted professionally and showed significant improvements in the speaking skills of students studying in the flipped classrooms when compared with non-flipped classrooms. However, at the risk of sounding critical—which is certainly not my intention—in future studies, I think we can start to consider research that has incorporated other techniques into the pre-class and in-class activities. Taking hints from the studies summarized earlier of using **concept mapping** (Chen & Hwang, 2020), gamification (Hung, 2018), and ASR technology (Jiang, 2021), there is room for further research that compares two groups that are both experiencing flipped learning, but with one group having an added teaching technique that have been proven successful in SLA research. This may produce even more improvements in the flipped learning model.

It has been proven time and time again that flipped learning is beneficial for improving students' speaking skills. As suggested by Ema Ushioda as part of her collaborated conference session at the JACET International Conference in 2017 (Kanaoka et al., 2017), in any research conducted in the classroom (e.g., case studies, action research), the students' learning still needs to be the principal focus. Keeping in mind that flipped learning brings about higher oral proficiency, I call for future research of flipped learning and speaking skills to avoid simply comparing the flipped and traditional teaching methods. Instead, future research needs to run comparisons of flipped learning when used with or without other pedagogical techniques. Such research will give us a clearer understanding of what works well with flipped learning while keeping our students' skills improving: the objective of education.

Pedagogical implications for teaching speaking

Well, after my little spiel at the end there, I am sure it is obvious that we need to incorporate some techniques to help students improve their speaking in addition to the videos that come with the traditional flipped classroom. Hmmm, a traditional flipped classroom might sound like a bit of an oxymoron.

In addition to the usual explanations provided to students via video or some other medium, we could look at making additional materials available for students to use in tandem with those explanations. A wide range of ASR technology is available for teachers and students. Some of the more sophisticated products give detailed and visual feedback on minor problems in students' pronunciation and the rhythm of their speech. These are, without doubt, extremely helpful, but at the same time, often costly for teachers and students. If teachers and students are willing to pay for this technology, that is great, but not everyone can afford such products. Most modern word processing software products have speech-to-text technology that displays students' utterances on their screens. These may not give the precise feedback on minor points that some of the more expensive software does, but students will be given an indication of which places they have been able to read with intelligible pronunciation and which areas they have not.

I must add a word of warning here, though. Sometimes, students will read words and sentences that are generally clear and understandable when spoken face-to-face, but the speech-to-text technology receives it differently. Technology is fantastic, but nothing is better than the human ear! When students see what they have said appearing on a computer screen as something utterly different from what they read, it can lead to a drop in their self-confidence. Upon closer inspection of the students' sentences on the computer screens, we often find that the sentences are not that different in sound but simply appear different when put into written text. A quick search on the Internet will show you a wealth of funny texting errors that have caused embarrassment for the sender and tears of laughter for the receiver. With common misunderstandings in speech-to-text software surrounding pronunciation errors and homonyms, it is essential to remind your students that what they have said might not be as bad as it first seems.

Some teachers encourage their students to use speech recognition applications on their smart devices that enable students to give demands to their smartphones, smartwatches, or smart speakers. If the student's English is intelligible, the device will follow the command. Although I have no qualms about this, in most cases, there is no direct feedback beyond whether what the students have said was understood or not. The visual feedback from speech-to-text software is likely to be more valuable for students' learning.

In the flipped classroom, the techniques used during face-to-face sessions are just as crucial for students' learning as what has been done beforehand. Techniques such as concept mapping and brainstorming encourage students to put their ideas on paper; they put together monologues, such as speeches and presentations, and dialogues through roleplays and interactive tasks conducted in front of classmates. It should be added here that concept mapping techniques should be just that: a map of the concepts that they will cover in their presentations mapped out for students to see. I discourage students from writing out complete sentences and memorizing scripts for presentations and roleplays. This may help give the students more confidence in the short term, but, as we saw with the joke related to the **Audiolingual Method** mentioned earlier in this chapter, when we think about students being flexible with language over the long term, having students use just a couple of words to prompt them when they need it is enough. In my own classes, I usually give students very little time to prepare for presentations and roleplays and, as part of that preparation, allow a maximum of six "cheat" words.

We can also consider using games in our classes to encourage students' speaking skills and verbal interactions. As Hung (2018) illustrated, the use of digital games seems to lower students' anxiety to speak English. However, teachers should not feel restricted to online materials; there is still an enormous number of analogue board games that encourage communication among students, a number growing every day. It has been shown that board games are also beneficial for improving students' oral performances and lowering anxiety (e.g., Cheng, 2018; Gaudart, 1999), especially with students of lower proficiency (e.g., Fung & Min, 2016).

However, teachers should be aware that not all board games are the same. Even if a game is fun and exciting to play in our **L1**, that does not necessarily mean it will have the same effect when playing it with our students in the L2. Before deciding on games to use in our classes, we need to ask ourselves several questions: Do the games encourage verbal interactions among students? Do the games present students with opportunities to use the target structure? (Presuming, of course, the lesson is focused on a particular grammatical structure or language **function**.) Are the students going to eventually fall back into using their L1 while playing the games? Are the winners of the games decided by ability or luck? (From a motivational perspective, winning by luck is often more effective for encouraging active participation, especially for those with lower proficiency.) Can the games be adapted to promote more purposeful use of the **target language**? Although it often takes a lot of time and energy, creating your own original games or adapting ideas from other games frequently results in the most effective results for your students.

Finally, we turn to post-class activities. Again, and I am going repeat this point a few times in the book, having students reflect on their learning and participation, followed by consideration of how to improve, is

Part II: Flipped Learning in SLA

Figure 2.1 *Summary of the pedagogical implications for flipping a speaking class*

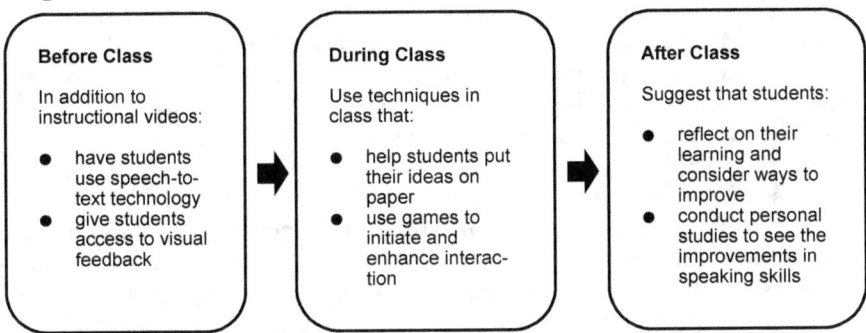

often the best way to use the time after class. If students can keep records of their results when using ASR and speech-to-text technology from before class, they can repeat the same activities after class to see their own improvements. In a way, students could conduct their own informal **pre-test-post-test** designed studies to see just how much they have been able to improve through the activities done before, during, and after the class sessions. A summary of the pedagogical implications discussed above can be found in Figure 2.1.

In the research summarized in this chapter, we have seen that flipped learning brings about many benefits when implemented in classes focused on improving students' speaking skills. First, as is seen in other language skills, because students feel more prepared as they come to the face-to-face class, they tend to feel less anxious. Reduced anxiety, as has been proven in studies related to speaking skills and flipped learning and in other areas of SLA, leads to higher self-confidence and ultimately improved performances in oral communication.

A clear pattern that has emerged in studies related to flipped learning and speaking skills is the importance of not only relying on the pre-class videos provided by instructors but also the implementation of other materials to assist students in their learning. Making use of multiple areas of **CALL**, such as **gamification** and ASR, either before class or during class, appears to work successfully with flipped learning to lower students' anxiety and develop their speaking skills. Thus, teachers could consider various materials and activities that complement the students' learning in English communication classes.

Despite the clear benefits of flipped learning in oral communication classes, language instructors may require the training to develop their teaching skills for teaching pronunciation before passing on advice and strategies to students. Ramírez (2015, 2018[11]) described the benefits of using the flipped learning model in teacher training to assist in-service

---

[11] A vignette for an edited book chapter summarizing this study (Ramírez, 2018) can also be found in Part III of this book.

teachers as they studied how to teach pronunciation. Ramírez (2015, 2018) illustrated how she provided the teacher-students with materials related to strategies for teaching pronunciation through an **LMS**. After working individually outside of class, the teacher-students then created lesson plans and implemented those plans in their regular language classes. Then, during the face-to-face sessions, they discussed how they had been applying the skills they had learned in their own classrooms and various difficulties that they had experienced in teaching pronunciation.

Ramírez's (2015, 2018) studies illustrate the importance of communication among teachers in order to improve the quality of their lessons. This does not have to be done in an official academic setting, as was the case in these studies. I understand very well that teachers are overworked and underpaid. This is a global issue. Even though we are busy, I still encourage language teachers to create opportunities to have study meetings to discuss techniques that have been successful and unsuccessful in their classes, share materials that they have been using with their students, and learn from each other to make the language learning process more enjoyable. Through the activities and materials shared in these meetings—formal or informal—the burden we face in this industry might be eased just a little. The sessions would be run ideally, of course, in academic settings, such as schools or rented offices, under the guidance of a leader, as we saw in Ramírez's (2015) study. But they could be just as effectively held in more casual settings, as a part of conversations over lunch or a cup of coffee, like the atmosphere I have been trying to establish in this book. Creating such study groups can result in higher quality education in all areas of language instruction, but I believe it is especially essential for teaching speaking, the skill that arguably causes the most anxiety for students, but at the same time is the one they want to master the most. For more ideas and discussions on improving your teaching standards, see *Insights into Professional Development in Language Teaching* (Farrell, 2022).

Writing

When I first came to Japan in 1997, I made a promise to myself to study Japanese as hard as I could. Even though I had a university degree in Japanese language (in fact, one of the editors of this series, Glenn Stockwell, was one of my Japanese teachers!), I was not the best student, and I will be the first to admit that my language ability was definitely not up to scratch at the time of graduation. One of the methods I used to work on my Japanese writing when I first arrived in Japan was to write a diary in Japanese every night before going to bed. I found it to be a fantastic way to work on my skills in the Japanese script as well as try out new words I had recently learned. At first, it was tough. I was only able to write about three lines each night. But I remained diligent, and after three years, I was able to scribble out a full page in Japanese just about every day. Even now, twenty years after no longer continuing the diary, I find that my writing fluency has not fallen away thanks to those habits I formed in my early years here. Keeping a journal is undoubtedly a way I can recommend from hands-on experience to improve your and your students' writing skills.

In this section, we will start with a brief look at writing research in SLA. This will be followed by a discussion of various research projects that focused on the effects of flipped learning on students' writing skills from the perspectives of writing fluency, writing proficiency, and attitudes towards writing. Finally, we will cover a few pedagogical implications and tips for improving our teaching of writing through flipped learning based on the discussions we saw in the research projects and other areas.

Just as a reminder, in this section, I am not going to cover writing accuracy from a grammar-teaching perspective; that will be discussed later, where I look at more structured writing through focus on form and focus on forms. In this section, I concentrate on communicative writing, where the students put their ideas and opinions onto paper through essays, newspaper articles, short stories, letters, and other written prose.

Writing research in SLA

One of the aspects of writing that makes it challenging—native speaker or not—is its permanency. What goes down on paper stays there once the ink has dried. That being said, though, in comparison to the other output-focused language skill, speaking (the conversation form, not the presentation form), we have more time to compose our essays, edit our blog entries before and after they go online, and check our Tweets for spelling mistakes (although, many people appear to forget to do this last one!).

In a similar way to the other language skills, the direction of teaching writing has seen various changes since the increase in the popularity of communicative language teaching in the 1980s. Whereas in the past, teachers mainly focused on what the final product would look like, in the modern era, more emphasis is put on the content of what students are writing and the message that they are trying to convey (Brown & Lee, 2015).

When we consider the styles of writing in the second language classroom, we generally look at freewriting, academic writing, and computer-mediated communication (**CMC**) (Horwitz, 2020). As much as I would like to discuss these in depth, this book is about flipped learning, not language learning in general, so I will try to keep these discussions to just brief introductions.

Although the papers were published decades ago, for me, the work by Vivian Zamel (e.g., Zamel, 1976, 1982, 1985, 1992) and Sondra Perl

(1980) has been immensely influential on the instruction of free writing in **ESL** and **EFL** contexts. In their papers, they discussed various techniques and processes that students use in writing their compositions, including "the act of seeing their ideas on paper" (Perl, 1980, p. 24), imitating highly proficient **ESL** writers (Zamel, 1982), the importance of inner dialogue (Zamel, 1982), and connections between writing and reading (Zamel, 1992).

In academic writing, much of the research has been focused around the work of Paul Kei Matsuda and his colleagues (e.g., Matsuda, 1997, 2015; Matsuda & Silva, 2014), who investigated various perspectives of writing, including translinguality (Matsuda, 2014), identity (Matsuda, 2015), the relationship between the reader and the writer (Hyland, 2008; Matsuda & Tardy, 2007), and how cultural background may affect the voice that is constructing in one's writing (Matsuda, 2001).

With increased access to computers and the Internet on a global scale, a trend towards increased **CMC** was inevitable. Research into **CMC** in writing has considered factors such as increased possibilities for collaboration and interaction (e.g., Godwin-Jones, 2015; Kurek & Hauck, 2014), influences on the writing process (e.g., Sun, 2010; Warschauer & Grimes, 2007), the use of social networking systems (e.g., Hattem & Lomicka, 2016; Malik *et al.*, 2019), and the effects on corrective feedback (e.g., Shintani, 2016). Zheng and Warschauer (2017) provide an excellent overview of how CMC has affected the instruction of writing in ESL and EFL environments.

Now that we have a bit of an awareness of how writing has been covered in SLA, let's move into research related to teaching writing in a flipped learning environment and what we can learn from research papers based on those studies.

Previous research of flipped learning and writing

Along with grammar instruction, using flipped learning to teach the skill of writing might bring the most benefits to students' learning. Because in a flipped environment the instructor is able to summarize the structure of how essays can be written, more class time can be spent concentrating on students putting pen to paper (or fingers to the keyboard if you prefer) with the help of their teachers and peers. The amount of research related to flipped learning and writing skills had a slow start but has increased dramatically since the mid twenty-teens.

Writing fluency

It is difficult to give feedback to students and help them improve their writing skills if they don't write or it takes them an hour to write a couple of lines. Speaking fluency is seen as vital, perhaps more so than grammatical accuracy, as it can lead to communication breakdowns if speakers take too long to say what they want to say. The same can be said for writing. Although we usually do have more time in the writing process, a speedy pen brings many advantages for the learner. Unfortunately, there has not been an enormous number of studies focused on writing fluency and flipped learning. In fact, as far as I know, there have only been two, both of which were authored by yours truly. Let's take a quick look at them.

In 2015, my colleagues, Simon Cooke and Aki Tohei (yes, Aki is the one that first introduced me to the concept of flipped learning), conducted a study with 22 Japanese university students (Leis *et al.*, 2015[12]), which was quite a small **sample** size. Of the sample, 11 students were studying English essay writing in a flipped classroom, and 11 were studying in a traditional classroom. The goal of the study was to measure the improvements in the writing fluency of students in the two groups and see whether or not there would be any significant differences between the two groups in how fluently they would write. At the beginning of the study, the number of words produced by the students was almost identical (i.e., about 135 words for the flipped group and 133 words for the non-flipped group), but at the end of the 10-week period, the students in the flipped group averaged 260 words. Those in the non-flipped group produced around 167 words. The flipped group became significantly more fluent writers ($p = 0.007$). The writing fluency of both groups of students improved, but the improvements seen from pre-test to post-test in the flipped group ($p < 0.001$) were far more significant than what was observed in the non-flipped group ($p = 0.219$).

In another study I conducted, I looked at students' writing fluency (Leis, 2015, 2018a). (There are two papers there because I used the same data and discussed the results from different perspectives.) Again, I looked at how the number of words students wrote in their essays in both a **pre-test-post-test** design and **longitudinal** fashion that looked at spikes and dips throughout the course. The study, once again, was conducted at a Japanese university, with a total of 17 students (four male, 13 female), who were around 19 years of age (average = 19.47). As had been seen in the Leis, Cooke, and Tohei (2015) study, a clear improvement was seen in students' writing fluency, as students were writing 131 words on average within the relegated time at the beginning of the course, but 255 words at the end of the course ($p < 0.001$). When the word counts were looked at for each week's essays—which were, of course, based on various topics—there were multiple spikes and dips based on the essay topic of that week. This isn't especially surprising. First, an immediate increase in fluency was seen in the first few weeks of the course, adhering to Penny Ur's prediction that the use of technology in a language course often results in immediate increases in students' motivation (Ur, 2013).

[12] A vignette for the Leis *et al.* (2015) study can also be found in Part III of this book.

Ur did, however, warn that this immediate spike in students' effort usually wanes just as quickly, as they soon get bored of the device, application, or whatever product is being used. In this study (Leis, 2015), however, their effort and fluency were maintained throughout the entire course. I argued, therefore, that it is vital that teachers considering implementing the flipped learning model to their courses be aware of the possibility of a declining drive in the latter half once the honeymoon phase has faded out.

Writing proficiency

There is no use, of course, in taking on an idea for your teaching unless you are seeing some improvements in the quality of your students' language ability. And there are quite a few more articles investigating writing proficiency than there are looking at writing fluency. As a reminder, we are not concerned with grammatical accuracy just at this point; that comes later on. Instead, we are looking at our students' ability to put a story, article, recipe, whatever they are writing down on a piece of paper. In the previous section, we looked at how much more they could write when studying under the flipped learning model, now let's look at just how good they can become.

First, based in the Korean EFL context, Lee and Wallace (2018) observed a clear trend in which students who were in a flipped classroom had improved average writing assignment grades than students who were studying in a non-flipped classroom, albeit not statistically significant ($p = 0.068$) by traditional standards ($p < 0.05$). The statistical analysis did not produce the result below the magical 0.05 standard. "Too often, however, the P value is degraded into a dichotomy in which results are declared 'statistically significant' if P falls on or below a cut-off (usually 0.05) and declared 'nonsignificant' otherwise" (Greenland *et al.*, 2016, p. 339); there is, therefore, still a lot to take out of this study. It was noted by Lee and Wallace that although those in the flipped classroom had had slightly lower average scores at the beginning of the course, they could improve to have higher average scores than their non-flipped counterparts at the end of the course. If this upward trend were to continue, one might say that the scores might have reached significant levels given a few more weeks.

In a study conducted by Kenneth Brown and me (Leis & Brown, 2018), we looked at whether or not students would make improvements in their writing skills under the flipped learning model. We also investigated the effects of the teacher. That is, if the videos that the students were watching before the classes were not made by their regular teacher, would the same effects be seen if they were made by their regular teacher? In the study, I made a series of videos related to essay writing which were uploaded to YouTube. Both the students in my class ($n = 17$) and Ken's class ($n = 21$) watched the videos in a flipped classroom. The study was conducted in a pre-test-post-test design, with students writing essays at the beginning of the course and again at the end of the course. The essays were rated by three evaluators using a rubric (**inter-rater reliability**: α = 0.95), and the average scores of the two groups were compared. We found that both groups improved significantly ($p < 0.001$). Then, we tested whether or not there were any differences between how much the groups improved, finding no significant difference ($p = 0.77$). This means that flipped learning proved to be successful in promoting the students' English writing skills, regardless of whether the teacher made the videos being watched by the students or not; teachers can expect significant improvements in their students' writing proficiency when using materials shared with students from the Internet or materials that they create themselves.

The effects of using flipped learning in writing classes have also been discussed in the Turkish EFL context. Using a mixed **qualitative** and **quantitative** approach, Ekmekci (2017) conducted a study with two groups of students: one group in a traditional classroom ($n = 20$) and the other in a flipped classroom ($n = 23$). Each student was required to write short essays at the beginning and conclusion of the writing course, which were marked based on an argumentative paragraph rubric. The average essay scores were compared both between the two groups and within the groups. In a similar pattern to what we have seen in this chapter already, the results show significant improvements in the quality of essay writing among all the students regardless of whether they were in the flipped group or not. However, the students in the flipped group improved vastly more—going from 42.02 at the beginning of the course to 71.49 at the end of the course—than the students studying in the traditional classroom (43.40 to 58.30). In the follow-up **semi-structured interviews** conducted with the students in the flipped learning group, the students generally showed positive reactions to their flipped learning experiences. Students remarked on how having details about the writing process included in the videos helped them remember and understand how to write better. Those who gave negative feedback mentioned the length of the videos and the content being boring as cons of flipped learning. The importance of using high-quality videos for our students has been and will continue to be a reoccurring theme throughout this book.

Writing attitudes

Unlike the spoken word, which is part of an **online** process and errors generally disappear as soon as they have appeared, the written word is permanent. Therefore, the confidence of students studying writing in L2 contexts has a great influence over the attitudes with which they approach learning this skill. The benefits of using flipped learning to increase the confidence students have in their writing ability have been covered in numerous studies.

Su Ping and her colleagues (2020[13]), for example, conducted interviews with 18 EFL students in Malaysia about their experiences studying under the flipped learning model. When comparing their flipped learning experiences with their regular classes, five clear themes emerged from the students' responses: 1) an increased amount of preparation; 2) higher quality in in-class engagement and interaction; 3) more opportunities for practice during the lesson and thus increased motivation; 4) immediate feedback from teachers and peers; and 5) increased feelings of self-efficacy. Overall, the students in the flipped classroom had more positive experiences than those in the non-flipped environments because "the flipped approach allowed them more time to reflect upon the content before class" (Su Ping et al., 2020, p. 313).

Pedagogical implications for writing

We have seen through the studies summarized above, conducted in various countries on different continents with participants of diverse cultural backgrounds, that flipped learning is indeed effective for improving students' writing abilities: their writing fluency, their writing quality, and their attitudes regarding actually wanting to write. So now, let's consider some pedagogical implications that we can take from these results. What should we be aware of when it comes to implementing flipped learning into our writing classes?

First, it should be noted that the use of technology in writing instruction is not anything particularly new. In fact, considering that the majority of written communication in the 21st century is digital, teaching a writing course that is not focused on typed prose might be questionable when it comes to its authenticity. There are many reference books, such as those by Stockwell (2012, 2022), Walker and White (2013) and Dudeney and Hockly (2007), available now that have a wealth of ideas for using technology in the language classroom. You can also find plenty of ideas about how to use technology in your writing class from published research papers and practical reports covering topics such as the use of blogs (Henry, 2019).

One of the interesting points that was made by some of the students in the Ekmekci (2017) study described earlier was that the videos were rather dull and took too long. We have already discussed the importance of considering the length of our videos in an earlier chapter. Creating attractive videos is just as important. After seeing students in my class enjoying one of my lessons a few years ago, I was once told by a former colleague, "Teachers are not entertainers!" Yes, he was right. We are not entertainers. But that does not mean our classes cannot be entertaining. This is true for teaching in the classroom, I feel, but even more so when creating videos for our students to watch. Our teaching doesn't have to be overly

---

[13] A vignette for the Su Ping et al. (2020) study can also be found in Part III of this book.

serious. Can't we use a few jokes and keep the content light-hearted? (I've been trying to do that throughout this book.) What we create doesn't have to be perfect, but we can still be professional by looking out for mistakes throughout our videos. When our students are accessing our videos, which is usually online, they are faced with multitudes of temptations from other videos and material that they would prefer to be watching. I give various tips about making videos throughout this book, but for now, I suggest keeping them quick, upbeat, and, perhaps most importantly, have a bit of fun.

A common theme we see in creating videos for flipped classrooms is the inclusion of many visual aids and animations. Visual aids have proven to be beneficial for students' learning as they increase the authenticity of the materials (Macwan, 2015), improve comprehension (Ulloa Salazar & Díaz Larenas, 2018), as well as strengthen learner motivation (Matthew & Alidmat, 2013), and decrease anxiety (Lee *et al.*, 2015). If you decide to make your own original videos for your writing classes, which, as we have discussed is quite time-consuming but effective for motivating your students, you probably don't need to include moving animation as much as you might in videos used in, for example, grammar instruction. (I will talk a little about that later when we discuss flipped learning and focusing on form.) However, using simple pictures or figures that clearly illustrate the main points you are making in the video will lead to a higher understanding of the content. For example, in the videos I made for my own English composition classes, I used a very basic drawing of a hamburger (Figure 2.2) to help explain the different parts of an essay and the importance of paragraphs. As you can see in the example I've given, when preparing the visuals to support your explanations, you do not have to be Michelangelo and create masterpieces. They are there to simply assist the students as they learn and complement the explanations you give as you help the students prepare for class. If you then use the same visuals as part of your face-to-face lesson, the students' memories will be more easily triggered, leading to better in-class activity.

In the two papers I mentioned earlier that were related to the **dynamics** of writing effort and fluency, even though there were a few dips here and there, we saw that I was able to maintain the number of words students were writing to a level significantly higher than at the beginning of the course. Increasing students' motivation or skills over a short period is not particularly difficult; it is keeping the intensity high for an entire course that is tricky. With your flipped classroom, I suggest not using all of your best material early on. Instead, keep a few of your more exciting writing topics, fun ideas for your videos, and practical strategies for writing until a little later, just before the students start to get bored.

Keeping with the ideas that cropped up in the **dynamics** of fluency study, it is also interesting to consider the topics that were given to students where those dips and spikes occurred. Students appeared to write

Figure 2.2 *The English essay hamburger*

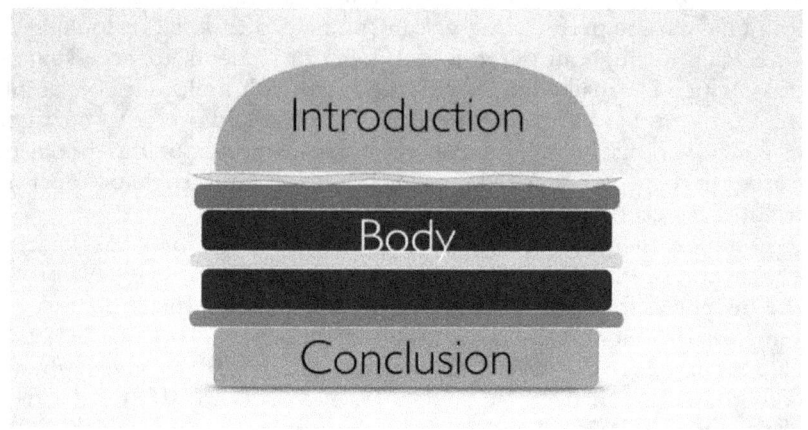

most fluently when they were required to describe various items (e.g., describe three unusual Japanese foods: 317 words) and events (e.g., write three diary entries for the past week: 352 words). When focusing on just one topic for the writing composition, making it somehow related to the previous multiple-entry theme may allow the pen and fingers to move more smoothly. For example, in one week of the course described in the study, I had students write their reactions to a magazine article that they had read. The average word count was 251. The week before that class was about a scary experience, which had no connection to the magazine article at all. However, in the week following the entries about unusual Japanese foods, I had students write a recipe for a dish that they could cook well. The average word count was 330. The topics covered in each week's lessons should not stand alone. Instead, teachers could choose issues that are related to previous or future topics that will be covered in the course to create a favorable syllabus for improving students' writing fluency and competency.

Although we are not talking about grammatical accuracy in this chapter, another major point that needs to be discussed when implementing flipped learning into your writing class is the role of corrective feedback. Written corrective feedback has received a tremendous amount of attention in the field of SLA (e.g., Bitchener, 2008; Bitchener & Ferris, 2012; Ferris, 2012; Li, 2010; Sheen, 2010), and covering it in detail would require an entirely new book. Similarly, the question of who gives the feedback has been addressed, but not anywhere near as much as how to provide feedback. The question of "who" asks whether it is more effective for teachers to give the feedback, peers to give feedback, or self-feedback—where students correct their own mistakes—that leads to the most benefits for students' learning. Birjandi and Haddi Tamjid (2012) discussed this issue in part from the perspective of assessment and it has also been investigated from the perspective of implicit theories (Papi *et al.*, 2019; Waller & Papi, 2017), but there is still much more room for research in this area. The amount of literature on the role of feedback in the flipped classroom is especially thin.

In proposing a framework for a flipped writing classroom that includes peer and teacher feedback, Luo and her colleagues (2020) suggested the flipped learning wheel as a process design for writing classes. The flipped learning wheel provides a straightforward procedure for effective flipped writing classrooms and is based on instructional design theories such as the Community and Inquiry Model (Garrison *et al.*, 1999) and First Principles of Instruction (Merrill, 2002). Luo and her colleagues' design incorporated the principles of "collaboration, reflection, learning community, engagement, accessibility and relatedness" (Luo *et al.*, 2020, p. 8), with accessibility being a critical aspect of among these principles; if students have insufficient access to Wi-Fi and device chargers, for example, the optimal level of out-of-class instruction will be problematic to achieve. On the other hand, if students are able to access the materials for flipped learning to satisfaction, increased interaction, collaboration, and peer and teacher feedback can be achieved during the face-to-face lesson. It is during the face-to-face lesson where Luo *et al.* suggest the jigsaw technique.

The jigsaw technique (Aronson, 1978) encourages group work, in which students collaborate on a task (e.g., writing a newspaper article, preparing a movie report, or composing a tourism pamphlet of their hometowns) and take on different roles in the group work (e.g., leading the group, taking notes, facilitating, editing). The groups of students include *home groups* (i.e., the students' original groups) and *expert groups* (i.e., students from other groups who have the same roles within their own groups). After doing the initial work on their writing projects in their home groups, students then join their expert group and get advice from other students who have taken on the same role in their home groups (i.e., facilitator, note-taker, etc.). The students then return to their home groups to discuss what they learned from their peers before making any necessary changes to their writing tasks. The process seen in the jigsaw technique encourages a high amount of collaboration: one of the main goals of flipped learning. Therefore, it may be especially ideal for implementing into a flipped writing class while also giving students more responsibility for their education, reducing students' anxiety, and increasing their learning motivation (Luo *et al.*, 2020). For more on the jigsaw technique, see, for example, Aronson (2002, 2004) and Darnon *et al.* (2012). For reports on the effectiveness of the jigsaw technique in EFL writing instruction, see, for example, Zahra (2014) and Esnawy (2016), and combined flipped learning in EFL teacher training, see Jeong (2021).

How about after the writing class? As we saw earlier in this book, once the face-to-face class has finished, students can be given the opportunity to evaluate and reflect on their learning as well as create new ideas through re-organization. In our flipped writing classes, we can encourage students to reflect on how they prepared for and participated in class. Did they understand the concepts of writing that we introduced in our videos? Did they participate in the jigsaw activity as much as they could have (if you have used the jigsaw technique, of course)? Because of the permanence of writing, just one draft is never enough; we need to revise and recreate our works constantly. Although the majority of students' efforts in flipped classrooms usually come before the lesson, in a writing class, the post-lesson reflection and revision of composition might be just as essential.

So, there we have it: the flipped writing class. We have discussed the effectiveness of flipped learning for improving students' writing skills, and I think we can pretty much agree that there are many benefits: increased fluency, improved writing proficiency, better attitudes towards writing. To achieve these, we have discussed the effects of using videos that are not too long and are a little entertaining for students. The use of simple visual aids also benefits students' comprehension, so teachers could consider how they include such figures in their videos. During the class, using highly interactive tasks, such as the jigsaw technique, and class designs that encourage peer instruction and peer correction, such as the flipped learning wheel, contribute to students' learning as there is a greater sense of agency among the students and the lesson is centered around the students and their ideas, not the teacher and the chalkboard. Finally, once the lesson is over, students can be encouraged to reflect on what they have learned and have another go at their compositions; the more students write, the more proficient they are going to become. Figure 2.3 summarizes of the main implications discussed in the chapter for flipping your writing class.

The purpose of compiling this book was to give you a brief encounter with flipped learning and introduce a few ideas that can be in teaching and in research. It would be impossible to cover every single paper written on flipped learning and introduce every single way of flipping your classroom. There are, of course, many, many more ideas out there. For more ideas on how to use flipped learning in your writing class, I suggest you start by checking out the book "Flipping your English class to reach all learners" (Cockrum, 2014). Although this book may not necessarily be written for teaching EFL, it has some excellent ideas within, especially in Chapter 5, which is focused on flipped writing instruction. I would also like to point you in the direction of Hassan Mohebbi's edited book, *Insights into Teaching and Learning Writing: A Practical Guide for Early-Career Teachers* (2023), which provides an excellent overview of teaching writing in **ESL** and EFL contexts. Although this book does not cover writing in

Figure 2.3 *Summary of the pedagogical implications for flipping a writing class*

Before Class	During Class	After Class
Instructional video that are:	Use techniques in class that:	Make sure that:
• not too long • are a little entertaining • include simple visual aids	• encourage interaction • encourage peer correction • use topics students are interested in	• students have time to reflect • students review the videos • students revise and rewrite

the flipped classroom, the chapters within describe a wide range of perspectives on writing, all of which can easily be given a flipped learning touch.

Listening

When my father passed away in early 2022, my siblings and I shared various memories we had of Dad, both personal recollections and stories of his own that he shared with us. One of my favorite stories that he told me from his childhood was the time when he and his younger brother, Errol, overheard the local life insurance agent talking to his parents—my grandparents—about life insurance policies for their children. Dad and Errol hid and listened to the conversation. When they heard the man in the suit offer a price for the lives of Dad and Errol, they thought that they had been sold into slavery and made plans for a daring escape from the country to the city. Eventually, quite a few years later, Dad ended up making a career out of helping others set up insurance policies and ensuring financial stability in their lives.

I think what this story tells us is the importance of **schemata**, especially when we are considering the **online** language skill of listening. The life insurance agent in the story above was most likely using simple enough language that children could understand, but because the two boys did not have knowledge of the terminology used in that field, misunderstandings occurred. Similar situations occur even more frequently in L2 learning, where students may have understood the words that have been spoken, but misunderstandings occur due to the context.

Listening is arguably the most difficult of the four language skills to teach, because of various issues including schemata and it being **online** in nature. In my opinion, it is especially difficult for native speakers of English to teach listening. For native speakers of English, or any language for that matter, little effort is required when listening to something being uttered in their L1. Listening to something spoken in one's L2, however, is much more cognitively demanding and listening strategies come to the fore. That's why, I think that when it comes to teaching listening skills, a non-native speaker of the target language will often—not always, of course—be more effective in passing on hints to improve students' listening proficiency.

As always, we will start this chapter by having a brief look at research related to listening in SLA, before moving onto what research in flipped learning tells us about improving students' listening skills.

Listening research in SLA

When looking at speech-processing theory, the concepts of **bottom-up** and **top-down** listening processes frequently arise. Many students believe that they must understand every single word that they are hearing (i.e., **bottom-up** listening process), which is, of course, not realistic (Horwitz, 2020). On the other hand, though, if students rely too much on top-down processes, which can lead to guessing what the other person is saying rather than truly listening and understanding, it can result in inadequate listening performance and miscommunication (Tsui & Fullilove, 1998). The use of **bottom-up** and **top-down** listening processes are intertwined when we listen to our L1. Thus, in the development of L2 listening skills, teachers of second and other languages need to balance tasks in classes that focus on bottom-up listening processes and top-down listening processes separately, as well as use tasks that train students to use both of these processes simultaneously.

It is difficult to talk about the skill of listening in SLA without referring to the work of Stephen Krashen. Krashen is probably one of the most well-known researchers in SLA and through his input hypothesis (Krashen, 1982, 1985), he argued that language learners could only become proficient in the target language through input which is slightly beyond their current level of understanding (i.e., comprehensible input or i + 1). Krashen's input hypothesis, like any hypothesis that receives much attention, was not without its critics, mainly from the lack of empirical evidence to support Krashen's claims (e.g., Ellis, 1990; McLaughlin, 1987) and arguments for the importance of output (i.e., speaking and writing) (e.g., Swain, 1985). A discussion of these points, however, is well beyond the scope of this book.

From the perspective of pedagogy, several teaching techniques appeared that followed the principle of focusing on input and not forcing learners to use the language until they are ready. Perhaps the first method used for teaching listening that grabbed the spotlight was James Asher's (1977) Total Physical Response (TPR). TPR focused on the "doing" of language and followed a teaching style in which the teacher would utter a command and students would follow that command. For example, if the teacher said, "Stand up," the students would stand up. If the teacher said, "Play the guitar," the students would pretend to play the guitar. If the teacher said, "Quickly run to the door and open it," students would quickly run to the door and open it. With the students' L1 rarely used, TPR encouraged students to connect the **target language** with an image or action rather than translating into their mother tongue.

As we can see from this extremely brief encounter with research related to listening comprehension in SLA, it is a very complex issue. Let's now delve into research directed at listening instruction in the flipped learning world.

Previous research of flipped learning and listening

There is not a lot of research in the literature focused purely on the implementation of the flipped learning model into a class targeted at improving students' listening skills. It is certainly an area that needs more attention from researchers. But from the research based on the effects of flipped learning on students' listening skills, scant as it may be, we do see these skills improving significantly. Let's have a look at a couple of studies.

First, we head to a study conducted in the Egyptian EFL environment. Recognizing the difficulties Egyptian students were having with academic listening, Ahmed (2016) implemented the flipped learning model to help ease the struggles her students were experiencing. Before the class, Ahmed had her students watch short videos based on the lesson that was to follow. Students were also given quizzes to check their understanding of the content and opportunities to comment on and discuss difficult parts of the videos. For the first 15–20 minutes of class time, the instructor held discussions based on comments made on the videos prior to class, before applying the concepts and strategies introduced in the videos in listening practice. After class, students reflected on their flipped learning experiences and the activities they had partaken in during the lesson. It is also interesting to note that students were required to create a technological tool to use in teaching as well as a lesson plan using that teaching tool. In this way, the students were encouraged not only join a flipped classroom but also think about how they might use such technology when they became teachers in the future.

To confirm the effectiveness of the flipped learning model for improving listening skills, a pre-test-post-test designed **quasi-experimental study** was conducted with the 34 third-year university students majoring in English education who were participating in the course. At the beginning and end of the study, Ahmed measured the students' listening proficiency by having them answer multiple-choice test items based on both short and long conversations. Using a **paired-samples** t-test, a statistically significant difference (i.e., $p < 0.05$) was observed when comparing the students' proficiency scores at the beginning of the course and at the end. Ahmed (2016) proposed various possible reasons for the improvements in listening proficiency, such as having an understanding of the content of the lessons before they started through watching the videos each week, which led to higher quality practice during class time, the use of quizzes to confirm whether or not students had accurately followed the content of the videos, and the collaboration work that was encouraged when students participated in discussions based on parts of the videos that they had not understood clearly. Although this study was conducted with only one group and did not run a comparison with a similar course that was not flipped, the results still show that using flipped learning can be effective for improving students' listening proficiency.

For understandable reasons, a large chunk of studies conducted by university professors and researchers based at universities use participants that are university students; it is not always easy to find other **subjects** for your study. An exception to this can be seen in the study conducted in Cambodia by Roth and Suppasetseree (2016), whose subjects were a little younger (ages 17–20) and were preparing to enter university. Roth and Suppasetseree used a **mixed-design** method for their study, in which they aimed to measure the benefits of flipped learning for students' listening proficiency and get students' opinions regarding its effectiveness. In the listening course, videos were shared with the students via the social networking system, Facebook. The students were able to view the videos at their discretion and post comments based on the contents of the videos.

Once again, the results of the data analyses showed the positive effects of the flipped learning model for students' language learning. First, using paired-samples t-tests to analyze the differences between the students' scores in the pre-test and post-test, a significant increase in listening proficiency was observed ($p = 0.009$) as students' scores increased from around nine to more than 11 (the maximum score was 15). As was mentioned earlier in the commentary of Ahmed's study, although there was not a control group studying the same content but without the flipped factor, which could have given highly reliable support for flipped learning, clear improvements were still observed.

In the second part of Roth and Suppasetseree's (2016) study, students' opinions of flipped learning were sought through **semi-structured interviews**. Overall, the students showed extremely positive views, commenting that it: 1) developed their listening skills, 2) helped them understand the spoken texts in the videos more, and 3) improved their listening comprehension. These three responses in particular appear to show that the students had increased self-confidence in their listening ability as a result of participating in the flipped classroom. The students also mentioned the advantages of the visuals that came with the videos used in the course for understanding differences between confusing vocabulary items: Roth and Suppasetseree give the examples of sleepover and oversleep. Finally, like many studies related to flipped learning, the students felt a higher sense of autonomy in their learning. They had control over where and when they watched the videos, as well as the ability to pause, rewind, and listen again to places that they had misheard or had not understood. The findings of this study provide many hints for teachers, many of which will be covered later in this chapter.

In a particularly interesting study by Mohammad Amiryousefi (2017[14]) in Iran, the listening proficiency of three groups of first-year university students who were studying English conversation was compared based on whether they were studying in a full-flipped classroom, a semi-flipped classroom, or a traditional classroom.

The idea of a semi-flipped classroom was something that especially caught my eye in Amiryousefi's study. The students studying under the semi-flipped classroom were broken into groups of five or six members and required to join a Telegram[15] group. There was also one large Telegram group to which all members of the semi-flipped group belonged. The students were first given a list of resources from which they had to choose audios and videos that interested them. Then, in their smaller Telegram groups, the students discussed which of the materials that each person had chosen was the most interesting before reporting which one they liked the most to the whole-class Telegram group. The entire class then decided which audio or visual material was the most compelling. Next, the students worked with the materials that they had chosen, while giving each other assistance in their small Telegram groups with the content and vocabulary items. This whole process was done under the guidance of the teacher, who provided assistance when necessary. During class time, the teacher was not required to explain or elaborate on the contents of the materials that the students had chosen, rather acted as an observer, only adding advice as needed while the students held discussions and debates. I really liked the idea of the semi-flipped model that Amiryousefi used in this study, as it encourages learner agency; students feel that they have choices to make in the lessons and those choices affect how the classes will be run and their learning as a result.

In Amiryousefi's study, listening proficiency was measured in two ways: a listening test that had been made public by **TOEFL** and an original teacher-made listening test. The listening tests were multiple choice and included items based on both short conversations and long conversations. Although no significant differences were observed among the

---

[14] A vignette for the Amiryousefi (2017) study can also be found in Part III of this book. Also, in Amiryousefi's study, comparisons of speaking proficiency, the amount of time students spent studying outside of the classroom, and students' attitudes towards their English lessons were investigated. A more thorough summary can be found in the vignette.

[15] Telegram is an instant messaging service that was popular in Iran around 2015–2018. Due to censorship and privacy issues, the application was blocked by the government in 2018 (BBC News, 2018).

three groups when the students' listening proficiency was measured using TOEFL ($p = 0.113$), quite a large difference was reported in the teacher-made listening test, with the students studying in the traditional group having much lower scores ($p < 0.05$) than the flipped and semi-flipped groups. There did not appear to be any significant difference between the flipped group and the semi-flipped group. A similar result was seen when students gave their opinions about how they felt flipped learning being used in their group affected their listening skills. Those in the flipped and semi-flipped groups gave very positive feedback (4.21 and 4.07 respectively [max: 5]), which were significantly higher than what was reported by the students in the traditional group (3.24). In line with Ahmed's (2016) and Roth and Suppasetseree's (2016) studies, we see here salient improvements in the listening skills of students studying under the flipped learning model.

The studies summarized above make it clear, once again, that flipped learning has the potential to be beneficial for students' learning, this time from the perspective of listening skills. There is a lot to learn from these studies, including what we could be doing in our flipped courses to benefit our students' learning and what we should perhaps be avoiding. Based on the topics covered in these studies, let's now have a look at a few ideas for teaching.

Pedagogical implications for listening

The first point I would like to make related to conducting a flipped classroom based on improving listening skills is not really based on the research we have discussed in this chapter, rather a point from me. At the beginning of this chapter, I talked about the importance of building students' **schemata** as a vital part of improving their listening skills; if you don't know much about the topic, you are going to have trouble comprehending what is being said, regardless of the language. Unfortunately, we have not really seen this considered in the research reviewed in this chapter. The same point could certainly be made about reading; it is also a language skill based on input. I think that covering a wide range of topics in our classes, especially those in which we are focusing on listening and reading, will contribute to not only improving students' language skills, but also their general knowledge about the world. This was something that I kept in mind when preparing the Ultimate Listening dictogloss[16] textbooks (Leis & Cooke, 2019a, 2019b), in which a wide range of topics from cows to bubble wrap to the *katakuri*[17] and Pluto is covered. Introducing your students to a variety of topics will help not only build their

---

[16] Although not directly related to flipped learning, the dictogloss technique, developed by Ruth Wajnryb (1990) is an excellent way to develop students' language skills. I mainly use it in my classes centered on listening and speaking skills, but as the original name of the technique—grammar dictation—suggests, it can also be used to help students with the grammatical accuracy of their language.

immediate language skills but also provide them with a wide range of knowledge required to participate more enthusiastically in future interactions.

Many students tend to feel that having advanced listening skills is an innate skill and there is not much that they can do to improve them. Indeed, researchers are still at a loss regarding how much an impact language aptitude—"the specific talent for learning foreign languages that exhibits considerable variation between learners" (Dörnyei & Skehan, 2003, p. 590)—has on students' listening proficiency. Studies are inconclusive, but the majority of research suggests weak to no **correlation** between language aptitude and L2 listening ability (e.g., Duman *et al.*, 2021; Li, 2016, 2019; Ranta, 2002; Sáfár & Kormos, 2008). Therefore, we can assure our students that advanced listening proficiency is not a birth-given gift, but a result of extensive practice, adoption of diverse strategies, and reflection on the success of those strategies (Rubin *et al.*, 2007). Passing on strategies in pre-class videos may be one of the keys to successful flipped listening classrooms.

We saw in the Ahmed (2016) study that the teacher explained various strategies to help students improve their listening skills. Introducing and sharing skills, either from your own experience as a L2 learner (presuming the teacher has studied a second language, whether that be English or another language) or based on strategies, has been proven effective in research. Language learning strategies are broken down into three mechanisms: cognitive strategies, **metacognitive strategies**, and socio-affective strategies (Lapkin & Swain, 2001; O'Malley & Chamot, 1990).

Cognitive strategies refer to what humans do when taking on a challenge and try to make it easier (Derry & Murphy, 1986; Serri *et al.*, 2012). Remembering the concepts of bottom-up and top-down listening processes, in listening comprehension classes, teachers might encourage students to take preparation notes of their background knowledge of listening topics (i.e., schemata), predictions of the content of the stories and discussions they will be hearing, and predictions of what English words they will hear. Dictogloss, which was touched upon a little earlier, is an especially effective technique for building students' listening skills as it trains the bottom-up and **top-down** processes (Cooke & Leis, 2018; Elahifar *et al.*, 2022) and presents opportunities for the teacher to develop students' cognitive strategies through the pre-class videos.

When using metacognitive strategies, students think deeply about their learning processes, considering what has been effective for them in their learning and what has not. Based on past listening comprehension experiences, students may choose to use metacognitive strategies such as

---

[17] The *katakuri* is a small flower that blooms in spring in some Asian countries.

"advance organization, selective attention, monitoring, problem identification, and self-evaluation" (Vandergrift, 2003, p. 466). In the flipped listening classroom, students can be encouraged to use these stratgies in the pre-class videos, as teachers have them reflect on previous listening comprehension classes, thinking about how to further develop their strengths and combat their weaknesses. If teachers share the topics of the listening comprehension tasks and some questions that will be asked in those tasks in the pre-class videos, students will be able to prepare their strategies more concretely.

Finally, socio/affective strategies encourage just what you would imagine from the name: increased interaction with others in the class and techniques to lower the anxiety of students as they prepare for the listening comprehension tasks (Vandergrift, 2003). In addition to regular strategies for lowering anxiety and increasing enjoyment (e.g., interesting topics, careful use of praise), discussions among students about ideas prepared before class for the listening tasks and checking answers with other group members can help create a more relaxed atmosphere for learning during face-to-face sessions.

Whilst the use of strategies has been shown as effective for improving students' listening performances (e.g., Movahed, 2014), at the same time over-teaching strategies may cause confusion for students and "distract listeners from the actual linguistic input itself" (Wang & MacIntyre, 2021, p. 508). Thus, introducing and encouraging the use of strategies can be effective, but teachers need to tread lightly as they bring these ideas into the flipped classrooms. For comprehensive discussions of strategies in language learning, see Cohen and Macaro (2007), Vandergrift (2003), and Gavriilidou and Mitits (2021). Figure 2.4 summarizes the above suggestions for planning your flipped listening classroom.

Another point to consider in flipped classrooms, which has already been discussed in this book but is especially valid for listening comprehension classes, is whether or not teachers include closed captions in their videos. Because students are able to watch, re-watch, pause, fast-forward, and rewind the videos used in flipped classrooms at their discretion, I imagine most teachers will use English as the language in their videoed explanations. Thus, closed captions can act as effective scaffolding for students as teachers create all-English environments for learning.

Research supports the use of closed captions in videos (see, for example, Vanderplank, 2016): They increase the chance of **incidental learning** as students are given opportunities to pick up language that is not necessarily being focused upon in that lesson (Van Lommel *et al.*, 2006) and lower students' anxiety levels (Leis, 2016). Therefore, I strongly suggest that teachers add closed captions to their videos—as time-consuming it may be—to **scaffold** the students in their learning. Furthermore, wherever possible, I suggest using the closed captions options seen in many video-sharing websites that enable the students to turn the cap-

Figure 2.4 *Summary of the pedagogical implications for flipping a listening class*

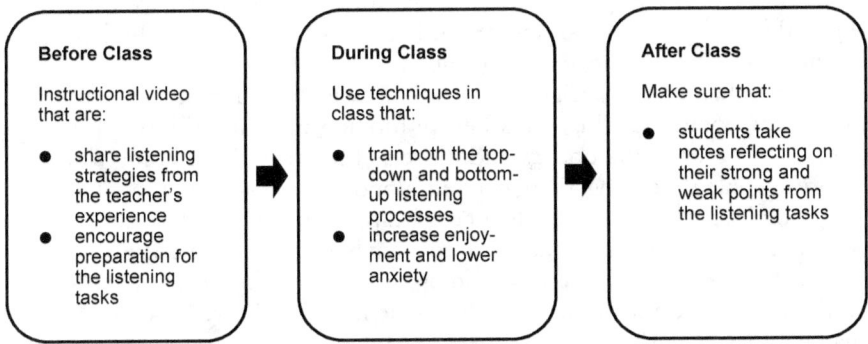

tions on when they are having trouble hearing difficult words and phrases and off if they so wish. Like many aspects of flipped learning, opening a range of options for students to choose from, as seen through strategies for listening and closed-caption options, create a higher sense of agency in their learning experiences.

Reading

Have you ever seen the film *You Got Mail*? It's a 1998 romantic comedy movie starring Meg Ryan and Tom Hanks, and in it, the characters were using the latest technology (at that time, of course) to e-mail each other. It's a fun movie: probably not in my top 10 all-time favorites, but the storyline is cute, and the old buzzing and whirring sounds that the computer makes as the characters log on to the Internet bring back many memories. Anyway, in one part of the movie, Meg Ryan's character, Kathleen Kelly, reads a picture book to some children who are visiting her store. The children's shining eyes tell you that they are immersed in the story and enjoying it a lot. This scene always reminds me of when my sixth-grade teacher, Ms. Omar, would read stories to us both for enjoyment and to learn various parts of the English language. One memory that really sticks out from then was when Ms. Omar was pointing out examples of similes while reading Roald Dahl's *The BFG* and started laughing so much she had to ask one of the students to read it for her.

I mention these two situations—reading stories in *You Got Mail* and my primary school teacher reading books to us—because I find that this scene of a group of children or students sitting down and enjoying a story with the adult who is reading it seems to be disappearing from our society. Adults are overworked and tend to have too little time to spend quality moments with their children. In the same way, many of us don't seem to have the time or energy to curl up on the sofa and indulge ourselves in a good novel. Children and adolescents (and adults, too) appear to have lost appreciation for books, preferring just to watch television or short clips on video-sharing websites. I really hope, as educators, we can bring back this enjoyment of sitting around and reading a book, whether it be alone, with a loved one, or in a group.

In this chapter, we are going to look at what SLA research has told us about improving reading skills before moving into how flipped learning can help our students understand more as they read. I am going to focus more on silent reading than reading aloud, as we saw in the situations described above and the influence of flipped learning on reading comprehension; as we understand more of what we read, we are going to enjoy it more. When we enjoy reading more, it's going to be much easier for us to pick up a book instead of reaching for the remote control or game console. Let's begin.

Reading research in SLA

Many principles surrounding L2 reading are similar to listening: bottom-up processing, top-down processing, schema. I've already covered those in the listening chapter, so I would like to focus on two main approaches related to reading in SLA: intensive reading and extensive reading. Intensive reading describes how students read somewhat short texts to analyze the grammar and vocabulary within in addition to understanding the content (Horwitz, 2020). Extensive reading, which seems to have captured a great deal more interest among SLA researchers in recent years, is more closely related to the idea that students learn language best through input; students should read as much as possible to "achieve a *general* understanding of longer texts" (Horwitz, 2020, p. 136). As you might well imagine, research involving intensive reading and extensive reading differ somewhat, so at the risk of going into too much detail, I am going to break this brief synopsis of reading research into intensive reading and extensive reading.

Intensive reading

In a typical EFL classroom environment, instruction through intensive reading is most likely the way that teachers will rely on to develop students' skills. Students will often be given short texts, such as magazine articles, short stories, or business reports to analyze for meaning. Two keywords that often appear in intensive reading instruction are *skimming* and *scanning*. Skimming refers to the action of quickly looking over a written text to get an overall understanding of the gist of the content. The reader will scan the text when looking for specific information (e.g., the answer to a question on a reading test or the amount of sugar you need in a recipe). Other strategies for reading comprehension include previewing, predicting, inferring, and guessing the meanings of words based on the surrounding discourse (Nunan, 1999).

Research related to comprehension in intensive reading and reading pedagogy has been conducted from a number of perspectives, such as strategy instruction (e.g., Gilakjani & Sabouri, 2016; Lopera Medina, 2012; Song, 1998), mental imagery while reading (e.g., Praveen & Rajan, 2013; Ushiro *et al.*, 2018), implementation of specific techniques (e.g., jigsaw technique) (Esnawy, 2016; Namaziandost *et al.*, 2020), and through the use of eye-tracking technology (Ushiro *et al.*, 2019).

Extensive reading

Without a doubt, research related to extensive reading has grown over the past 20 years, especially after the publication of Bamford and Day's (2004) book, *Extensive reading activities for teaching language*. Since then, there has been a growing number of teachers who have applied extensive reading to their classes, as well as an ever-developing library of graded readers, which allow students to partake in extensive reading at a level that suits their language proficiency.

Extensive reading has been shown as effective for improving students' language skills in various areas, such as grammatical accuracy (Lee *et al.*, 2015), writing proficiency (Azizi *et al.*, 2020; Mermelstein, 2015), and students' attitudes towards reading in general (Birketveit *et al.*, 2018). For more on extensive reading, see, for example, Nation and Waring (2019), Day and Bamford (2002), and Renandya *et al.* (2021).

How many words do we need to know?

Another critical area we think about when it comes to reading comprehension is the relationship between the extent of our vocabulary banks (i.e., the number of words we know) and how much of the text we are reading we are able to comprehend. The majority of research suggests that if we understand between 95% (e.g., Laufer, 1989) and 98% (Hu & Nation, 2000; Nation, 2006; Schmitt *et al.*, 2011) of a piece of writing, we will be able to understand what we are reading without having to consult our dictionaries.

There are also studies discussing the actual number of words and phrases readers need to know to comprehend a written text confidently. These figures, of course, change depending on the difficulty of the text and the content (i.e., whether it is a novel, a research paper, or an instruction manual for a new phone). For example, Nation (2006) suggested that knowing between 8000 and 9000 words and word families would enable the learner to read and understand just about any text without encountering many problems. Based on scores in reading comprehension tests correlated with scores in vocabulary tests, Laufer (1992), on the other hand, suggested that the more words students understand, the higher scores they will get in the reading tests, but that the reading comprehension scores leveled out at a vocabulary bank of 7000.

Several techniques to improve students' vocabulary understanding and production have been investigated in SLA, such as L1 translations through flashcards (either analogue or digital) (e.g., Ashcroft *et al.*, 2018; Elgort, 2010; Nation & Webb, 2011), using dictionaries[18] (e.g., Rezaei & Davoudi, 2016; Zou, 2016), and, in more recent years, through gamification (e.g., Chen *et al.*, 2019; Waluyo & Bucol, 2021).

For more on developing EFL reading skills, see, for example, Dixon (2016), Hudson (2007), and Watkins (2017).

Previous research of flipped learning and reading

Because reading is a relatively passive skill[19] (e.g., Nunan, 2015), it may seem more reasonable for students to do the reading in their own time and at their own pace, rather than in the classroom with interruptions from the teachers and interactions with other students. Therefore, you might be thinking that of the four language skills (well, five, if we want to include grammar instruction) we teach in the classroom, reading will probably work the least effectively. If you have been thinking this, then you are not alone. There has not been a lot of research done on reading in the flipped classroom. But perhaps there should be a lot more, because "many students get frustrated when reading alone because they either read too slowly, cannot comprehend what they are reading, or lose interest in the text" (Mehring, 2016, p. 7). From the studies that have been conducted to date, there is a lot to learn.

One area in which flipped learning may especially suit reading instruction is in the teaching of academic reading. Research articles, for example, often contain a lot of specific terminologies and jargon. Therefore, having understanding of these is essential to getting through scholarly papers without becoming stuck every few sentences. Brown (2018) recognized the difficulty students might face with academic reading, therefore flipped her Academic Reading Across the Disciplines course with her second-year university students in Japan. The students in the course had relatively high English proficiency (i.e., B2/C1 on the **CEFR** Scale) and had completed an introductory course to English for academic purposes. In the course described by Brown, the goals included further improvement of students' academic reading skills, learning to self-assess progress, and improving their academic learning skills through collaboration and discussion.

In Brown's (2018) study, the teachers of the academic reading course

---

[18] The effects of using dictionaries for vocabulary acquisition have, in fact, quite mixed results, with some studies suggesting using a dictionary is ineffective (e.g., Chan, 2011; Koyama & Takeuchi, 2004).

[19] I use the word passive here rather loosely. Reading can be very cognitively demanding, so even though students may not appear to be active in the sense that they are in speaking and writing, they are going through various thought processes as they recognize words on the page, think about their meanings, and interpret the writer's message, making it "an active—even interactive—process" (Thornbury, 2017, p. 238).

combined the flipped learning approach with a group leader discussion activity (GLDA). Students were required to act as group leaders twice throughout the course, providing them with opportunities to practice reading skills and demonstrate their mastery of what had been covered in the course. The GLDA worked together with flipped learning using 1) pre-class videos and preparation activities and 2) feedback, discussions, and evaluation activities conducted during the face-to-face sessions. By flipping the class with GLDA, all students, not just the weekly leaders, needed to "engage fully with the material and key concepts prior to the lessons, which necessitates them taking responsibility for managing their learning themselves" (Brown, 2018, p. 154).

The pre-class activities in Brown's course included videos related to the content of the following lesson, strategies for discussion leadership, academic reading and writing strategies (students were required to write summaries of lesson content), and worksheets. Weekly leaders were also required to create handouts for their group discussions, which included written summaries of the weekly topic, information related to that topic showing the student had gone beyond the textbook and videos given to them (e.g., other related research papers), comprehension questions, and critical thinking questions for discussion.

During the face-to-face class sessions, the teacher acted as an observer while students led discussions in their groups for around half of the designated lesson time. The group discussions included time for perusing the handouts made by the group leader, brief explanations of materials that the leaders had found, and interaction among the group members related to the content of the materials. The remainder of the class time was spent on peer and self-evaluation in addition to other student-focused activities related to the course content.

Brown's (2018) study gives an excellent guide to running a reading course with a flipped learning aspect. The pre-class videos assisted students in understanding the content of the course better—"It was very helpful (to) me to understand such a difficult reading with so many special terms" (Brown, 2018, p. 158)—which also allowed more in-depth discussions during the face-to-face class sessions. Some negative feedback was received from participants in the course, but these were mainly directed at the lack of preparation of group leaders than the flipped learning component of the course. Although Brown's study was based on teaching academic reading, the ideas of summarizing the content of the readings and passing on reading strategies, tips for discussion leadership, and suggestions for summary writing through the pre-class videos could be transferred to other reading genres. Now that we have looked at an example of intensive reading, how about extensive reading?

Flipping an extensive reading course might seem complicated, and rightly so. In many courses that focus on extensive reading, students often work at their own pace and read different books depending on their language proficiency. This is especially true for courses that use graded readers (i.e., books that range in difficulty from beginner to advanced, depending on the level of vocabulary, the complexity of language within, and the number of words in the book); how can teachers create videos for students to watch before class when they are all going to be reading different books?

Zhan (2019) identified two major problems with traditional approaches to courses focusing on extensive reading. First, similar to what was mentioned above, it is challenging to meet the needs of all of the students in classes of large numbers. Second, the limited time that teachers have with students in class is not satisfactory to establish a solid foundation for developing reading proficiency. Zhan (2019) suggests the flipped learning model as ideal for overcoming these problems, as it is easier for teachers to provide students with various materials that match the students' individual levels, and students can study in their own time at their own pace. Second, the pre-class videos allow teachers to have a running start to face-to-face sessions; students are not coming to the class with zero knowledge about what is going to be covered during the lesson. The pre-class videos act as "information transfer" while the face-to-face sessions provide opportunity for "absorption internalization" (Zhan, 2019, p. 52). Third, the teacher can easily pass on reading strategies to students. These strategies can be related not only to strategies to understand the content, but also to give evaluations of the content and encourage more critical reading.

The amount of research related to flipped learning in an extensive reading course is very minimal. Still, from the ones that have been published, we can get some hints about how to flip our own extensive reading courses and conduct research to measure the success of what we do. Although to my knowledge there are no studies to date, the flipped mastery model (Johnson, 2018) appears to suit extensive reading perfectly. I encourage researchers and language instructors using extensive reading to consider the flipped mastery model for their classrooms.

One example of flipping an extensive reading class was conducted with university students in Indonesia (Yuvita *et al.*, 2022). The teacher made a number of videos—both self-made and found on the Internet—available for students that were related to the books students used for extensive reading. During the in-class sessions[20], the teacher checked the students' understanding of the story, and the students summarized the story in discussion groups. Although at the beginning of the course the teacher chose which story students should read and review, as the course progressed and students became used to reading and reviewing the books, students decided the books they wanted to read, and discussions were

---

[20] It should be noted here that although the authors described the "in-class session" in their study, these were not held face-to-face in-person, but conducted online due to the Covid-19 Pandemic.

held in groups of students choosing that same book. The groups of students also were required to present summaries of the stories and their discussions in front of the class. The course, therefore, was run over four-week cycles per book read, with the students 1) individually retelling the stories they had read in front of class members, 2) reviewing the movie version of the book they had read followed by writing a movie review, 3) discussing and comparing the movie and book versions of the stories in groups, and 4) summarizing their groups' ideas and opinions of the movie and book versions of the stories in front of the class. The videos that the teacher had prepared for students included example summaries and hints for discussion to assist students throughout the program.

In Yuvita *et al.*'s (2022) study, a comparison was run between the students studying in the flipped extensive reading class and a non-flipped class. The non-flipped control group did not receive any pre-class video materials, and the in-class sessions were conducted in a regular online way. The students were given reading tests before and after the course in a pre-test-post-test design, with the results indicating the students in the flipped-learning group had significantly ($p = 0.035$) higher scores at the end of the course than the students in the non-flipped class. Higher student-student engagement and more opportunities for students to be active in their learning with the flipped-learning model were discussed as reasons for its success in this study.

Other examples showing how flipped learning was effective for improving reading proficiency were reported by, for example, Karimi and Hamzavi (2017), who distributed one-hour-long videos of full lessons for students to watch before class. During the face-to-face sessions, the students took part in reflection activities, discussions, and practice based on the content of what they had learned before each class. The same lesson content was given directly to students in the control group that had been viewed in the videos by students in the flipped learning group. The researchers reported significant improvements for the students in the flipped learning group as well as, despite the pre-class videos being so long, positive attitudes towards this way of learning among the students. Abaeian and Samadi (2016) concluded that regardless of the proficiency levels of the students (i.e., intermediate or upper-intermediate), flipped learning was beneficial for students' reading proficiency. Finally, Rachmat *et al.* (2021) also provide an interesting discussion of their class, in which pre-class videos giving suggestions for various reading strategies were sent to students' smartphones via social media.

The third area related to reading in SLA research that we looked at earlier was vocabulary acquisition. Again, there has not been a huge amount of research sharing ideas pertaining to vocabulary teaching via flipped learning. Still, we can undoubtedly get hints for our teaching and further research from what is out there. The two studies I'm going to introduce successfully used flipped learning to help students strengthen their vocabulary banks, one with university undergraduates in Serbia, the other with high school students in Türkiye.

First, Knežević and her colleagues (2020) implemented flipped learning to improve their students' understanding of academic vocabulary. As is often the case for first-year university students (Carkin, 2005), the students in Knežević et al.'s (2020) study lacked the required knowledge of academic vocabulary that is needed at college. The students studying in the flipped classroom were provided with two online resources as part of their pre-class activities, an LMS on which the teacher uploaded words lists and definitions, and a learning laboratory website, which instructed students on the form, meaning, spelling, and collocational use of the target vocabulary items. The website included gamification aspects, with various activities, games, and quizzes to check students' understanding. Two days before the face-to-face sessions, students were required to rate the vocabulary items according to how well they had understood them before the lists and online materials had been distributed. If students indicated any confusion regarding the target items, teachers gave supplementary explanations via the LMS. The face-to-face sessions were focused on discussions, practice, group work, collaborative activities to encourage creative use of the target items, and critical thinking. The control group (i.e., non-flipped group) simply received printed copies of the word lists before the face-to-face sessions. Class time included similar activities to what was conducted in the flipped learning group, but with less time devoted to collaborative study.

A post-test comparing the performance of two groups of students revealed that those in the flipped learning environment had significantly higher scores ($p = 0.005$) despite their pre-test scores being almost identical. Furthermore, the results suggested that studying the vocabulary items was less cognitively demanding for the flipped learning students than for the non-flipped students, meaning that flipped learning used the students' time more efficiently. Like Stockwell (2013), Knežević et al. (2020) especially credited the use of technology as a stimulant for students' **intrinsic motivation** as they enjoyed the gamification aspect of learning vocabulary outside of class and the increased amount of interaction among students during the face-to-face class sessions in comparison with a traditional method of teaching.

Second, Kırmızı and Kömeç (2019) noted lack of classroom time and low motivation to study autonomously as reasons for the insufficient lexical knowledge among Turkish high school students. To counterattack this, they employed flipped learning to introduce vocabulary to students and encourage them to take responsibility for their learning. The students in the flipped learning group were required to watch videos that gave definitions of weekly vocabulary lists along with visual representations and example sentences to show how each word would be used in a natural context. The videos also gave explicit instruction on the pronuncia-

Part II: Flipped Learning in SLA

tions of the words. During the face-to-face classroom sessions, the students played games to allow the teacher to check students' understanding of the vocabulary items before the students did practice exercises in groups (including **cloze tests** and picture stories) while the teacher monitored students' progress and helped when needed. Finally, students were given quizzes to assess how much they had fully understood the target vocabulary items for that week. The control group received the same instruction as the flipped learning group, but during the face-to-face sessions. The practice exercises were done individually after class as homework.

To measure the success of flipped learning, Kırmızı and Kömeç (2019) conducted four quizzes throughout the course, analyzing the results of the students in the flipped learning group in comparison to those in the control group. Although there were no significant differences reported in the first quiz ($p > 0.05$), the flipped learning group did significantly better ($p < 0.05$) in both productive vocabulary (i.e., being able to demonstrate the ability to use the vocabulary items accurately and in appropriate ways) and receptive vocabulary (i.e., being able to understand the meanings of the vocabulary). The students in the flipped learning group were also given open-ended questionnaires to gain insights into students' attitudes toward this new way of learning. The reactions from the students were very positive, with around one-third noting that flipped learning allowed them to learn at their own pace: "I can watch the videos over and over" and "I can pause the videos if I need a break" (Kırmızı & Kömeç, 2019, p. 444). Students' intrinsic motivation also appeared to have been strengthened, as was seen in comments such as, "Now, we have more time for more enjoyable activities in class" (Kırmızı & Kömeç, 2019, p. 444). It should be noted, however, that some students ($n = 7$; 28%) commented that a negative point of flipped learning was not being able to ask questions to the teacher immediately.

As we have seen with all the studies covered in this book, once again, flipped learning appears to triumph when it comes to teaching L2 reading skills. This is true for intensive reading, extensive reading, and vocabulary acquisition. Based on the findings and discussions of the results, we can now create an image of how we might conduct a flipped reading lesson with similar success to what has been reported above.

Pedagogical implications for reading

As has been a common theme throughout this book, the pre-class videos, materials, and activities have a massive influence on the setup of the in-class reading sessions. Based on what we have seen in the studies summarized above, for successful flipped reading learning, pre-class videos explaining and giving examples of strategies for reading the text and discussions that will be held during the class based on the content of the

Figure 2.5 *Summary of the pedagogical implications for flipping a reading class*

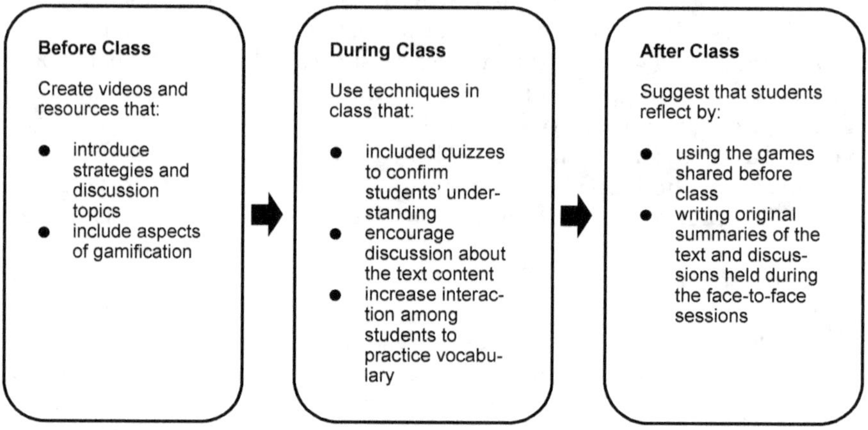

Before Class

Create videos and resources that:

- introduce strategies and discussion topics
- include aspects of gamification

During Class

Use techniques in class that:

- included quizzes to confirm students' understanding
- encourage discussion about the text content
- increase interaction among students to practice vocabulary

After Class

Suggest that students reflect by:

- using the games shared before class
- writing original summaries of the text and discussions held during the face-to-face sessions

readings are essential. In Brown's (2018) study, the students made mention of the lack of preparation by some students in the course. It may be beneficial to have students submit worksheets earlier (e.g., one week before class) to ensure students are fully prepared both as discussion leaders and participants.

Regardless of the type of reading that is being focused on in class, whether it be academic reading, extensive reading, or intensive reading for a deep understanding of the content, the strength of one's vocabulary is going to have a major influence on comprehension and reading fluency. Helping students learn vocabulary through videos made by the instructor appears to be effective, but risks being boring for students. With an abundance of smartphone applications and computer programs now available that use games to increase the enjoyment of studying vocabulary, teachers could consider making gamification part of the pre-class materials for studying vocabulary in fun ways.

As with other language skills, a simple quiz at the beginning of the face-to-face sessions helps teachers assess any difficulties students may have had with the pre-class materials and address any noticeable problems either through explicit instruction or guidance throughout the lesson. Groupwork that includes discussions based on topics arising in the reading passages and practice exercises of using the target vocabulary items again bring the focus onto the students rather the teacher: one of the main objectives of the flipped learning model.

Finally, as part of post-class activities, students could be encouraged to continue reviewing the vocabulary learned in the class. With repeated practice and rehearsal being seen as essential for retention of the vocabulary items (Ellis, 1996; Schuetze & Weimer-Stuckmann, 2011), what students do after the flipped class might be the most important for reading of all the language skills. This is another reason why I believe the introduction of the gamification aspect is crucial in this area; students can play the games anywhere and at any time that they like and the games are fun!

As we saw in Brown's (2018) study, linking reading and writing can be an effective activity to have students do after the class. By writing summaries of the text students had read and including opinions shared through the discussions held in the face-to-face sessions, teachers will be able to measure students' understanding of the content of the lesson, and the students themselves will be able to visualize their progress throughout the course.

Figure 2.5 summarizes the main points to keep in mind when flipping your reading class.

Grammar

Even though I first had the dream of becoming a teacher when I was in grade two of elementary school, there were days in high school when I thought about becoming a chef. I was accepted to a cooking school, where I was planning to study culinary skills for 12 months and then look for an apprenticeship at a restaurant. The plans were looking great until I told my parents, who were completely against the idea. It was only a few days after my parents expressed their objections to my studying at cooking school quite sharply that I was accepted to the Japanese language department at Griffith University. Thus, my life changed, and here we are today.

Even though I didn't take on a career as a chef, I have always been, and still am, interested in cooking and when the opportunity arises, you might find me in the kitchen at home or perhaps grilling a few steaks on the barbecue. One thing I should mention here very clearly is that there is a difference between enjoying cooking and being good at it. As much as I love whipping up a meal, I am guilty of not always exactly following the instructions in the recipe book. Although being creative may work for the experts, for a beginner like me, the results can be disastrous: like the time I forgot to put yeast in the pizza dough, resulting in what could be described as cooked glue. If I read and followed the recipes correctly, my dishes would be much more delicious. I think the same could be said about studying grammar when learning a second language. When we reach an expert level, it is okay to be creative and play around with sentences patterns; we see a lot of this in song lyrics, for example. However, when we are still at the learning stages of language, it is often best to stick with the recipe and follow the grammatical rules.

For many language students, grammar is probably the least enjoyable part of studying. In fact, having to study grammar has been named as one of the major factors in language learning **demotivation** (Kikuchi & Sakai, 2009). But, and it goes without saying, speaking and writing with grammatical accuracy is a vital aspect of language learning. The meaning one is trying to convey can completely change if incorrect grammar is used. Not only that, and I say the same thing to my students about pronunciation, it can gain you a lot more respect[21]. Even if you speak your chosen foreign language with some slight errors in pronunciation or grammar, the other people with whom you are communicating are still likely to understand. This is especially true in verbal communication, where meaning can be clarified. But I think that being articulate and using the correct grammar are vital for gaining just a little more respect from those you are communicating with. In this chapter, we are going to take a look at focusing on form and focusing on forms—the teaching of grammar—and how flipped learning has played a role in this vital area of language education.

Grammar instruction: Research in SLA

When talking about grammar instruction, two common terms that almost always arise are focus on forms and focus on form. Focus on forms (with the "s") refers to the teaching of grammatical structures. Teachers choose the grammar points that they want to teach in their courses or they are laid out neatly in order in a textbook. These grammar points are then taught explicitly as individual structures. Focus on forms is often seen as the traditional way of teaching language. On the other hand, with focus on form (without the "s") the fundamental target is meaning[22]. The students are learning the meaning of what is being spoken and written rather than the underlying grammatical rules. Language instruction through focus on form is often taught through **focused tasks** in task-based language teaching or **incidental learning** (e.g., **unfocused tasks** and discussions) in which students are using the language to convey meaning rather than analyze the structure. For more on the distinctions between focus on forms and focus on form, see Long (1988, 1991) and recent discussion by Ellis (2016).

There has been much debate over the effectiveness of grammar instruction in language learning. The grammar-translation method, which was popular for centuries, made full use of the students' L1 to translate text (both spoken and written text) and analyze the structures of the target language. Despite more communicative methods proving to be effective for students' learning (e.g., the direct method), the grammar-translation method has remained popular because "it requires few specialized skills on the part of teachers" (Brown & Lee, 2015, p. 18). Some

---

[21] As I mentioned in the chapter on speaking, I am not meaning here to speak like a native speaker. I encourage speakers to be articulate when using the L2. If that means they have a slight accent or their speech is affected by their L1, that's fine. As long as what they are saying is clear.

[22] There is also the concept of focus-on-meaning, which, as the name suggests, still puts the focus on the meaning of what is said or what is written, but without attention given to the linguistic features within the discourse (Doughty & Williams, 1998).

studies suggest that the explicit instruction of grammar and metalinguistic explanations do indeed bring some benefits to the language learning process (e.g., DeKeyser, 2007; Sato, 2009, 2010; Sheen, R., 2002, 2005; Sheen, Y., 2007; Shintani *et al.*, 2014; Suzuki *et al.*, 2019). Other studies campaign for more implicit instruction of grammar, preferring the focus to be on communication (e.g., Ellis, 2002; Ellis *et al.*, 2002; Fotos, 1998; Shintani, 2015). Then, there is research that suggests there is no difference, and students' success in language learning is not necessarily due to whether grammar is taught explicitly or implicitly, but various other factors, such as language aptitude, age, and motivation (e.g., Graus & Coppen, 2016; Norris & Ortega, 2000).

Research and debates related to the teaching of grammar in the language continue to this day and a clear-cut conclusion is yet to be reached. Thus, the correct question to ask might be not, "Which way is better?" but "Which way is more effective for what kind of student and under what kinds of circumstances?" I touch on focus on form in the next chapter where we briefly look at task-based language teaching, so for now, we are just going to concentrate on explicit grammar teaching (i.e., focus on forms) and how flipped learning might help make your grammar classes just a little more attractive for your students.

Previous research of flipped learning and grammar instruction

It makes sense that flipped learning is used for explicit grammar instruction. Although teaching grammar and teaching mathematical equations are different fields, they do hold some similarities in having formula or sentence structures in which learners can place and replace numbers and, in the case of English, words. As was mentioned in the early stages of this book, mathematics teachers were some of the first ones to get on board with the idea of flipped learning (e.g., Strayer, 2007), and it has been used effectively in that field since (e.g., Strayer *et al.* 2015; Sun & Xie, 2020). The amount of research using the flipped classroom as a means to teach grammar is certainly increasing as teachers recognize that explicit instruction of the grammatical equations can be conducted outside the classroom, leaving face-to-face sessions for practice and communicative tasks.

Recognizing the benefits, the flipped learning model could possibly bring to language students' grammatical accuracy, one of the earliest studies in this area was conducted by Webb and Dorman (2016), which involved a total of 64 university students studying in EFL contexts (Macau, China) and ESL contexts (the United States). The study aimed to investigate the effects of a flipped grammar class on students' grammatical accuracy (measured through both a grammar test and students' self-evaluations of their grammar skills). Although the students were in EFL and ESL contexts, this was not a comparison of these two learning environments, rather an observation to see if flipped learning would be favorable for students' grammar skills or if the traditional classroom would bring about similar or better results. Thus, the students were divided into four groups: one group from each learning context acting as the control group (i.e., traditional learning; $n = 25$) and one group from each context acting as the experiment group (i.e., flipped learning; $n = 39$).

Although the students in Webb and Dorman's (2016) study were estimated to have high-intermediate English skills, the instructors recognized that the students made numerous grammatical errors[23] in their academic writing classes. Thus, the teachers agreed that there was a need for explicit grammar instruction to improve the quality of students' writing skills. Students in the experiment group received explicit grammar instruction via video lessons and follow-up online quizzes. The students in the control group received the same explicit grammar instruction via mini-lectures and quizzes both conducted during class time. To run the comparison between the two groups, grammar tests and surveys with items related to students' self-confidence and knowledge of English grammar were conducted in Weeks 2 and 14 of the pre-test-post-test designed study.

The results of the study showed that the flipped group made significantly greater improvements in grammatical accuracy throughout the course in comparison to the control group ($p = 0.012$; $\eta^2 = 0.10$). Analyses of the students' self-confidence in their grammar knowledge and skills revealed that both groups were significantly more confident ($p < 0.01$) at the end of the course, suggesting that explicit grammar instruction, whether taught in a flipped context or not, might be helpful in strengthening students' self-confidence. Overall, the findings of the study support the idea of flipping a grammar class.

Al-Harbi and Alshumaimeri (2016) conducted a similar study to Webb and Dorman (2016), by investigating the improvements of the grammatical accuracy of students in a flipped classroom compared to a traditional classroom, but with 43 high school students (ages 16–17) in Saudi Arabia. Al-Harbi and Alshumaimeri realized that because the EFL environment gave few opportunities for students to experience English outside of the classroom and they were taught English in the traditional grammar-translation method, Saudi high school students were often very passive in their language learning and anxious to speak due to concerns about grammatical accuracy. With grammar being taught separately from communication classes (Assalahi, 2013), it results in students knowing about the language, but unable to use it correctly and confidently in real communication (Al-Hamlan & Baniabdelrahman, 2015).

Like a regular flipped learning structure, in this **quasi-experimental**

---

[23] Although the difference between "mistake" and "error" is often considered in research related to grammatical accuracy and corrective feedback, I am not going to dwell on the distinction here. That is a topic for another day.

study, students in the experiment group ($n = 20$) were required to watch videos explaining each grammar point, which were distributed via the educational networking system Edmodo. When students joined the face-to-face sessions, the teachers began with discussions about the content of the videos to judge whether they had understood the main points or not. After this, students participated in collaborative activities and games, as well as group work which gave opportunities for peer correction. The control group ($n = 23$) received the same explanations of the grammar structures, but in a traditional manner. Classes were run in a present-practice-produce (**PPP**) style, with students passively listening to the teacher clarify the main points of the grammar structures, before moving onto group work. However, because the 45-minute lessons did not allow enough time to complete the group work activities (due to the amount of time spent on grammar explanations), students were usually required to complete these activities after class as part of their homework.

The students' knowledge of grammar was measured through a pretest and posttest to justify whether or not flipped learning was effective. At the end of the seven-week period, although a clear trend for the experiment group making improvements in their grammatical knowledge was observed, there was not a statistically significant difference ($p = 0.285$). Al-Harbi and Alshumaimeri (2016) also used a questionnaire (Johnson & Renner, 2012) and **semi-structured interviews** with students in the experiment group to gain some understanding of their opinions towards flipped learning. Although the students generally had positive views of flipped learning, they did express dissatisfaction with what they saw as having to do extra homework outside of the classroom.

When reading this study, I feel that the results may have been different if two small adjustments had been made. First, if it had been conducted for a little longer, a significant difference may have reported. Studies have shown that at least one university semester (i.e., three months) is the minimum period of time needed before we can expect any salient changes (e.g., Freed, 1990; Sasaki, 2011). Second, although a discussion was held at the beginning of the face-to-face sessions with the students in the experiment group, students may still have been hesitant to share their misunderstandings. If the teachers had used an online quiz—and there are plenty out there now that give immediate feedback to the teacher about students' strengths and weaknesses in the quizzes—they might have been able to narrow in their comments and guidance to the students during the group work to those weaker points. Using a quiz at the beginning of face-to-face sessions to grasp students' understanding of the videos and their content is one of the features of the original designs of a flipped classroom. In a flipped grammar classroom, adding the quizzes or a focused task at the beginning is imperative for teachers to pinpoint their students' strengths and weaknesses with the target structure. Then, directing the students' attention to those weak points enables teachers to get the most out of the limited time they have with their students.

A similar study to the one described above, conducted with 28 university students (aged 18–20) in the neighboring country of Oman, showed positive results for flipping a grammar classroom (Al-Naabi, 2020). In Al-Naabi's quasi-experimental study, run over eight weeks, a statistically significant improvement ($p < 0.001$) was reported in students' grammar skills, albeit without a comparison conducted to a non-flipped group. The responses from the students in the semi-structured interviews were also very positive, with comments being centered around the usual benefits of flipped learning: being able to watch the videos anywhere and at any time, being able to pause and replay videos when needed, and videos being useful for future reference.

What was especially interesting in Al-Naabi's (2020) study was the amalgamation of explicit explanations of the grammar structures through the videos watched before class and opportunities for **incidental learning** through **TBLT** conducted in the face-to-face sessions. The relatively short videos—the longest was 9:32, which students still said were too long—contained clear explanations of grammar points given by their teacher. Then, the face-to-face sessions followed a TBLT lesson plan framework (Willis, 1996), which included pre-task activities to introduce the topic and activate students' **schemata**, the actual task conducted while teachers oversaw the students' performances, and a language focus stage, in which the students received feedback and extra practice related to the target structures where necessary. Although this lesson structure did not feature the quiz at the beginning of the lesson, as was recommended a few paragraphs ago, the teacher was able to assess students' ability to use the target structure successfully through the communicative tasks. Based on the students' performances, practice could be pinpointed to the places students were still finding difficult.

The three studies summarized above support the use of flipped learning for teaching grammar. There are plenty of other studies conducted in a variety of learning contexts that agree: Lubis and Rahmawati (2022) with university students in Indonesia; Philippines and Tan (2020) with adolescents in Philippines; El-Bassuony (2016) with adolescents in Egypt; and Asaka *et al.* (2018) with Japanese junior high school students. However, as we have seen, we cannot just go out there and do anything we like to flip our grammar classes; there seems to be a clear format to follow. Let's look at some ideas for using flipped learning successfully as part of our grammar instruction.

Pedagogical implications for flipping grammar instruction

Considering the advice of Norris and Ortega (2000) that a combination of implicit and explicit grammar teaching may lead to more significant results in the accuracy of what students say and write, flipped learning might be an ideal way to teach grammar. There are several pedagogical implications we can take from Norris and Ortega's advice and from what we have discovered through the research projects discussed above.

First, one of the differences between the Al-Harbi and Alshumaimeri (2016) and Al-Naabi (2020) studies that were discussed earlier was related to the videoed explanations of the grammar points. Although Al-Harbi and Alshumaimeri (2016) used videos available on video-sharing websites, Al-Naabi (2020) created his own videos and explanations to share with the students. I have discussed in previous research that it doesn't really matter who is giving the explanation in the pre-class videos (Leis & Brown, 2018), however, that was for a writing class. For grammar instruction, it might be better for the teachers themselves to create the videos for students. These videos do not need to be of such a high quality that you'll be nominated for the cinematography prize at the next Academy Awards, but they could be a little entertaining, right? (Remember, the mundane process of studying grammar is often seen as a reason for students' **demotivation**.) A video of the teacher standing in front of a whiteboard simply explaining a grammar point might not be interesting, unless you are artistically talented and can include drawings and effective use of colors. Using presentation and video editing software may take a little extra time to make your videos, but it may help students understand the content better (and help the students enjoy the videos a little more) if you include pictures, animation of words changing place within a sentence, and other tools in editing software, without going overboard with it[24].

A second point we need to consider is whether we use the L1 or the L2 when giving explanations of the grammar points in the pre-class videos. The students in Al-Naabi's (2020) study gave a suggestion that some parts of the videos could be translated into Arabic (i.e., the students' L1). However, this is in fact quite a controversial topic. In ESL environments, where students usually come from different cultural and linguistic backgrounds, it is a no-brainer that only English should be used. In EFL contexts, however, it gets a little trickier. Of course, we don't want to go back to the old grammar-translation days and simply use the L1. But at the same time, it is almost unavoidable to teach grammar without using technical terms (e.g., complement, conjunction, and past participle). These terminologies are important if we want to become experts of linguistics, but in the majority of cases, our students just want to learn to be able to use the L2 to communicate with others; they are not aiming to write dissertations or books on the formation of the English language.

---

[24] The point of not going overboard is important here, I think. Although we all want to motivate our students and be the best teacher our students have ever had, as we learn from the Yerkes-Dodson law (Yerkes & Dodson, 1908), doing too much can also have a negative impact. For interesting reading about the Yerkes-Dodson law, see, for example, Teigen (1994).

There are quite a few studies supporting the use of students' L1 when teaching grammar (e.g., Chen, 2006; Galali & Cinkara, 2017; Jingxia, 2010), and I believe that we are wasting a valuable tool if we completely discard it from our grammar explanations. When it comes to classes on speaking, listening, writing, and reading, yes. Absolutely. Our videos and classes should be conducted all in English. Well, let me change that. They should be *almost* all in English. There are still times when we can use the L1. But when it comes time to provide descriptions of grammar through the pre-class videos for our students, a little use of the L1 can clarify the finer points to help students prepare for class better.

The next point for us to consider is what we do in the face-to-face sessions. Even though the debate regarding whether **PPP** is an ideal way to teach grammar or TBLT is more effective is still raging, there is quite a strong backing for TBLT. I agree with the TBLT method to a certain degree. I still believe, though, that some explicit explanation of grammar is important as it gives students a foundation to work on when studying autonomously. This is why I often push for a lesson structure that begins with a **focused task**, followed by some explicit instruction of the grammar directed at the points where the students made mistakes in the **focused task**. Then, a little practice—communicative drills if you like—can be done to encourage **automaticity**, with an **unfocused task** to finish off. The flipped learning model works perfectly with this structure, as the opening focused task used in the face-to-face session provides the guidelines for how teachers need to run the remainder of the lesson and where to concentrate their feedback.

When you have judged that the students are not able to use the grammar structure satisfactorily and a further explanation is necessary, whether you slide that explanation in between tasks as I have suggested above, or leave it until the end of the class, as suggested by Willis (1996) and was used in Al-Naabi's (2020) study is entirely up to you. Use what works best for your students and your style of teaching. But to avoid the dangers of **fossilization**, and if time allows, my suggestion is to induce speech (or through writing if the lesson is using written tasks) that utilizes the target structure. Later in the class, opportunities through unfocused tasks, while calling upon that target structure when needed, encourage students to go beyond the restrictions of that one structure into more authentic language, an aspect of language learning that should appear in every lesson (Nunan, 2004).

After the face-to-face session has finished, students can of course review the grammar videos as necessary. Encouraging students to retake online tests to check their understanding of the grammar is also a way to review the content of the class. Another option, whether the class is focused on the skill of speaking with grammatical accuracy or writing with grammatical accuracy, is to have students actually write out the kinds of conversations they participated in during the face-to-face session. With

Figure 2.6 *Summary of the pedagogical implications for flipping a grammar class*

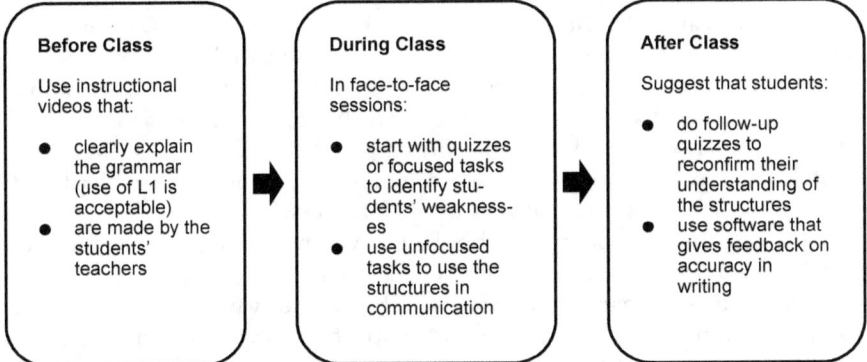

writing being more permanent, it gives students opportunities to visualize their language and discover any mistakes they may have made by themselves. The use of digital tools to provide computer-mediated corrective feedback has also been discussed as an effective way for students to improve their language skills in their own time (Barrot, 2020). Students can, of course, use either the spelling and grammar check tools found in the majority of word processing software or downloadable digital writing tools to check the accuracy of their writing without their teachers being alongside them. Figure 2.6 provides an outline of the pedagogical implications for flipping a grammar class.

I think that if you are going to start anywhere with flipping your English classes, flipping your grammar classes might be the best place to begin. Like the success that was seen in mathematics in the early years of the flipped model, even before the ideas of sharing videos online were suggested by Bergmann and Sams in 2012, the possibilities are endless for teaching grammar. I think that we would all agree that mastering grammar is an indispensable part of the language learning process but studying it in a teacher-led way appears to simply result in students developing a dislike for language, not a love for it. Flipping the grammar class might be one way of solving this dilemma, as it "helps promote cooperation, academic curiosity, responsibility, and active and deep learning" (Filatova, 2015, p. 65).

The possibles

I really enjoy sports and I always try to keep active. I have run a couple of half-marathons, try to get out for a round of golf whenever I can, and love hitting the tennis courts, if time allows. When I was a teenager, I played a lot of cricket. I was passionate about cricket (probably a little too passionate from time to time). A few times, I was invited to trials for representative teams. About 40 or so boys joined these trials, which were run over a few days, and all of us were vying for 15 positions in the representative team. On the last day of the trials, there was always a game played between the *probables*—those who were most likely going to be chosen in the team—and the *possibles*—the boys who the selectors wanted to see play just a little more as they had shown potential of making the final team. Those who were not chosen for the Probables vs. Possibles match were moved to another field where a friendly game was played among the leftovers. I was always in the leftovers.

So far in this section of the book, I have shared some ideas and research related to previous studies related to speaking, listening, reading, writing, and grammar instruction, which are the ways I think you will probably think about when you develop your flipped classrooms: the probables. In this, the final chapter of Section 2, I would like to introduce a couple of ideas related to other areas of language teaching that have received a lot of attention in SLA to which you might possibly consider adding a flipped-learning touch in your teaching and research: the possibles. The research related to these topics in SLA is plentiful, so I aim to keep explanations of the concepts discussed here to a minimum. However, the literature in these areas is still rather thin when it comes to flipped learning. Thus, there are opportunities here for further research, especially if you are interested in conducting action research. Of course, there are other ideas that are not included here: the leftovers. I hope you will be creative and come up your own original plans for research as well; the deeper our understanding of flipped learning is, the higher quality of education we will be able to provide for our students.

Task-based language teaching

TBLT in SLA

The concepts of task-based language teaching (TBLT) are generally credited to Prabhu (1987), who had been using this teaching method in his own classes since the late 1970s (Oxford, 2006). Since then, TBLT has received much attention from various corners, including its supporters and critics. In a nutshell, TBLT encourages language teaching that is conducted under five main principles (Ellis, 2009): 1) Tasks should encourage students to use language that is purposeful and functional; 2) More importance should be placed on the meaning of what students produce (i.e., through speaking or writing) than grammatical accuracy; 3) There should be a gap that students attempt to fill or complete through the task; 4) Students should be able to complete the tasks relying on their own resources (i.e., without having to open a dictionary every two minutes); and 5) There should be an outcome beyond simply using the language (e.g., solving problems, answering questions, figuring out mysteries). The tasks used in TBLT are typically either focused tasks (i.e., tasks that force students to use a particular grammatical structure) or unfocused tasks (i.e., there is no specified grammatical structure that the students are pressured into using).

Whether or not TBLT brings about increases in students' linguistic performances in comparison to other teaching methods, such as the traditional **PPP** structure, is still up for debate. In a meta-analysis of 52 studies presented through various media (e.g., journals, book chapters, and dissertations), Bryfonski and McKay (2019) suggested positive learning outcomes in courses taught using the TBLT method over a long term. On the other hand, Harris and Leeming (2022) reported that although improvements were noted in Japanese university students' proficiency and self-efficacy, similar improvements were also observed in the classes using the PPP structure of language teaching. What is unquestionable, however, is that TBLT is gaining popularity, and its concepts may be interesting to blend into a flipped learning environment. For more on TBLT, see Anderson & McCutcheon (2019), Ellis *et al.* (2019), Khezrlou (2022), and Lambert and Oliver (2020).

Flipped learning and TBLT

Despite TBLT being such a popular topic in SLA circles, research projects focusing on TBLT in a flipped format are almost non-existent. In fact, I was only able to find one study[25]. Rachayon and Soontornwipast's (2019)[26] pre-test-post-test study described a course conducted with one group of 23 undergraduate nursing students at a university in Thailand. The students participated in an English for specific purposes (**ESP**) course designed to have students practice English language used in a hospital setting. The study combined three aspects of language teaching (flipped learning, TBLT, and gamification) in an attempt to ease difficulties (i.e., L2 speaking anxiety, increasing speaking proficiency to standards to work at an international hospital) identified by nursing students in Thailand (Rachayon & Soontornwipast, 2019).

The combined TBLT, gamification, and flipped learning model was used to give students more opportunities to experience the language and vocabulary that would be covered in the face-to-face sessions as they prepared for class. The classes followed four-stage procedures, with the students 1) [face-to-face session] doing preview activities including the teacher explaining how to play the game for that week (i.e., clarifying topics and activating schemata); 2) [at home] playing an online game designed to practice and develop vocabulary and conversations required for

---

[25] The study cited here is a summarized version of the Ph.D. dissertation of one of the authors of the paper, which also provides an excellent discussion of combining flipped learning and TBLT. See Rachayon (2018) for the full dissertation.

[26] A vignette for the Rachayon and Soontornwipast's (2019) study can also be found in Part III of this book.

the follow class's tasks (i.e., the flipped learning and gamification components working as pre-task activities; 3) [face-to-face session] participating in tasks and reporting results to the teacher and receiving feedback; and 4) [at home, face-to-face session] repeating tasks at home and then reporting their results either in the next face-to-face session or via videos shared on the class LMS (i.e., post-task activities).

Students' speaking proficiency was measured through 15-minute one-on-one interviews and roleplays between the students (playing the role of nurses in an international hospital) and a native speaker of English, who played the role of a patient. In the speaking tests, students demonstrated their skills through greetings, asking about symptoms, asking for personal details, giving directions, and other necessary language **functions** used at hospitals. Assessment of the students' speaking proficiency was based on their ability to successfully complete the tasks given during the interview, their listening comprehension, fluency, and pronunciation. Analyses of differences between the pre- and post-test results saw statistically significant improvements in all tasks given during the interviews ($p < 0.001$), listening and fluency ($p < 0.001$), and pronunciation ($p = 0.005$). These results indicate that the combination flipped learning, TBLT, and gamification were indeed beneficial for students' speaking performances.

Several reasons for the success seen in Rachayon and Soontornwipast's study were discussed in the paper. The main focus of the discussions was based around how flipped learning enabled students to prepare better for the tasks, and this led to lower anxiety and higher quality performance during the face-to-face sessions. Whether or not these results were purely due to the gamification aspect, the TBLT aspect, the flipped learning aspect, a combination of two of those, or indeed the fusion of all three requires further study in what would be a massive project. But I think we can all agree that the Ph.D. study of Rachayon and the subsequent collaborated paper summarized here have provided an excellent basis on which further research can be conducted in this area.

Pedagogical implications for flipping TBLT

There really isn't much for me to add here. Combining TBLT and flipped learning is completely workable and appears to be successful in an EFL environment. My suggestion would be to wait until your students have become accustomed to flipped learning and TBLT before adding the gamification facet to the class. When you do decide to incorporate gamification, there is no need to aim for the professional standard that was used in Rachayon (2018) and Rachayon and Soontornwipast (2019). Having students learn and practice vocabulary items, phrases, and grammar structures before class through videos and games can provide a solid foundation to prepare students for the face-to-face session tasks. If unfocused tasks are being used, introducing topics to build students' back-

Figure 2.7 *Summary of the pedagogical implications for flipping a TBLT class*

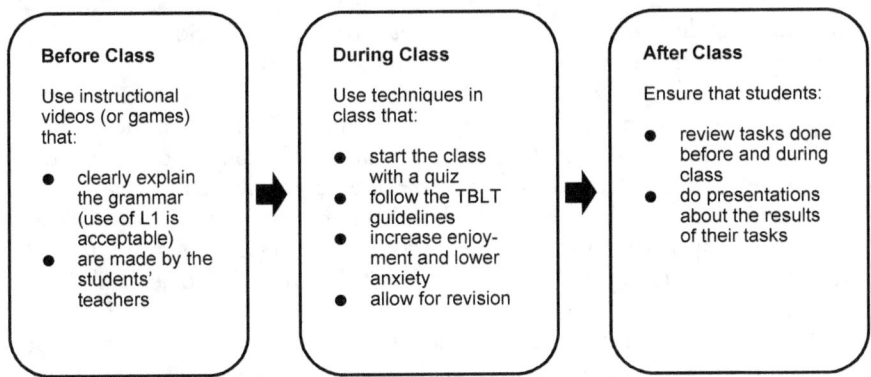

ground knowledge (i.e., schemata) can also be useful.

During the face-to-face sessions, regular TBLT procedures could be used after conducting a short quiz at the beginning to check students' understanding of the vocabulary, phrases, and grammar structures that have been introduced before the lesson. Opportunities for students to revise and check their progress in the tasks with other group members can also be effective in lowering anxiety that might be felt throughout the session. Finally, having students present the final results or answers of their task, which as mentioned earlier, should go beyond language use (e.g., Who is the criminal? Which holiday course is your group going to choose?) can ensure a strong finish to the session. Whether these presentations are done in the final moments of the face-to-face session or through videoed presentations uploaded to a class LMS is, of course, up to the discretion of the teacher. Figure 2.7 summarizes suggestions for implementing TBLT into a flipped classroom.

CBLT

CBLT in SLA

Both content-based language teaching (**CBLT**)—also often referred to as content-based instruction (**CBI**)—and content and language integrated learning (**CLIL**) originate from concepts related to immersion. Met (1998) provides a spectrum describing various contexts in when CBLT is taught, but with different focuses in language learning and teaching. At one end of the scale, what Met (1998) refers to as being the content-driven side of CBLT, we see total immersion, in which students are learning content while developing language skills: Both language and content are highly valued as parts of the learning process. At the other end of the scale, what Met (1998) refers to as being the language-driven side of CBLT, "language-driven programs focus on the development of TL [target language] proficiency but entail no high-stakes assessment of content knowledge" (Lyster & Ballinger, 2011, p. 280). So, even though language is being taught through reading passages or videos, for example, the objectives of the course and assessment are based purely on language progress and understanding, not on whether or not the students have understood the content of the passages that they have read or videos that they have viewed. CLIL, which started appearing in academic institutions throughout Europe in the 1990s, has been defined as "a dual-focused educational approach in which an additional language is used for the learning and teaching of both content and language" (Coyle *et al.*, 2010, p. 1).

Although some academics describe CLIL as being one part of the CBLT spectrum with no salient differences between the two (Cenoz, 2015), others suggest that a difference does exist depending on the teacher. According to de Boer (2015), in CBLT classrooms, instructors are language teachers; in CLIL classrooms they are experts in the content that is being taught. Thus, if a music lesson is being taught in English by a specialist music teacher, it is CLIL. If the music lesson is being taught in English by an English teacher, it is CBLT. For ease of understanding—and because this is not a CBLT/CLIL book—I am going to keep it simple and just use the umbrella term of CBLT.

Whether it is used in a strong content-focused way or weak[27] language-focused way, CBLT has received much positive response from language instructors and researchers alike. It does, after all, offer an opportunity for students to experience an immersion schooling environment even if they are in an EFL context. Furthermore, as described by Genessee and Lindholm-Leary (2013), it encourages cognitive and social development as students learn the target language, provides a basis for students to learn the target language and its linguistic systems, and creates prospects for students to tie new information learned in the target language to previous knowledge. CBLT and CLIL settings have shown to bring increases in both students' language proficiency (e.g., Lasagabaster, 2011; Sylvén & Ohlander, 2015; Yang, 2014) and their motivation (Lasagabaster, 2011).

Flipped learning and CBLT

Like the other methods of language teaching being focused on in this chapter, there has not been a lot of research conducted combining the CBLT and flipped formats. Of the studies conducted thus far, positive results have been reported in flipped-CBLT classes focused on teaching, for example, foreign cultures with university students in Japan (Leis,

---

[27] Although I used the word "weak" here, there is no intention to give a negative feeling to the language-driven side of CBLT. It is simply an indication that the focus is weak in comparison to the other end of the CBLT scale.

2018b), physics with high school students in Italy (Capone *et al.*, 2017), and science pedagogy with university students in Italy (Gallo, 2017). Gallo quite rightly observes that "the traditional lecture is no longer adequate for the new generations of students who need different stimuli in order to get the skills and competences required for their future profession" (2017, p. 156). With the popularity of the CBLT and CLIL methods steadily increasing and the benefits that merging these methods with the flipped learning model bring (e.g., Birdsell, 2020; Finardi, 2015; Finardi *et al.*, 2016), I believe we will see more scientific studies and action research of the hybrid flipped-CBLT model emerging over the next decade.

In fact, the trend of combining CBLT and flipped learning has been reported for a couple of years, but has not received the attention it could have. The *Inverted CLIL approach* (Finardi, 2015; Finardi *et al.*, 2016), for example, provides excellent ideas for teachers looking to give their students guidance in preparing for content-based classes. Finardi (2015) made use of videos that had been made openly available through **MOOC**s. Using such videos, she was able to access a wealth of topics related to what was being covered in the lesson. Finardi (2015) had her students first do tasks and practice exercises related to the background information of the topic and vocabulary appearing in the videos students would view in future classes. Once students were sufficiently prepared and confident with the necessary vocabulary, they would watch the videos and read materials made available through the MOOC outside of class time. The students were encouraged to watch the videos at least twice, the first time without closed captions and the second time with closed captions presented in their native language[28]. Then, during the face-to-face sessions, students were encouraged to work on their language production skills (i.e., speaking and writing) through discussions and writing tasks related to the topics that had been covered in the **MOOC** study videos and materials.

The inverted CLIL approach provides many opportunities for teachers to bring a content-focused structure to their language classes. Finardi (2015) mentions that flipping CBLT contributes to students' learning in many ways, such as giving freedom for where and when they would like to study the out-of-class materials (i.e., the flipped component), and increased access to authentic use of the target language. With more research and evidence gained though empirical studies, we may reach a clearer understanding of how a flipped CBLT class can benefit language students' learning.

---

[28] I think the way in which teachers encourage students to use closed captions really depends on the proficiency and motivation of the students. There are several options, such as 1) no closed captions followed by L1 captions; 2) L1 closed captions followed by L2 closed captions followed by no closed captions; and 3) L2 closed captions followed by L1 closed captions, followed by L1 closed captions, and no closed captions when students are ready. Each student will have different preferences. Ask your students to try various ways to find out which way works best for them.

Pedagogical implications for flipping CBLT

Finardi's (2015) inverted CLIL approach is certainly interesting and gives language instructors a concrete structure to consider when looking at flipping a CBLT course. Although there is a wealth of knowledge waiting in video-sharing websites, the idea of using a MOOC brings an extra advantage in that reading materials and other activities to help students understand the content better are also commonly made available. Because these materials are often created for native speakers of the target language, not language learners, scaffolding students before class through introducing vocabulary—especially specialist terminology—and topics appearing in the videos (e.g., topics that are related to cultural issues) will help students prepare for the content better. Teachers could contemplate using vocabulary tests that students have to pass before they are able to view the videos to ensure they have sufficient understanding of these words and phrases.

With input being the focus of the out-of-class preparation, the face-to-face sessions can be spent encouraging output from students. Students can share their opinions about topics arising in the videos, discuss places that they found difficult, and have debates about issues pertaining to the themes. Writing practice can also be done during class, as students create, for example, newspaper articles, opinion essays, or descriptions of course materials from various perspectives.

Finally, and what is probably often given the least amount of attention in the flipped classroom by many teachers including me, we need to think about what students do after the class. Reviewing the videos, perhaps without closed captions, and materials and redoing the vocabulary tests that had been given to students before the class may give the teachers and students themselves indications of how much they have understood the materials that had been covered in the lesson. Figure 2.8 gives an overview of a structure that teachers could use when thinking about

Figure 2.8 *Summary of the pedagogical implications for flipping a CBLT class*

Before Class	During Class	After Class
Instructional videos and materials that: • introduce phrases and vocabulary related to video content • are available through online courses (e.g., MOOCs)	Use techniques in class that: • focus on production skills such as writing and speaking • help students understand the content better	Ensure that students: • review videos and materials to confirm their understanding • redo vocabulary activities and tasks giving before class to reconfirm their understanding

combining flipped learning and CBLT (or CLIL if you prefer) in their classes.

Young learners

Research in SLA

Teaching English to young learners has received much attention in various learning environments over the past few decades. In Japan, where I am based, the amount of literature skyrocketed after 2011, when teaching foreign languages was included as part of the national primary school curriculum. It isn't easy to give a brief overview of teaching English to children because there are so many areas to look at. So, I'm just going to keep it short and focus on two areas: picture books and songs. The discussion of implementing flipped learning with young learners considers a third area: CLIL.

Picture books

Telling stories has been part of education since the beginning of time. Whether they be stories of gods from Greek methodology or Dreamtime stories from Aboriginal Australia, stories have been used to pass on life lessons from generation to generation. It makes sense, therefore, to use stories as part of teaching English to younger learners. Not only can they be entertaining when used in the right way, but they can also motivate, give children opportunities to think deeply and find meaning in the stories, improve children's listening skills, increase their awareness of the target language itself, act as stimuli for speaking activities, boost opportunities for teacher-student communication as well as student-student communication, and develop a wide range of students' abilities from predicting through to reflecting (Wright, 2008).

When choosing what kinds of pictures books to use in EFL classes with younger learners, Mourão (2016) lays out three main points for teachers to consider. First, the relationship between the pictures and words should assist the listeners to understand what is being read; we could not expect children to understand a picture book that is being read over the radio (Shulevitz, 1985). Picture books such as *Brown Bear, Brown Bear, What Do You See?* (Martin & Carle, 1967) and—my personal favorite—*The Water Hole* (Base, 2004) give listeners the information they need without relying on translations or further explanations.

Second, the design of the picture book, including the title page, front and back covers, and dedication pages provide opportunities for children to retell the story in their own words and go beyond the content of the book into a deeper discussion (Mourão, 2016). Final illustrations after the story of *The Gruffalo* (Donaldson & Scheffler, 1999) depict a forest scene, and *The Monster Bed* (Willis & Varley, 1963) shows the mother and child sitting and enjoying a hot chocolate together. Such illustrations can instigate discussions, particularly among older primary learners, such as, "Why do you think the illustrator chose a forest scene?" and "What do you think the mother and child are talking about?" taking the picture beyond the content within the pages and into the students' original ideas and opinions.

Finally, picture books can be used not only for language learning but also as a way of introducing social, cultural, and historical features of language. Mourão (2016) discusses the example of *Yo! Yes?* (Raschka, 2007), which introduces the colloquial greeting of "Yo!" as is often heard among American youths, and the friendship between an African American child and a Caucasian child. Students can hold post-listening discussions regarding the cultural differences between the two children in the story, as well as conversations about the meaning of friendship. Another example can be seen in the book *Edwina the Emu* (Knowles & Clement, 1996), which opens opportunities for discussions about the roles that mothers and fathers play in raising children.

There are a number of studies investigating the benefits of using picture books in English education with younger learners, focusing on the areas of vocabulary acquisition (e.g., Hashemifardnia *et al.*, 2018; Joyce, 2011; Kalantari & Hashemian, 2016), listening (e.g., Peck, 2001), and bilingual education (e.g., Lyster *et al.*, 2009; Lyster *et al.*, 2013). For discussions on classroom techniques for using picture books, see Hasegawa *et al.* (2020) and Hasegawa (2021).

Songs

I'm sure we have all found ourselves singing in the shower or humming away to our favorite tunes while doing some chores around the house. Singing is relaxing and makes us feel good. Going to karaoke to sing a few songs, whether it be alone or with friends, has even been proven as an effective means of reducing stress (Matsumoto *et al.*, 2012). In the language classroom, songs can be used as a way to start the lesson or to practice pronunciation, stress, and intonation (Slattery & Willis, 2001). The use of songs probably began to really capture the attention of language teachers in the 1980s through Carol Graham's (1978) series of jazz chants that introduced "everyday natural spoken language…with an awareness of the rhythm" (Dirección de Formación Inicial Docente, 2010, 0:29).

Chants and songs bring many advantages to the classroom. They implicitly encourage students to use a natural rhythm in their English, they are fun, and they can be used with actions and dance. Also, because they are easy to remember, children will often go home singing the songs in their head, creating an effective way for us to bring our classes into the students' out-of-class lives (Forster, 2006). When choosing songs to use in the classroom, it is vital for teachers to remember that we are teaching language, not music. It is easy for teachers and students to be infatuated with whether the singing is in tune or not; keep in mind that the teacher's "main responsibility is not to teach singing skills, but to teach the target language" (Şevik, 2012, p. 12). When choosing songs to use in the EFL classroom with younger learners, keeping principles such as 1) choose songs with simple lyrics; 2) connect the vocabulary with children's regular English lessons; 3) include repetition; and 4) include easy actions, will lead to high success with the song (Ersöz, 2007).

Research investigating the use of songs and chants in EFL classrooms has been discussed the effects from the perspectives of vocabulary acquisition (e.g., Chou, 2014), speaking (e.g., Millington, 2011), and learner motivation (e.g., Şevik, 2014). For more on teaching English to younger learners, see, for example, Cameron and McKay (2010), Slattery and Willis (2001), Vale and Feunteun (1995), and Wright (2008).

Previous research of flipped learning and young learners

As far as I know, there is very little research related to flipped learning with younger learners. This is kind of understandable because, in the digital age of flipped learning, students are generally required to access the Internet through tablets or smartphones. In many cases, parents are not willing to purchase such devices for their children due to concerns related to the dangers of the Internet. There is, however, the option of referring back to the analogue era of flipped learning for ideas. For example, teachers could share words cards for vocabulary that will appear in picture books, lyrics and sheet music for songs that will be sung in class, and actions that will be used in total physical response activities. With CLIL increasing in popularity worldwide, especially with younger learners, hints for creating a flipped classroom with younger learners may lay in that area. One example of how CLIL and flipped learning were combined with younger learners is in a study conducted in a rural area of northeast Italy by Alessandra Imperio.

Imperio's (2018)[29] action research was conducted over a two-year period with elementary school students. Recognizing the limitations of the school environment, the teachers implemented three main strategies to create an ideal learning environment: re-organization of the classroom, conducting a number of classes as CLIL, and implementing the flipped learning model. Flipped learning was used for history, geography, mathematics, and science, and CLIL was used in mathematics and science classes. Thus, the combined flipped and CLIL methods were used for mathematics and science.

Like many teachers implementing the use of technology into classes with young learners, the teachers in this study found that most students were only able to access the Internet by using their parents' smartphones

---

[29] A vignette for the Imperio's (2018) study can also be found in Part III of this book.

or tablets. Also, because most LMS platforms are designed for older learners, they are too complex for children who do not have experience studying online. Thus, the teachers developed a simple and secure bulletin board on which they could share links and other information related to the content of the face-to-face sessions. Students were also able to add to the bulletin board, including giving advice and editing each other's contributions. Throughout the study, the students collaborated to create a glossary of English terms related to their mathematics and science classes.

Observations of the students' participation in the bulletin board posts and face-to-face sessions suggested to teachers that the students were highly motivated by the combined CLIL and flipped learning in their classes. The teachers also recognized increases in students' proficiency, both in the content of the lessons being taught and the English language. Many hints can be taken from Imperio's (2018) action research, and I believe the implications from this study can be adopted into classes that use picture books and songs as well.

Pedagogical implications for young learners

Although the number of studies related to flipped learning with English education for younger learners is very minimal—I could find only one—there are plenty of ideas coming out of that one study. First, in the pre-class videos, as we saw in Imperio's (2018) study, keeping it simple for the students is best. Although we may find challenging our students tempting, especially with younger learners where there tends to be a significant difference of proficiency levels among the students, it is not the time to throw them in the deep end. (Refer back to Part I, where I talked about **scaffolding** and deep end learning.)

Like a typical flipped classroom, pre-class videos can introduce games and songs that will be used in the face-to-face sessions or language structures and phrases for language functions if this is more the focus of your lesson. What I especially liked from Imperio's study was the way the students were given the responsibility in groups to collaborate and create glossaries of terminologies they had learned in their mathematics and science classes. Of course, in a non-CLIL environment, this can still be done as students work together using a bulletin board to build a bank of words, phrases, songs, or even mini encyclopedias related to cultural topics that they learned through their English lessons.

Again, as is one of the fundamental purposes of flipped learning, the face-to-face sessions need to be focused on the students and their ideas. Teachers can play the role of supervisor or moderator, as they oversee the students' progress and intervene to give hints as they see fit. While reading pictures books, for example, the teacher is most likely going to be the one reading. However, the students can still play the lead role, as

Figure 2.9 *Summary of the pedagogical implications for flipping a class for younger learners*

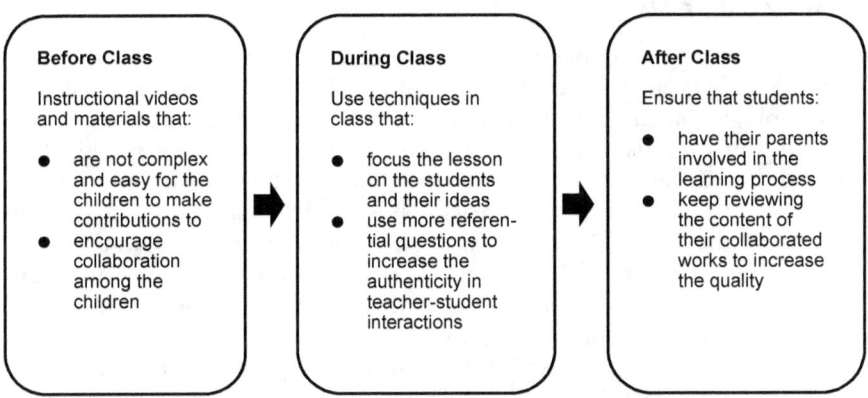

teachers use **display questions** to confirm whether students have understood the vocabulary that had been introduced prior to the class and **referential questions** to check students' comprehension of the content of the book and whether they are able to read between the lines and apply what they have learned into their everyday lives, giving the face-to-face session more "communicative authenticity" (Ur, 2012, p. 229).

Finally, we look at what happens after the class. Although parental support is vital at any level of education, with younger learners, when students are just beginning to get a feel for studying, the support from their parents and guardians can make or break the children's learning experiences. Parents' support does not just come from letting their children use their smartphones but from sitting down with them and being part of the learning process. The teacher may need to give some hints and pass on some scaffolding techniques to parents (e.g., let the children discover and edit their own mistakes) to keep the learning centered around the child, but this can also be done in a flipped way. If teachers can create short videos sharing scaffolding techniques, the content of which can be confirmed and discussed as part of usual teacher-parent conferences, it will go a long way to creating an ideal flipped learning experience for the students.

As children continue collaborating to work on their glossaries and mini encyclopedias, they may find misunderstandings from pre-class work during the face-to-face sessions. Students can continue to edit their group work post-class as they aim for their best end products. Figure 2.9 summarizes the suggestions for pre-class, during-class, and post-class activities when flipping a classroom with younger learners.

Assessment

Assessment in SLA

One of the biggest concerns many teachers seem to have in the classroom is how to assess their students and evaluate their progress. Despite terminologies such as testing and assessment being used as the same meaning in everyday casual conversations, in the academic world, they refer to two different systems. *Assessment* tends to be more of an umbrella term used to describe anytime teachers notice what students are good at and what they are struggling with. *Testing* is focused more on official judgements of students' English proficiency or how much they have understood of what has been taught in the classroom. When referring to theories related to testing in language learning, the three most prominent principles[30] that are discussed in most reference books are reliability, **validity**, and washback[31].

Reliability asks the question of how much we can trust the test, especially the scoring. If the teacher were to mark the test tomorrow, would the student get the same score? If a different teacher were to mark the test, would the results be different? Brown and Lee (2015) suggest that when tests are not well-balanced in terms of difficulty, the design of the test is defective, or the tests are not distributed to students fairly (e.g., some students have more time to do the test than others) the reliability of the test is affected. When checking the reliability of a situation in which two or more teachers are marking the tests (commonly known as inter-rater reliability), multiple choice items generally have high reliability, but items that allow more freedom for students, such as essay tests and speaking tests, require the use of rubrics with descriptions of each criterion to ensure strong reliability (Jonsson & Svingby, 2007).

Validity in testing covers how much the test reflects what was actually done in throughout the course. For example, a test is said to have high face validity when, for example, the topics of reading passages or grammatical structures that appear in the test are actually the same as what had been covered in the course. Does the test look like what the students did in class? Content validity is measured by looking at whether or not the test is in fact measure what it set out to measure. If I am testing students' speaking proficiency, for example, have items asking them to write out a script for a conversation is not going to have high content validity because too many aspects of speaking are not possible in this kind of test item (e.g., pronunciation, fluency, body language).

The third principle of testing that is given much importance is wash-

---

[29] Some researchers add other principles, such as authenticity and practicality, but for the sake of space, I am just going to focus on reliability, validity, and washback here.

[30] I have seen some researchers and authors of reference books for teachers call washback "backwash," but my own personal preference is "washback."

back. When considering the washback of our tests, we need to ask ourselves the question, "How is my test going to affect the way my students study and their attitudes in class?" If our tests are mainly comprised of multiple-choice items, there is a good chance that students won't focus on producing language in their everyday studies, because multiple choice items generally test comprehension rather than production. Then, in our regular classes, students might be less inclined to speak out in class. If, however, we encourage output from students through, for example, open-writing tasks, and develop rubrics that reward effort for writing more than a certain number of words in addition to other criteria (for example, see Leis, 2021b), students might be more willing to speak out in class, without the fear of making grammatical mistakes. For me, the concept of washback is always in the back of my mind when creating tests; it is one of my biggest opportunities to really make a difference to the way my students feel about English, especially those whose motivation is lower than others.

As always, there is a lot more to discuss when it comes to testing and assessment, much more than I can put in here. If you are interested, I recommend books related to language testing such as Bachman (1990), Hughes and Hughes (2020), McKay (2006), and Winke and Brunfaut (2020).

Flipped learning and assessment

Adding flipped learning to assessment is quite a challenge, but very possible. Assessing students' understanding of the content of pre-class materials is a vital part of the flipped classroom. The testing done through quizzes at the beginning of face-to-face sessions, for example, can be done by using technology and online applications to give teachers immediate feedback on students' comprehension and whether or not there are any areas that need to be addressed.

One example of assessment in a flipped learning environment is that of Graney (2018) who suggests that in post-class videos, teachers can give feedback to students based on observations that were made while students were performing tasks and other activities conducted during the in-class session. These post-class videos can give explicit explanations of places students were unable to use correctly as well as point students in the direction of other materials to assist with extra studies. Graney (2018) admits that such feedback may not guarantee that students will be able to master the points being focused upon, but "we should be willing to adjust the feedback until the students are capable of using it" (p. 66).

Lin (2019) looked at the possibility of using peer assessment in a mind-mapping based flipped writing classroom. In the study, students watched the teacher's explanation videos prior to class, which were distributed via an LMS. Using a mind-mapping application downloaded from the Internet, the students organized the paragraphs for their writing and prepared to practice the writing task. The principal concept of Lin's (2019) proposal for the flipped component of assessment, was the introduction of an online peer assessment module, which enabled students to give feedback to each other based on their writing before class. By doing this, students were not only able to get feedback from their peers, but also see multiple examples of how to write the required essays.

In previous studies in this book (e.g., C. J. Brown's study in the chapter about reading), we have discussed the possibility of teachers giving examples of summary writing. This proved effective as students were given a good model to work with. Lin (2019) provides us with another opinion in giving students access to as many examples as there are students in the class. There are, of course, dangers of plagiarism and copying among students, but there was no mention of this in Lin's (2019) study and the results showed improved performance and increased autonomy.

The two studies mentioned above show how assessment in regular classes can be made possible through assessment and feedback from the teacher, as seen in Graney's (2018) study, and peer assessment, as was the focus of Lin's (2019) study. But what about more formal tests, like achievement tests that check how much of what we have taught the students has been understood and to what degree? To my knowledge, there hasn't been any discussions about how an achievement test might be flipped. In the next section, I will give my suggestion on how this might be possible.

Pedagogical implications for assessment

The principle of washback was mentioned earlier as one of the most important aspects of language testing. Another concept, which is much less well-known, is that of "wash *forward*" (Brown & Lee, 2015, p. 498). Brown and Lee (2015) suggest that it is beneficial for teachers to pass on strategies to their students before the test to help them prepare. "Sometimes, preparation and reviewing before a test is even *more* instructive than the test itself!" (Brown & Lee, 2015, p. 498). From a flipped learning perspective, this means we can consider providing students with videos explaining what kinds of items will be on the test. This, of course, is not telling the students exactly what will be on the test but showing the students the instructions for the test items and passing strategies to help the students study. I think that we would generally agree that students dislike tests; they believe that the teachers are out there to show them how much they don't know, rather than helping them find guidance for future studies, which should be the real meaning of giving tests to our students. With the right kind of advice and encouragement for our students, we can help ease their anxiety and perform to their best.

Following the principles of the four pillars of F-L-I-P™ (Flipped

Figure 2.10 *Summary of the pedagogical implications for flipping assessment*

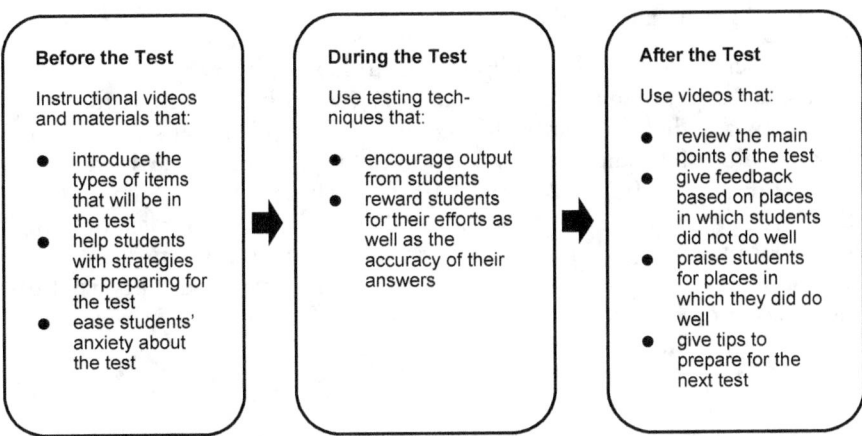

Learning Network, 2014a), our tests need to be flexible and encourage as much output from students as possible. Our tests should be opportunities for students to show us their proficiency in the target language skill. Creating test items and using rubrics that have been shared with the students before the test and are focused on effort as well as how accurate their answers are may bring about more meaningful tests. In my 2021 paper focused on strengthening students' growth mindsets for language learning, I discussed rubrics designed to have a washback effect leading to less anxiety about taking risks and making mistakes (Leis, 2021b). Using the right test items and marking with an effective rubric can make a difference to your students' attitudes towards their language learning experiences later on.

Finally, taking a leaf from Graney's (2018) suggestions, a post-test video giving explicit feedback to students based on their test performances, example answers, praise for places in the test in which the students did well, and passing on tips for the test next will encourage more post-test reflection: the part of the test when the real learning happens. As was mentioned earlier, there still hasn't been much done regarding assessment in flipped learning and nothing, as far as I know, related to flipping tests. The suggestions in Figure 2.10 might be constructive for your students in giving them a better language experience with their language assessment.

SOFLA®

The final *Possible* we are going to look at is that of the *SOFLA®*: an approach to flipped learning pioneered by Helaine Marshall, who was kind enough to contribute this section. Many thanks to Helaine and Chizuko

Wallestad for sharing their research!

Previous research of SOFLA®

The Synchronous Online Flipped Learning Approach, or SOFLA® (Marshall, 2017; Marshall & Kostka, 2020), describes two separate learning pathways that, in combination, can result in robust instruction: the Community of Inquiry framework for online teaching (Garrison, 2016; Garrison *et al.*, 2000) and flipped learning (Bergmann & Sams, 2012). SOFLA® is a distance learning model that most closely replicates actual classroom teaching and includes structured, interactive, multimodal activities in an eight-step learning cycle with both asynchronous and synchronous components that create fertile spaces for students now learning online. The eight steps of SOFLA® include:

1) Pre-Work;
2) Sign-In Activity;
3) Whole Group Application;
4) Breakouts;
5) Share-Out;
6) Preview and Discovery;
7) Assignment Instructions; and
8) Reflection (Marshall & Kostka, 2020).

This section describes an implementation of this model in a literacy methods course, along with the results from student course evaluations and questionnaires.

Classroom setting and participants

The literacy methods course took place from September to December 2020 at a large, private university in the U.S as part of an online cross-campus program. Participants were 14 graduate students in teacher education, studying to earn a public-school credential in either TESOL or Bilingual Education. This was a required course in their respective programs. Classes met synchronously in an Adobe Connect virtual classroom, where students used audio devices and webcams, as well as the chat feature and whiteboards, to communicate with each other and complete learning activities. Class sessions provided two and one-half hours of instruction each week for 15 weeks. In addition, students were required to complete at least five hours of work per week asynchronously.

Online pedagogy in practice

Each class session followed the 8-step SOFLA® learning cycle. Following is a brief description of each step, adapted from the Holistic Rubric for SOFLA® designed by Heather Rubin (2021).

Step 1 – Pre-Work: Prior to the synchronous session, the teacher assigns a short video with embedded interactions, related readings and/or activities to introduce the content to students.
Step 2 – Sign-In Activity: The session begins with an open-ended prompt related to the pre-work, posted in a shared space where students respond and sign their name.
Step 3 – Whole Group Application: The teacher guides the class as they collaborate on an activity that applies concepts from the pre-work, clarifies misconceptions and/or deepens their understanding.
Step 4 – Breakouts: The teacher provides explicit instructions for a timed and structured group activity that reinforces and extends student learning.
Step 5 – Share-Out: Groups share their work by presenting their product or findings. The teacher elicits peer feedback using the SHAC (Share, Help, Ask, Comment) Protocol (Fethi & Marshall, 2018).
Step 6 – Preview and Discovery: The teacher shows the students selected content from the next pre-work and introduces key terms and concepts.
Step 7 – Assignment Instructions: The teacher explains each assigned task for the next pre-work, indicating the timeframe and the location of resources.
Step 8 – Reflection: The session ends with an open-ended prompt. In a shared space, students write something that resonated with them and sign their name.

In each step of SOFLA, both the teacher and students have specific roles to play that maximize interaction, feedback, and accountability.

Results

Survey data from student course evaluations and questionnaires indicate that most students responded positively to a course utilizing SOFLA®. When asked about the likelihood of recommending this course structure to other students, 71.42% of the students, or 10 of the 14 students, indicated they would do so. Regarding the synchronous sessions, 100% of the students reported that the class sessions were organized, interesting and engaging, and that participation was encouraged. A key finding from the final course questionnaire demonstrates how students benefited from the course structure, both in terms of their level of participation and their level of mastery. When considering this course relative to other college courses the students had taken, 86% of the students rated the intellectual challenge as higher and 100% responded that their level of involvement in the course was greater. One student's comment in particular exemplifies the effectiveness of SOFLA®: "Online learning has turned me into a better student" (Final Questionnaire, Literacy Methods, Fall 2020).

Significance

Overall, in assessing the implementation of SOFLA® in this literacy methods course, it is clear that the course structure contributed to the students' positive experience. What SOFLA® provides is a highly structured sequence of learning activities that, seemingly paradoxically, also provide freedom for both the teacher and the students to be creative and to think critically. SOFLA® serves to create fertile spaces for teaching and learning in an online setting and therefore should be considered when designing instruction for higher education.

PART III

VIGNETTES

Introduction

Well, here we are in the third part of the book. Kudos to you for making it this far. I understand how tough it can be to get through academic books from time to time. In this part of the book, I turn it over to the most important person in this interaction: you. It is your turn to take some of the ideas that have been presented in this book so far and conduct your own research project. I probably shouldn't say that so lightly; you need to be inquisitive and be asking questions to get the ball rolling in research projects. I've had several conversations with research students in the past that go something like this:

Student: Professor, I want to do a research project.
Adrian: That's awesome. I'm here to help if you need it. So, what are you going to study?
Student: I don't know. What do you think I should do?
Adrian: Oh, okay. Well, perhaps you should read some papers and look for some ideas there.
Student: Okay, thanks. What papers do you think I should read?
Adrian: Well, what topic are you interested in?
Student: Please give me a topic to research.

And so on, where the student continually asked me to decide their topic for them. It is frustrating because we shouldn't be doing research just for the sake of doing research. We should be seeing research as fuel to feed our curiosity. Whether we are talking about research or just looking to improve our language skills, I always encourage students to follow the OIRCA pattern. (I really should have come up with a better acronym!)

Observe

For starters, we need to be observant. What is happening around us? What has been successful for us or our colleagues in their studies? What hasn't been successful? From there, we can start to develop an interest in specific topics and do some research on those topics using academic search engines, such as Google Scholar, Academia, and Research Gate. As we are reading through the papers, we need to have a critical mindset. Now, I don't mean critical in a negative sense, but critical in a way that we are asking ourselves questions, such as, "What about . . .?"

These questions should act as the springboard to our own study. They help us find gaps in previous research that give us hints about our own studies. Often, these questions and gaps will be mentioned when the authors discuss the limitations of their own study. They might include factors such as, the age of the **subjects** ("What about older subjects?"

"How about younger students?"); cultural background ("Okay, this study was conducted in the Japanese **EFL** context. Would I see similar results in an **ESL** context, such as in New Zealand?"); or the design of the study ("This study used only surveys to gather **quantitative** data. What if we conducted a similar study but used diaries or interviews to get **qualitative** data?" "This study was conducted in a pre-test-post-test design. If we did more of a **longitudinal** study, gathering data multiple times over a longer term, we might get a better understanding of the **dynamics** of when and why students' efforts rose or dropped."). We can develop the critical **research questions** for our own investigations from these questions that we are asking ourselves as we read.

Imitate

A few years ago, there was a fascinating episode of Last Week Tonight hosted by political commentator and comedian John Oliver. As part of the episode, Oliver ran a section on scientific studies and the dangers of false information being reported from experiments due to pressure on younger researchers to produce mind-boggling historical research findings (Oliver, 2016). This episode really stuck with me because it is true. So many researchers feel pressure to create something new or produce ground-breaking data that the importance of replication studies seems to have been lost. Even though they are just as important, replications studies do not seem to have the same appeal for many researchers or academic journals as ambitious state-of-the-art investigations. In my opinion, this is an extremely regrettable situation that we find ourselves in.

My point here is that it is fine to do replications studies; in fact, we *must* do replication studies (and I don't use the word "must" very often!). In my OIRCA acronym, I purposefully used the word *imitate* instead of *copy* because 1) OCRCA is even more difficult to read than OIRCA, and 2), jokes aside, the word "imitate" gives a feeling that we have included our own touch in the study; there is a bit of us in the research we are doing. "Copy" suggests that we are just doing it in exactly the same way someone else did it. That's why those machines are called photocopiers, not photo imitators. Anyway, when we imitate the studies conducted by other researchers, we are still following the same ideas of the research that caught our attention. However, we are looking at the topic from a different angle, that is, the angle of the questions we were asking ourselves while reading the paper: the gaps we are trying to fill.

If you are having trouble coming up with some ideas for replications—what might often be called writer's block—I always suggest that it's a good idea to take a step back and get away from it all. Just sitting and staring at the paper or your computer screen isn't going to be much help at all. Instead, it's always helpful to go for a walk or a run. In fact, most of the ideas for what to write in the section of this book you are reading right now come to mind as I was taking Jake for a walk. (You remember Jake, right? My dog, the staffy.) If you're stuck, go for a change of scenery. Grab a coffee. Go to the beach. Do some work in the garden. You'll be surprised at the ideas you come up with when you're not even trying.

Reflect

Once we have completed our study, it is time to look back on what we have done and how we did it. Reflection is an essential part of learning any skill, but particularly language learning. We have all heard the phrase *practice makes perfect*, but I personally don't believe in this. For me, it is, as one of my cricket coaches from my playing days used to say, *perfect practice makes perfect*. Quality is more important than quantity. This is closely related to the concept of **deliberate practice** (Ericsson *et al.*, 1993; Hambrick *et al.*, 2014). We need to use **metacognitive strategies** (Chou, 2017; Efklides, 2006) to not only look for strengths and weaknesses in what we have been doing—and as a reminder, although I am referring to our research projects here, this is also relevant for our language studies, getting better at golf, losing weight, or whatever your goal is—but, more importantly, think of strategies and ideas to do better next time. In your research paper, you do not necessarily have to report these as limitations to your study, of course. However, reflecting on how you conducted your study and how you could do better often leads to more success in the future.

Challenge Again

The final part of OIRCA is to challenge again. We can't expect to produce the perfect study and perfect results first time, every time. If you have done your reflection and discovered the places where you need to improve, you should have plenty of things to do in your next challenge.

Another vital part of the challenge again stage isn't necessarily related to how you actually do your study, rather how you react to results when you submit your paper to be published. It's no secret: When it comes to getting your article published in academic journals, it's a tough, tough world out there. Sometimes, you'll get comments from reviewers that just make you want to cry. I remember one time having a paper returned from a journal, with one reviewer saying, "Loved it! Fantastically written with many interesting and valid points." Then the second reviewer commented, "Very poorly written. This brings nothing to the field of language education." If this happens to you, try to remember that the comments are not personal. Just try to pick yourself up—and it's not easy, I know—and say to yourself, "I guess the reviewer was having a bad day." We all get rejected. It's a part of life in the academic world. Look at the reviewers' comments, try not to be too hard on yourself, and take on the challenge again. Positive results will come!

In this part of the book, I share a series of summaries of research articles related to flipped learning that have been published in academic journals over the past 10 years or so. I have tried to make the summaries as brief as possible. Some of the vignettes have been provided by the authors themselves, and others are ones that I have written. All of them come with suggestions for replication studies to help you get your research project started. It goes without saying, but if you plan to replicate any other of the studies, it needs to be referenced appropriately. If you are going to use questionnaires created by the researchers, contact the author to ask permission first. You might feel a little nervous contacting researchers at first—I know I was—but generally, people in academia are friendly and will be more than happy for you to use their materials. Just make sure you ask their permission first and acknowledge that they allowed you to use their materials.

As you read through the vignettes, you will come across some terminologies often used in data analyses. These include letters and symbols, such as p, **Cronbach's alpha** (α), and SD. I haven't put these letters and symbols in bold—it looked a little strange when I tried it—but you will find them explained in the glossary if you are unsure of what they mean. Methods of analyzing data that appear in the vignettes (e.g., **ANOVA**, t-tests), though, have been kept in bold. You'll find them in the glossary, too. (I've made just the first three of each bold.)

A final word about research I should make is related to ethics. There are many issues in doing research that we need to be careful of in the modern era, that scientists could 'get away with' in the past. One example is research that compares male and female students. In the modern era there are many discussions related to **LGBTQ** and that one's physical sex may not be the same as one's psychological gender. Therefore, in research, it might be questionable to ask the gender of the participants in the **sample**. If you feel it is necessary to ask a sex/gender item to get a better description of the demographics of your participants, it is advisable to provide more than two options (e.g., male, female, other, prefer not to say).

When it comes to the research itself, some researchers tend to create their research questions after they have analyzed the data. This way, it appears like all their hypotheses are correct, and none of their results are "bad." In research, there are no bad results. Disappointing results? Yes. Unexpected results? Yes. But bad results? No. There is no such thing, provided the research design is sound. Although it is possible to conduct **post hoc** theorizing, to be a professional in your academic career, I strongly recommend being honest in your paper and admitting that your theorizing was done after analyzing the results. This is the way to earn—not demand—respect in your field.

Okay, that's enough from me. Go and flip through the vignettes (pun intended). If there is something that attracts your interest, have a closer look at it and the ideas for replication studies. If you are even more interested, find the paper online, read through it, create your research questions, and start your research. Good luck!

Vignette 1

Mohammad Amiryousefi

Title

The incorporation of flipped learning into conventional classes to enhance EFL learners' L2 speaking, L2 listening, and engagement

Reference

Amiryousefi, M. (2017). The incorporation of flipped learning into conventional classes to enhance EFL learners' L2 speaking, L2 listening, and engagement. *Innovation in Language Learning and Teaching*, *13*(2), 147–161. https://doi.org/10.1080/17501229.2017.1394307

Research questions (RQs)

RQ1. In comparison to conventional teaching, how does flipped learning influence EFL learners' L2 speaking and listening?
RQ2. How can conventional vs. flipped learning influence EFL learners' out-of-class participation and engagement with course materials and contents?
RQ3. To what extent can the opportunities given to EFL learners play a role in the selection of course materials influence their participation and performances?
RQ4. How do EFL learners perceive their flipped learning experiences?

Participants

Data from 67 first-year university students attending two different universities in Iran were analyzed in the study. There were 38 females and 29 males, and the average age was around 22. The participants' English proficiency was described as either intermediate (i.e., 44 students) or high-intermediate (i.e., 23 students) according to their results in an Oxford Placement Test. In addition, the students were all participating in a compulsory conversation course called Conversation 2, a requirement of which was to pass the previous Conversation 1 course.

Method

This **quasi-experimental study** was conducted over a span of four months in three compulsory conversation classes. One group received instruction under the flipped earning method. Another group was conducted in a semi-flipped way. In this group, the students were broken into groups of five or six members and encouraged to interact with each other outside of the classroom using an instant messaging system to choose and discuss various videos that the instructor had shared with them. Finally, the third group was taught in a traditional classroom-only style.

To measure students' listening proficiency, the researcher used two listening tests. One of the tests was a standard listening test released by TOEFL, which included 50 multiple-choice items based on both short and long conversations. The other listening test was a teacher-made test, which was reviewed by colleagues for **validity**, and **Cronbach's alpha** coefficient ($\alpha = 0.86$) confirmed that the test was appropriate to use in the study.

The participants' speaking proficiency was measured through interviews conducted by two experienced teachers. A scale based on **CEFR**'s speaking rating scale and an original scale was used to measure students' speaking proficiency. At the end of the interviews, the raters' scores were analyzed for **inter-rater reliability** ($\alpha = 0.81$). The scores were seen as satisfactory for data analyses.

Third, the participants were asked to keep a log of the amount of time they spent outside of the classroom dedicated to revision of the previous class and preparation for the following lesson. The students were required to submit this log to their teacher at the end of each session.

Finally, to measure students' attitudes towards flipped learning, the participants were asked to complete questionnaires related to their learning experiences, the usefulness of techniques used for improving listening and speaking skills, and their opinions regarding materials used in the course.

Data analysis

First, based on the results of their listening and speaking tests at the end of the previous conversation course (i.e., Conversation 1), the author confirmed that there were no significant differences among the three groups in terms of listening or speaking skills.

To investigate the effects of the flipped and semi-flipped models, the students' scores in listening tests and speaking tests, an **ANOVA** was used with **post hoc Tukey tests** to confirm which group or groups had improved more significantly than others. The results showed that although no significant differences were observed between the flipped or semi-flipped groups for any of the listening or speaking tests (i.e., the teacher-made test, standardized listening test, and interview test), both of these groups did significantly better ($p < 0.05$) in the final teacher-made listening test and interview-style speaking test.

When the amount of study time outside of the classroom was analyzed, the semi-flipped group spent significantly ($p < 0.05$) more time than the flipped group, which in turn spent longer ($p < 0.05$) than the traditional group. In fact, the students in the flipped group reported spending more than double the amount of time spent reported by the students in the traditional group. Furthermore, the students in the semi-flipped group said that they had spent almost three times more studying and preparing for class than those in the traditional group. However, satisfaction and motivation based on engagement with the materials was reported highest in the flipped group ($p < 0.05$). This was followed by the semi-flipped, which was still significantly higher ($p < 0.05$) than the traditional class.

In their responses to the questionnaire related to their experiences with flipped learning, there were significant differences among all three groups ($p < 0.05$), with the flipped group having the most positive experience, followed by the semi-flipped. Although there were no differences between the flipped group and the semi-flipped group regarding their feelings about the effects on their listening and speaking skills, both groups reported the effects as significantly more positive than the traditional group.

Main conclusions

Overall, it is evident through the results that the flipped and semi-flipped groups had much more positive experiences in this course. Moreover, adding the flipped component, regardless of whether it was a complete flip or a semi-flip, led to higher proficiency scores at the end of the study.

Possible replication studies

Flipped learning was looked at from a number of angles in this study, which gives us a wealth of ideas for replication research and future development.
- This study focused on listening and speaking: input and output language skills. A potential further development would be to consider comparing just the output skills (i.e., speaking and writing) or just the input skills (i.e., reading and listening).
- This study looks at how active students were outside of the classrooms. Observations of how students behave in the classroom (e.g., willingness to ask questions, active participation in group work, number of utterances by students in the class) may give us further insights into the differences among these three kinds of groups.

Vignette 2

Mei-Rong Alice Chen, Gwo-Jen Hwang

Title

Effects of a concept mapping-based flipped learning approach on EFL students' English-speaking performance, critical thinking awareness and speaking anxiety.

Reference

Chen, M. A., & Hwang, G. (2019). Effects of a concept mapping-based flipped learning approach on EFL students' English-speaking performance, critical thinking awareness and speaking anxiety. *British Journal of Educational Technology*, *51*(3), 817–834. http://dx.doi.org/10.1111/bjet.12887

Research Questions (RQs)

RQ1. Can the concept mapping-based flipped learning approach contribute to the significant development of EFL learners' listening comprehension achievement in comparison with the conventional flipped learning approach?

RQ2. Can the concept mapping-based flipped learning approach contribute to the significant development of EFL learners' speaking performance in comparison with the conventional flipped learning approach?

RQ3. Can the concept mapping-based flipped learning approach contribute to the significant development of their critical thinking awareness with the conventional flipped learning approach?

RQ4. Can the concept mapping-based flipped learning approach help students reduce their speaking anxiety in comparison with the conventional flipped learning approach?

RQ5. Do the students learning with the concept mapping-based flipped learning approach make progress in terms of their concept map scores?[31]

Participants

A total of 72 first-year university students (average age 19) studying English participated in the study. The students were studying in a compulsory Oral-Aural Drills English course, with both groups taught by the same instructor.

Method

This quasi-experimental study aimed to investigate the effects of including the idea of concept mapping in the flipped classroom. The Experi-

---

[31] A second question was included in RQ5 in Chen and Hwang's study: What are the relationships between the concept map scores and the scores for students' speaking performance, critical thinking awareness, and speaking anxiety? In order to keep the summary closely related to flipped learning, it was not included in this vignette. Please refer to the original paper for information regarding the **correlations** between concept mapping and students' speaking performance, critical thinking awareness, and speaking anxiety.

ment Group ($n = 37$) and the Control Group ($n = 35$) were based on the class groups, and **Moodle** was used as a platform for sharing videos and learning materials with the students in both groups. The same materials were used, and both groups followed the flipped learning model of watching videos before class (in this study, students were required to watch videos of **TED Talks**) and contributed to online discussions about the presentations on the Moodle forum. However, the Experiment Group had the added feature of concept mapping, and the Control Group followed a conventional flipped learning process. The construction of the concept map was conducted during class, meaning the only difference between the two groups was the inclusion of the concept map construction during the face-to-face class time.

The study used a pretest-posttest design and was conducted over 18 weeks. The first eight weeks were spent training the students to get accustomed to learning in a flipped classroom and introducing the idea of concept mapping. In the pretest, conducted in Week 9 of the study, the students had two listening tests and a speaking test in addition to being given a survey related to their anxiety when speaking English and their critical thinking skills. Over the following seven weeks, while using the same materials, the two groups followed conventional flipped learning (i.e., the Control Group) or flipped learning with the inclusion of concept mapping during face-to-face class time (i.e., the Experiment Group). In Week 17 of the study, the posttests (i.e., two listening tests and a speaking test) were conducted, and in the final week of the study, students once more responded to a survey related to L2 speaking anxiety and critical thinking.

Data analysis

In this study, the effectiveness of adding concept mapping to a flipped classroom focused on improving the students' speaking and listening skills was investigated from five perspectives: listening comprehension tests, speaking tests, a survey related to critical thinking, a survey related to L2 speaking anxiety, and the Closeness Index Concept-Mapping for Scoring (a scoring index proposed by Chang *et al.* [2005] to compare a learner's concept map and one created by an expert).

RQ1. Listening Comprehension

An **ANCOVA** was conducted to measure whether the inclusion of concept mapping would improve students' note-taking skills, thus leading to greater improvements in their listening comprehension. The **ANCOVA** reported that the Experiment Group had significantly higher scores ($F = 9.31$, $p < 0.01$) in the posttest listening tests (**ANCOVA** adjusted posttest mean = 74.09) in comparison to the Control Group (ANCOVA adjusted posttest mean = 68.59) with medium **effect sizes** ($\eta^2 = 0.12$).

RQ2. Speaking performance

Again, an ANCOVA was conducted to confirm whether adding the concept-mapping experience would enhance students' speaking proficiency. The ANCOVA reported once again that the Experiment Group had significantly higher scores ($F = 28.85$, $p < 0.001$) in the posttest speaking tests (ANCOVA adjusted posttest mean = 8.23) in comparison to the Control Group (ANCOVA adjusted posttest mean = 7.01) with large effect sizes ($\eta^2 = 0.30$).

RQ3. Critical thinking

The participants' critical thinking awareness was measured using surveys. The ANCOVA reported that the Experiment Group had significantly higher scores ($F = 7.42$, $p = 0.01$) in the posttest speaking tests (ANCOVA adjusted posttest mean = 3.98) in comparison to the Control Group (ANCOVA adjusted posttest mean = 3.63) with medium-to-large effect sizes ($\eta^2 = 0.10$).

RQ4. EFL speaking anxiety

The anxiety students feel when speaking English was investigated through surveys. The ANCOVA reported that the Experiment Group had significantly lower anxiety ($F = 30.23$, $p < 0.01$) in the posttest speaking tests (ANCOVA adjusted posttest mean = 2.45) in comparison to the Control Group (ANCOVA adjusted posttest mean = 3.07) with large effect sizes ($\eta^2 = 0.31$).

RQ5. Closeness index concept-mapping for scoring

Although the Control Group did receive some training in concept mapping, this was not included in their in-classroom room activities during the **intervention**. Therefore, rather than comparing the two groups, only the Experiment Group's pre- and post-test scores were considered in this part of the analysis. A **paired-samples** t-test was conducted with statistically significant improvements ($p < .001$, $d = 0.704$) being reported from the scores in the pretest ($M = 60.12$) to the scores in the posttest ($M = 73.41$).

Main conclusions

Chen and Hwang's supports the flipped learning model as a beneficial way of conducting language teaching. By adding the concept-mapping feature, it appears that students receive a double dose of good medicine; even more significant improvements were seen in their speaking and listening scores, as well as greater awareness of critical thinking and lowered anxiety. Utilizing a strategy such as concept mapping in tandem with flipped learning, or other similar methods, can be highly recommended for teachers who find their students struggling to improve their oral and aural language skills.

Possible replication studies

- This study was conducted in an Asian EFL context. It would be interesting to run a replication in an ESL environment or with a non-Asian EFL class.
- The students in this study were first-year university students with quite solid linguistic proficiency at the beginning of the study. Performing similar research with younger learners or beginner-level students may bring different results.

Vignette 3

Alessandra Imperio

Title

Flipped classroom, C.L.I.L. and classroom setting: Innovative learning experiences in an Italian primary school class

Reference

Imperio, A. (2018). Flipped classroom, C.L.I.L. and classroom setting: Innovative learning experiences in an Italian primary school class. In M. Carmo (Ed.), *Education and new developments 2018* (pp. 346–350). InScience Press. https://end-educationconference.org/wp-content/uploads/2020/02/Education-and-New-Developments_2018.pdf

Research question (RQ)

Although no clear research question is mentioned in the paper, the objective of the action research was to increase students' motivation and improve their skills in the subjects being taught by implementing innovative teaching methods and going beyond the traditional face-to-face style of teaching.

Participants

The participants in this study were 28 students attending a primary school in a rural area of northeast Italy. The students attended school for 40 hours per week, from 8:30 to 16:30 each weekday. The students were studying in a classroom that was reported as unsatisfactory for learning purposes, as it was too small for the number of students and the furniture was old.

There were two teachers leading this class. One of the teachers was proficient in teaching under the CLIL method, and both had had experience studying in a flipped classroom as university students. The former teacher had also previously visited schools in foreign countries to observe teaching various methods and techniques.

Method

This action-research study was conducted over two years with the same group of students. Flipped learning was used for history, geography, mathematics, and science classes. Of these four subjects, mathematics and science were used as part of the CLIL program with the goal of improving students understanding of the content and language skills at the same time.

To overcome the challenge of students not having devices to access the Internet, the teachers had students use their parents' smartphones or tablets or they provided some additional materials on paper. Because many LMS platforms were deemed too complex for the students, the teachers created a simple secure online bulletin board on which the students could access pictures, websites, and new phrases that were uploaded by the teachers. Students were also able to upload and edit materials to the shared site, eventually creating a collaborative glossary of words and phrases that were used in classroom cooperative-learning activities.

Data analysis

Like in many action research studies, both teachers used classroom observations along with rubrics as part of assessing the value of implementing flipped learning combined with CLIL in primary school classes. The teachers took notes of what they observed and kept them in logbooks, sharing their notes on a regular basis. Through the observation logbooks and the students' performances appraised through rubrics, the teachers aimed to gain a deeper understanding of the advantages and disadvantages of creating a flipped classroom with primary school students.

Main conclusions

Several advantages of using the flipped classroom with primary school students were noted by the teachers. For example, the flipped component enabled students to collaborate more easily on tasks that had been given outside of class time and, more generally, contributed to the development of computer skills and life skills. During the face-to-face classroom sessions, students often commented that time seemed to pass quickly, suggesting the students may have been intrinsically motivated by combining flipped learning and CLIL. The teachers also noted that the students' English proficiency improved throughout the study period. In addition, benefits were achieved in students' inclusive practices, as learning activities were more individualized.

The only two disadvantages that were reported were the need for a longer time for running the same amount of content in comparison to a traditional class and the students often being noisy while working on group tasks[32].

Possible replication studies

- This study was conducted in a rural area of northeast Italy. It would be interesting to see if similar results would be observed in urban and metropolitan regions. (For an excellent example of a study comparing rural and urban areas, albeit with motivation research, not the flipped classroom, see Martin Lamb's 2012 study conducted in Indonesia.)
- This students in this study were taught in a CLIL environment. An investigation focusing on implementing flipped learning in classes using picture books and songs, for example, will also generate much interest among researchers and language teachers.
- The teachers in this action research had received intense training in CLIL and were experienced in a flipped learning environment. A discussion of a flipped EFL classroom at the primary school level in which teachers had not received such extensive training would give interesting insights to a wide range of educators.
- No empirical data was used to measure students' progress in this study. In replication studies, researchers might consider implementing regular questionnaires related to students' anxiety or motivation to give statistical support in addition to the teachers' observations. It should be noted, however, that when using questionnaires especially with young students, there are several ethical issues to be aware of.

Vignette 4

Michael Yi-Chao Jiang, Morris Siu-Yung Jong, Wilfred Wing-Fat Lau, Ching-Sing CHAI, Na WU

Title

Using automatic speech recognition technology to enhance EFL learners' oral language complexity in a flipped classroom

Reference

Jiang, M. Y. C., Jong, M. S. Y., Lau, W. W. F., Chai, C. S., & Wu, N. (2021). Using automatic speech recognition technology to enhance EFL learners' oral language complexity in a flipped classroom. *Australasian Journal of Educational Technology*, *37*(2), 110–131. http://dx.doi.org/10.14742/ajet.6798

---

[32] I personally don't find any problem with a noisy or slightly chaotic classroom. A noisy classroom shows that students are being active and working together. A line does have to be drawn, of course, if the chaos and noisiness does affect students' learning or interrupt other teachers' lessons. Alessandra tells me that she agrees!

Research question (RQ)[33]

RQ1. Do students that prepare themselves with automatic speech recognition technology outperform their counterparts in the control group in terms of oral English complexity in a flipped EFL setting?

Participants

The data from 128 university students were used in this study. The average age of the students was a little over 18, and the majority of the participants were female (i.e., 78.7%). Although the students reported having, on average, a little under 11 years of experience studying English, because their high school English classes were focused on university entrance exams (i.e., reading and writing skills), they generally had low confidence in their speaking proficiency. The students were studying in a 14-week compulsory integrated English course, which was conducted in four parallel classes. The objective of the course was to improve participants' general and academic oral communication skills. The students had had little experience studying under flipped learning prior to joining this course.

Method

This quasi-experimental study was conducted over 14 weeks. Before the course began, two of the four classes were randomly designated as the Experiment Group ($n = 68$). During the **intervention** of the study (i.e., Weeks 2–13), these students were given automatic speech recognition tasks as well as classwork materials that were distributed via the class LMS. This study's automatic speech recognition software gave students real-time transcriptions and translations. As the students used the software, feedback was given on the intelligibility of what they had said through transcripts, which indicated to students the errors in their pronunciation and speech. The other two classes, acting as the Control Group ($n = 60$), were not required to do any automatic speech recognition tasks. The same classwork materials were uploaded to the LMS before class for both the Experiment Group and the Control Group. The students in both the Experiment Group and the Control Group were taught using the flipped classroom.

At the beginning of the study, before the English course began, all the students were given a pre-intervention survey and placement test. This was followed by the 12-week intervention period, during which the students in the Experiment Group received the automatic speech recog-

---

[33] In Jiang *et al.*'s study, there were, in fact, three research questions. However, considering the limited space of this vignette, I have kept the summary to the first RQ. Access the full article for further information regarding this study. The remaining two RQs were:
- Does students' oral English proficiency in flipped EFL classrooms change significantly over time?
- Is there any interaction effect between group and time on students' oral English proficiency?

nition technology treatment, and all students (i.e., those in the Experiment Group and the Control Group) engaged in weekly communicative tasks during face-to-face classes. Throughout the intervention, eight units of the designated textbook were covered. At the end of each unit, students were required to submit their opinions or experiences related to the theme that had been covered in that unit via verbal presentations. The recordings from Units 2, 4, 6, and 8 were used for the data analyses. In the final week of the course, the students took a post-intervention exam.

Data analysis

The researchers used a tool downloaded from the Internet for audio and video recordings to document and subsequently analyze the lexical complexity and syntactic complexity of students' linguistic performances. A **two-way repeated measures ANCOVA** was conducted to investigate differences between the groups and within each group[34].

The results indicated that the Experiment Group's lexical complexity scores over the four analyzed recordings (39.04, 42.12, 40.57, 45.14, respectively) were significantly higher (F (1, 125) = 3.95, p = 0.049) than those of the Control Group (32.48, 30.62, 39.09, 43.75, respectively). The effect size (η_p^2 = 0.03) was reported as small to medium.

Syntactic complexity was investigated from three perspectives: overall complexity, phrasal complexity, and subordination complexity. The ANCOVA reported a significant difference between the groups for overall complexity (F (1, 125) = 12.34, p < 0.001) with medium effect size (η_p^2 = 0.09), phrasal complexity (F (1, 125) = 8.11, p = 0.005) with medium effect size (η_p^2 = 0.06), and subordination complexity (F (1, 125) = 5.15, p < 0.025) with medium to small effect size (η_p^2 = 0.04).

Main conclusions

This study illustrated the positive effects that using speech recognition technology in coordination with flipped learning has on students' speaking proficiency. Although flipped learning itself brought about improvements in students' speaking skills, the addition of the speech recognition software resulted in even higher standards, especially the complexity of their utterances. The authors assumed that these improvements resulted from extra opportunities to practice outside the classroom, emphasizing that "immediate feedback from reliable resources is a crucial element for an effective self-learning in a flipped setting" (Jiang *et al.*, 2021, p. 124).

Possible replication studies

- This study focused on the complexity of what students said. In replication studies, investigating other aspects of spoken English, such as accuracy and fluency, may give us a deeper understanding of

[34] The within-group analyses will not be covered in this vignette.

the benefits of using speech recognition technology together with flipped learning.
- The participants of this study were enrolled in only one public university in China who had studied English for more than 10 years. It may be interesting to see if similar results would be seen with students of lower proficiency, less experience with English, and in other EFL or ESL environments.

Vignette 5

Adrian Leis, Simon Cooke, Akihiko Andrew Tohei

Title

The effects of flipped classrooms on English composition writing in an EFL environment

Reference

Leis, A., Cooke, S., & Tohei, A. (2015). The effects of flipped classrooms on English composition writing in an EFL environment. *International Journal of Computer-Assisted Language Learning and Teaching*, *5*(4), 37–51. https://doi.org/10.4018/ijcallt.2015100103

Research questions (RQs)

RQ1. Do students in a flipped classroom environment produce more words in their compositions in comparison to students in a regular classroom?

RQ2. Do students in a flipped classroom environment show a greater increase in proficiency in comparison to students in a regular classroom?

Participants

A total of 22 Japanese students studying English composition (i.e., writing) at two different universities in northeast Japan participated in the study. The students in one group received instruction in flipped learning (i.e., Flipped Group; $n = 11$), and the other students received traditional instruction (i.e., Regular Group; $n = 11$).

Method

The study was conducted over a 10-week period with students in the Regular Group being taught with the instructor using Keynote Presentation software. Identical slides were converted into movie format and shared with students in the Flipped Group via YouTube. The two classes were taught English compositions using the same teaching schedule and textbook.

The study used a pre-test-post-test design. To answer the first RQ (i.e., number of words produced), the authors compared the average number of words produced in the students' essays in Week 1 with the number of words produced in Week 10. To answer the RQ about proficiency, three English teachers who were not involved with the study gave a score to each composition based on a marking rubric. Then, the proficiency scores were averaged, and comparisons were made between the scores at Week 1 for both groups and the scores at Week 10 for both groups.

Data analysis

To answer RQ 1, **independent-samples t-tests** were first conducted to confirm there were no statistically significant differences (i.e., $p > 0.05$) between the two groups at Week 1 of the study. Because no differences were reported ($t(10) = .06$, $p = 0.954$), paired-samples t-tests were conducted to compare Week 1 and Week 10 words counts of each group to measure whether there were significant improvements (or lack thereof) for each group. The analysis showed that the Flipped Group produced significantly more words in Week 10 ($m = 260.45$, $SD = 49.30$) than in Week 1 ($m = 134.73$, $SD = 39.42$): $t(10) = 3.37$, $p = 0.007$, $d = 1.44$. The Regular Group, however, showed no such improvements: Week 1 ($m = 133.45$, $SD = 38.50$); Week 10 ($m = 167.36$, $SD = 76.75$); $t(10) = 1.31$, $p = 0.219$.

To answer RQ2, again **independent-samples t-tests** were first conducted to confirm there that were no statistically significant differences (i.e., $p > 0.05$) in the proficiency of the students in the Flipped Group ($M = 11.09$, $SD = 3.19$) and Regular Group ($M = 7.67$, $SD = 2.73$) at Week 1 of the study. A significant difference was reported: $t(32) = 4.24$, $p < 0.001$, $d = 1.15$. Therefore, a one-way ANCOVA was conducted to compare the proficiency levels at Week 10 with the proficiency levels at Week 1 being adjusted to be the same. The ANCOVA showed that when pretest scores for both groups are adjusted to 9.38, the proficiency of students in the Flipped Group in the posttest ($M = 14.67$) is significantly greater than those in the Regular Group ($M = 10.57$), $F(1, 63) = 13.50$, $p < 0.001$, with strong **effect sizes** ($\eta^2 = 0.18$).[35]

Main conclusions

The students studying under the flipped learning model showed significantly greater effort and writing fluency than those in a regular class. Furthermore, although the writing quality of students in both groups did improve, those in the Flipped Group were able to improve to a greater degree. Thus, the authors argued that flipped learning is an optimal model to use in English writing classes.

[35] It should be noted that in a re-analysis of this study, I conducted a **split-plot ANOVA** (also known as a mixed-design analysis of variance), which was a more appropriate way of analyzing the data.

Possible replication studies

- The sample size of this study was minimal. A similar study with a larger number of students would be ideal.
- Only half of the students were able to experience flipped learning. A future study could be extended for another 10 weeks with students in the Regular Group receiving instruction under flipped learning and students in the Flipped Group studying in a traditional way to a obtain more reliable understanding of whether flipped learning is indeed effective.

Vignette 6

Jeffrey Mehring[36]

Title

Present Research on the flipped classroom and potential tools for the EFL classroom

Reference

Mehring, J. (2016). Present research on the flipped classroom and potential tools for the EFL classroom. *Computers in the Schools*, *33*(1), 1–10. https://doi.org/10.1080/07380569.2016.1139912

Research questions (RQs)

None

Participants

None

Method

This is a practical report summarizing research related to flipped learning in EFL environments up until the time the study was conducted.

Data analysis

None

Main conclusions

There are many effective tools available that enable teachers to create a communicative, English as a foreign language learning environment. The tools presented here give ideas on how to incorporate and use technology when developing an active, communicative learning environment. Shifting the focus from teacher-centered to an engaging student-centered

---

[36] Many thanks to Jeffery Mehring for contributing this vignette of his study.

classroom is difficult, but technology makes the process easier when used effectively. Technology enables the teacher to gather pre-class data which can inform them on what to do during the in-class sessions, thus enabling the in-class session to work on Bloom's higher levels of thinking, analyzing and evaluating information. After class activities can be developed that required students to demonstrate competence of new concepts and ideas by creating an artifact.

Possible replication studies

- A comparative study of two similar tools (e.g., Zoom and Google Meet) to determine which is most effective from students' and cost perspectives.
- Examine tools that create higher levels of engagement.
- Examine how data from the tools can inform educators on how to proceed during the in-class time, such as analyzing output from teachers in comparison to output from students.

With findings from scientific studies always being updated, there are many opportunities to publish practical reports and conduct meta-analyses of current research in your chosen field. This is especially true for a field like flipped learning, which, is still very young.

Vignette 7

Jeffrey Mehring

Title

Examining learner motivation during new teaching practices: An action-based research study

Reference

Mehring, J. (2015). Examining learner motivation during new teaching practices: An action-based research study. *Perspectives*, *23*(2), 5–11. https://issuu.com/tesolarabia-perspectives/docs/perspectives_june_2015

Research questions (RQs)

RQ1. What were the students' impressions and opinions about using video for self-reflection?
RQ2. What were the students' impressions and opinions about using knowledge surveys to assess learning outcomes?
RQ3. What were students' perceived benefits and challenges of learning in this format?

Participants

The participants of the study were 13 Japanese first-year students studying EFL in a women's university. The students, aged 18 to 19 years, had been studying English between four and six years before entering the university, and had graduated from both public and private high schools. Participants had Test of English for International Communication (TOEIC) scores between 200 and 420.

Method

This was an exploratory study that investigated how technology and knowledge surveys used in combination could lead to higher levels of motivation and attention among EFL students in a Japanese university setting. The research provides an understanding of student motivations and challenges.

Students were enrolled in a skills-based course, Communicative English I, which aimed to develop the students' ability to express themselves verbally and to acclimate them to the requirements and expectations of college life. The course met once a week during the 15-week semester for 90 minutes each week.

During the second week of the semester, students were interviewed in order to have a starting point for students to refer back to at the end of the semester. The recorded interview consisted of the instructor asking each student a number of questions individually whilst recording the interview.

At the beginning of the third week, students were given their first knowledge survey and asked to read it with a partner. After reading the knowledge survey, the instructor and students discussed any unknown vocabulary, making sure that questions were fully understood. Students were given 15 minutes in class to complete the survey, and then the instructor collected them for safekeeping. At the beginning of Week 9, students completed a new knowledge survey that the instructor collected.

In Week 14 the instructor informed participants that they would have an individual interview during Week 15 using the same questions from week two. After the individual interviews were conducted, students were asked to review all four videos, the two individual interviews, and the two group videos, and to complete the final reflection. All thirteen students who participated in the study completed and returned the knowledge surveys and reflections.

Data analysis

To answer RQ 1, participants' reflections were **coded** to find common themes. To answer RQ 2, data from the knowledge surveys was examined and reviewed. To answer RQ3, participants' reflections and videos were reviewed, coded, and looked for common themes.

Main conclusions

There were instances where students found the videos very helpful for both language development and motivation. The videos enabled students to watch themselves speaking English and recognize their weaknesses. Since students were able to recognize their weak points, they could work on them and improve their overall fluency. Videos motivated them to keep practicing in order to improve. Motivation extends from the students' ability to gauge success, and from the videos, students were able to witness themselves interacting and using the target language in authentic situations, witnessing both positive achievements and negative areas for further improvements.

The knowledge surveys did not seem as beneficial to the students. When the knowledge surveys were first introduced, the instructor found that students had trouble understanding what the knowledge surveys represented and how to correctly answer the questions. Upon further discussions, the instructor realized that students had never been asked to assess their learning using this type of system before, and that it would take students time to comprehend the benefits of the knowledge surveys.

The written reflections and videos point to instances where the students felt this new learning environment was beneficial. Videos afforded students opportunities to witness themselves communicating in English, encouraging them to remain motivated and improve. Comparing their English abilities at the beginning of the semester and then at the end enabled students to visualize actual progress. It also helped students to assess their weak areas and devise a plan for continual improvement.

Possible replication studies

- Replicate the study using a different methodology that would identify improvement.
- A comparative student of students using this model with others who use the traditional way of teaching.
- Replicate the study using different technology, possibly flip grid, to determine if different technology provides stronger outcomes.

Vignette 8

Suphatha Rachayon[37] and Kittitouch Soontornwipast

Title

The effects of task-based instruction using a digital game in a flipped learning environment on English oral communication ability of Thai undergraduate nursing students.

---

[37] This paper was a condensed summary of Suphatha Rachayon's Ph.D. Dissertation (see Rachayon, 2018).

Reference

Rachayon, S., & Soontornwipast, K. (2019). The effects of task-based instruction using a digital game in a flipped learning environment on English oral communication ability of Thai undergraduate nursing students. *English Language Teaching, 12*(7), 12–32. https://doi.org/10.5539/elt.v12n7p12

Research question (RQ)

To what extent does task-based instruction using a digital game in a flipped learning environment (TGF) improve English oral communication of Thai undergraduate nursing students?

Participants

The participants in this study were 23 second-year undergraduate nursing students (22 females and one male) at a university in Thailand. All the students studied in the same class in an oral communication **ESP** course. Overall, based on their grades in a previous course, the students' English proficiency was described as low-intermediate.

Method

This quasi-experimental study, combining TBLT, gamification, and flipped learning was conducted over a period of 11 weeks. For each unit studied throughout the course, the researcher—who was also the teacher of the course—followed a four-step learning structure.

The Preview Stage took place at the end of the previous lesson in each unit. Here, the students participated in pair work or group work activities during the face-to-face sessions to activate students' schemata and understand the topic area. The teacher also explained and showed how to play the game that would be done outside of the classroom.

Second, referred to as the Flip Stage, students played a game[38] that gave them opportunities to study and practice vocabulary items and phrases that would be required in various situations in an international hospital in which English would be necessary (e.g., giving directions, asking the patient's condition). This stage acted as the flipped learning part of the lesson as students were studying and practicing the English language that would be required in the following class tasks wherever and whenever they wished.

Third, during the face-to-face sessions, students participated in roleplay tasks with their classmates. Keeping in line with the principles of TBLT, these tasks included information gap tasks and problem-solving tasks. During the roleplays, the teacher observed and gave guidance when necessary. Once the tasks had been completed, students worked in pairs

---

[38] Although access is limited, I had an opportunity to see a video about the *Cool Nurse* game, and it is indeed very cool!

or groups to write scripts for the roleplays that they had just completed. The students presented the results of their tasks (e.g., how they solved problems) through these roleplays to the teacher and others in the classroom. The teacher was then able to give corrective feedback when necessary.

After the class, the students played the games once again and rewrote their roleplays based on feedback given to them in the face-to-face sessions. The students presented their roleplays to the other students by uploading videos to a shared social network page or in the following class.

Data analysis

This quasi-experimental study used a pre-test-post-test design. The students' English proficiency was measured through 15-minute oral communication tests, in which the students participated in seven roleplays as nurses in an international hospital, and the examiner performed the role of a foreign patient. Measurements of the students' oral English proficiency were based on how well students could complete the tasks, pronunciation, listening comprehension, and fluency.

Paired-samples t-tests were conducted to measure changes in the students' oral proficiency at the beginning of the course compared to at the end of the course. The tests proved significant ($p < 0.001$; $d = 3.057$) with very large **effect sizes** as students' scores increased from 23.53 ($SD = 4.44$) to 34.17 ($SD = 5.86$) out of a maximum of 50 points. It was noted that significant improvements with large effect sizes were reported in all areas of the oral communication test. However, although a significant improvement was still observed, the students' pronunciation ($p = 0.005$; $d = 0.647$) did not see quite the same rise as the other areas.

Main conclusions

Five main reasons were given for the large improvements seen in the students' oral proficiency over the 11 weeks.

As is often mentioned in studies showing the benefits of flipped learning, students were given the knowledge to access and develop their background knowledge of the topic before weekly classes.

Students were able to practice the target vocabulary and structures through the gamification aspect before performing them online in the face-to-face sessions. This is a little different from a typical flipped classroom; with the added facet of gamification, students were given opportunities to produce language in their own time rather than passively listen to the teacher's explanation of the textbook content, as is often the case.

The gamification aspect allowed students to learn through a digital game. Using games made the out-of-class part of learning more enjoyable for students.

The TBLT aspect gave students chances to speak more during the class. Because the flipped component had been added to the TBLT sessions, the pre-task activities—often involving input from the teacher—had already been completed when students entered the classrooms each week. This resulted in more interaction among the students and less time in which the students were passively listening to the teacher.

The feedback that the students received from their teacher and peers in the face-to-face sessions gave opportunities for improving grammatical accuracy through corrective feedback such as **recasts** or explicit correction.

Possible replication studies

- As the authors mention in this paper, it was not practical to conduct a comparison with students in a control group due to too many factors that might affect the results (e.g., different teachers, different textbooks). Conducting a study comparing the results with a control group may clarify whether the effects seen in this study were incidental or not.
- This study was conducted with nursing students. A similar study could be conducted with students studying **ESP** in different fields, such as hospitality and business.

Vignette 9

Martha Ramírez Rodríguez

Title

Flipping a pronunciation lesson for a teacher training course[39]

Reference

Ramírez, M. (2018). Flipping a pronunciation lesson for a teacher training course. In J. Mehring & A. Leis (Eds.), *Innovations in flipping the language classroom* (pp. 45–57). Springer.

Research question (RQ)

How can Colombian in-service teachers of English successfully learn about the teaching of pronunciation within a communicative approach through a situated **blended learning** environment?

Participants

The participants in this **case study** were 10 Hispanic English teachers

---

[39] In this edited book chapter, one complete lesson from the eight-week course is described in detail. In case studies, such as this one, illustrating how one full session was run can give readers a clearer idea of how regular classes were conducted for the entire course. A full overview of the study can be found in Martha's Master's thesis (Ramírez, 2015).

who had experience in language teaching in high school or university contexts. They had obtained either bachelor's degrees or master's degrees, and their English proficiency levels were described as between B2 and C1 on the **CEFR** scale.

Method

This course was run over eight weeks, consisting of two-hour face-to-face sessions per week. In addition, the participants were expected to do four to six hours of independent study each week. In order to allow for the large number of topics and pronunciation features that had to be covered in the course, materials were shared with the teacher-students through an online platform. Materials included explanations of the pronunciation features, articles, presentations, videos, audio, teaching tasks, pronunciation recording tasks, and interactive tasks to practice the pronunciation features.

The participants in the course worked individually outside of the classroom. During the face-to-face sessions, the teacher-students[40] joined discussions about difficulties they had had understanding the out-of-class tasks and explanations in addition to **microteaching** in which they practiced teaching pronunciation to other students in the course. The teacher-students also shared information with each other about how they had been applying what they had learned in the course in their regular classrooms. This enabled the participants to give and receive feedback to improve their lessons.

Data analysis

Qualitative data and quantitative data were collected through surveys, pre - and post-diagnostic pronunciation recordings, semi-structured interviews, reflections written by the participants, diary entries, focus groups, and lesson plans. Qualitative text analysis software was used in the analyses of participants' reflections, **reflexive diaries**, and focus group.

Main conclusions

One of the main findings of the **case study** was that the participants made remarkable improvements in their English pronunciation, especially in consonants and linking words. This second area of linking words is critical in speaking English, as the native language of the participants (i.e., Spanish) is described as **syllable-timed**, whereas English is a **stress-timed** language. It has been argued that when speaking English with a syllable-timed rhythm, the speaker's utterances will be unintelligible for native speakers of English who have had little experience interacting with those whose first language is syllable-timed (Nishihara & Leis, 2014).

---

[40] Teacher-students is often used as a term to describe in-service teachers who have joined a course to study and improve their teaching techniques.

The author also concluded that the flipped classroom helped increase the amount of time centered around the students and their ideas, increasing a sense of learner agency. Explanations of pronunciation points, for example, that should take only five minutes or so, often end up taking a large chunk of lesson time in a traditional classroom. Another advantage of using flipped classroom for this pronunciation-teaching course with in-service teachers was that it enabled situated learning to take place; the participants were able to go back, review the content, and set their own pace for learning, which allowed them to take advantage of the face-to-face sessions for application of the content.

Possible replication studies

- This study was conducted with teacher-students who already had quite a high command of English. A similar study with, for example, first-year university students majoring in language pedagogy who do not have such classroom experience may bring different results and experiences for the participants.
- The total number of participants in this study (i.e., 10) was relatively small. Such a class size would allow more interaction among the teacher and students during face-to-face class time. It would be interesting to see if similar experiences and results would be reported in a larger class of around 40.

Vignette 10

Rebecca Lee Su Ping, Elena Verezub, Ida Fatimawati bt ADI Badiozama, and Wang Su Chen

Title

Tracing EFL students' flipped classroom journey in a writing class: Lessons from Malaysia

Reference

Su Ping, R. L., Verezub, E., Adi Badiozama, I. F. B., & Chen, W. S. (2020). Tracing EFL students' flipped classroom journey in a writing class: Lessons from Malaysia. *Innovations in Education and Teaching International*, *57*(3), 305–316. https://doi.org/10.1080/14703297.2019.1574597

Research questions (RQ)

RQ1. What are the experiences of the EFL learners in the flipped writing classroom?

RQ2. What areas does the flipped classroom model foster EFL students' learning in?

Participants

A total of 18 students (i.e., nine male, nine female) studying in a foreign university branch campus in Malaysia volunteered to participate in this study. The students' ages ranged from 19 to 36. The students came from various cultural and linguistic backgrounds: Malaysia, Pakistan, Sri Lanka, Korea, Indonesia, and Kazakhstan. Although a concrete description of the students' English proficiency is not provided in the paper, it is mentioned that the students had not met the English language requirements to enter university degree courses. With an IELTS score of 6.0 being the norm to enter the majority of universities in Malaysia, it can be assumed the students had IELTS scores of around 5.5.

Method

The study was conducted over a span of three terms in 2017. The researchers used a qualitative study design based on interviews with the students. In the interviews, the participants were asked to describe their experiences of studying under the flipped learning model—in this case, it was in a writing course—and compare these experiences to studying in the traditional classrooms as they had done before entering this intensive language course.

Data analysis

This study used a semi-structured interview approach. Students were asked to describe their flipped classroom experiences in comparison with learning in a traditional classroom. They were also asked to comment on their writing skills after they had finished their training. The interviews lasted between 20 and 30 minutes. The interviews were audio-recorded and later transcribed. The transcripts were repeatedly read by the researchers and **coded** for qualitative analysis.

Main conclusions

Five main themes emerged from analyses of the interview transcripts:

1) *Increased preparation.* The students remarked that not only the quantity, but also the quality of their class preparation improved. Because students were able to pause the videos to take notes, and fast-forward or rewind when necessary, they better understood the content of the lesson, thus felt more confident when attending class.
2) *Enhanced engagement and interaction.* Reflecting one of the main advantages of the flipped learning approach, the participants in this study voiced their appreciation of the extra opportunities to interact with their teachers and peers in the flipped classroom. Unlike a passive traditional classroom, in the flipped learning environment, students were encouraged to contribute and discuss their ideas.

3) *Increases in in-class practice and students' motivation.* Because the students already had the knowledge about the lesson content before coming to class and the majority of classroom time in a flipped learning environment was dedicated to individual writing practice, students felt more motivated to write and to write well: "The videos motivate me to try" (p. 311).
4) *Immediate feedback.* Students commented that because of the increased opportunities to speak directly with the teacher in a flipped classroom environment, they were able to get immediate feedback on their writing as the teacher walked around and checked their essays. In a traditional classroom, such opportunities were rarely seen.
5) *Self-efficacy.* The majority of students (i.e., 90%) reported feeling more confident that they would be able to write essays with accurate grammar, structure, and cohesion. This confidence spilled over to the feeling that they would successfully achieve their goals of entering the university of their choice.

Possible replication studies

- This study focused on students' experiences in a writing course. It would be interesting to investigate students' experiences in writing classes—such as we see in this study—in comparison to their experiences while learning other language skills (e.g., reading, speaking, listening, grammar instruction) in a flipped learning environment. The results of such a study would give us a clearer understanding of whether or not their flipped learning journeys differ depending on the skill being taught.
- Consider holding in-depth semi-structured interviews with the teachers involved in flipped writing classes. By preparing interview questions based on the five main themes emerging from this study, a different perspective of the flipped classroom could be achieved.

Vignette 11

Mark Feng Teng[41]

Title

Flipping the classroom and tertiary level EFL students' academic performance and satisfaction

Reference

Teng, F. (2017). Flipping the classroom and tertiary level EFL students' academic performance and satisfaction. *The Journal of Asia TEFL, 14*(4), 605–620. http://dx.doi.org/10.18823/asiatefl.2017.14.4.2.605

---

[41] Many thanks to Mark Feng Teng for contributing this vignette of his study.

Research questions (RQ)

RQ1. To what extent do participants experience improvement in academic performances due to the structured flipped classroom model, semi-structured flipped classroom model, or traditional classroom model?
RQ2. What attitudes are reported by participants toward their learning experiences in each format?

Participants

A total of 90 students—50 females and 40 males—aged 18–20 years old, attending three classes at a university in China, were invited. The participants were English majors who had been studying English for at least six years. At the time of this study, they were first-year university students, who were taking a cross-cultural communication course. This course was selected because it included a large number of sections and students. Furthermore, it was representative of a robust, challenging course with broad content. Participating in the course required deep understanding and thinking. The students received two 40-minute class periods per week, in an audio-visual classroom where each student was allotted a computer. Based on National Matriculation English Test (NMET) results, the 90 participants selected were intermediate English language learners ($M = 102.34$; $SD = 1.34$). There were no significant differences among the three groups in terms of English proficiency level ($p = 0.78$).

Method

Learners who were assigned to Experiment Group 1 (EG1), which received structured flipped classroom instruction. This included WebQuests and online videos. The students in EG1 read all materials through WebQuests, viewed online videos, and took notes before attending class. Students then worked in class on inquiry-based assignments. For the present study, four WebQuests were created through QuestGarden (http://questgarden.com), an online authoring tool and hosting service for the creation and sharing of WebQuests.

Learners in Experiment Group 2 (EG2) were assigned to a semi-structured flipped classroom used the videos as learning tools. The affordability and effectiveness in supporting the flipped classroom were the two key factors that contributed toward the inclusion of online videos in the semi-structured flipped classroom. In terms of material delivery, in EG1, in- and out-of-class learning materials were organized in the QuestGarden format, and all the materials were delivered to the students before each lesson. In EG2, out-of-class learning materials were printed and distributed to the students before class, while in-class learning materials were printed and distributed to the students in class (semi-structured). During classroom time, EG1 worked on inquiry-based assignments and homework, wherein teacher and students worked in a collaborative manner, the instructor provided assistance, and students could ask questions directly. EG2 students worked on assignments individually during class.

Learners in the Control Group received traditional instruction. They attended lectures, with similar contents of the same mini lectures that had been recorded for the flipped classroom groups. The instructor printed and distributed materials that were identical with those in EG1 and EG2 at an appropriate time during class. These materials were used as a supplement to teachers' lectures. Students then reviewed the materials and completed their homework at home.

Data analysis

The quantitative data—academic assessment and questionnaire responses—were analyzed using the SPSS 19.0 statistical software. An ANOVA was applied to examine any group differences with a significance level of 0.05. The **F-ratios** and p-values were determined to see if there were any statistically significant differences between and among the groups. The assessment included three facets: learners' comprehension of the course content, comprehension of the distributed learning materials, and learners' overall performance of an oral presentation.

The qualitative data—interview transcripts—were **coded** on the basis of thematic analysis. As the procedures for interview data analysis mainly included grouping verbal responses into categories according to the emerging themes, thematic analysis was appropriate. Based on the thematic analysis, the author examined and coded the data. Five themes emerged from the interview data.

Main conclusions

The present research contributed to the development of flipped teaching as an approach to helping English language learners in blended-learning settings. Structured flipped teaching, augmented by the use of WebQuests, exerted positive effects in academic performance when engaging students in the learning process.

Students in the structured flipped classroom had more positive attitudes toward flipped teaching than those in the semi-structured flipped classroom. Additionally, students in the semi-structured flipped classroom expressed a higher level of satisfaction than those in the traditional classroom. The flipped approach is likely to satisfy students' needs for autonomy, competency, relatedness, and thus, create greater conditions for **intrinsic motivation**, which lead to empowerment, development, engagement, and an ability to learn independently or at their own pace.

Possible replication studies

- The sample size of this study was minimal. Future studies could be conducted with a larger number of students.
- The assessment in future studies could focus on more specific language skills.
- Students with a higher language proficiency level may have had a higher level of autonomous learning than lower proficiency level students (see Teng, 2019). If students with lower English proficiency were invited to this study, the results obtained from the current study might have differed significantly.

Vignette 12

Adrianne Verla Uchida[42]

Title

Integrating the four-dimensional education framework into an EFL course curriculum

Reference

Uchida, A. V. (2020). Integrating the Four-Dimensional Education Framework into an EFL course curriculum. *Relay Journal*, *3*(1), 25–47. https://doi.org/10.37237/relay/030103

Research question (RQ)

How did the integration of tasks and projects based on the Four-Dimensional Education Framework impact student learning?

Participants

The participants in this study were 78 first-year university students at a private university in central Japan. The students were not English majors, however they all had majors dealing with international relations. Approximately half of the students were also studying a foreign language in addition to English. The students were all enrolled in English II, a course required for graduation

Method

The university requires students English II to cover all sections in the Oxford English Grammar Course Intermediate textbook (Swan & Walter, 2011). The textbook is divided into 22 sections based on different grammar structures. To make the class more learner-focused, a flipped learning approach was implemented (Bergmann & Sams, 2012; 2014).

---

[42] Many thanks to Adrianne Verla Uchida Teng for contributing this vignette of her study.

The grammar tasks were assigned as homework, allowing students time in class to engage in various tasks and projects. The course included five one-lesson tasks and six multi-lesson projects.

Each in-class activity was designed to develop the student's English language skills while also fostering their sense of learner agency and learner autonomy. These tasks and projects were designed for students to "engage in activities that they find personally meaningful" (Noels, 2013, p. 27). All activities required the students to formulate a plan, complete it, and then assess the outcomes through self-reflection, similar to what Little *et al.* (2017) refer to as the teaching-learning cycle in the autonomy classroom. Moreover, the activities required student communication and collaboration to help develop their L2 identities and increase motivation.

Data analysis

The data used for this study were collected and analyzed using mixed methods. A teaching journal from the course (Farrell, 2015) was used to document class observations, reflect on the various tasks and projects, and note any additional concerns or ideas gathered during the course. Students were asked to record their feelings and observations on an open-ended reflection at the conclusion of every class. That data was coded by noting key words, patterns, and repetitive phrases, and then were matched to the CCR's Four-Dimensional Education Framework. Finally, an online Google Forms survey was administered to gather students' impressions about the course design, the various activities, and their perceptions of their English abilities.

Main conclusions

The overall conclusions of this study showed that most students reported anxiety about taking English classes, especially with a "native" teacher, but also excitement to study English in university. Many students said their motivation level had improved over the course of the semester. Students who felt their motivation increased stated the activities and how they were completed during class as reasons for their increased motivation.

While the students were not explicitly aware of the CCR framework and why the classroom had been flipped, at the conclusion of the semester student survey data showed that cited that the students had learned digital literacy, improved their writing and grammar knowledge, and became able to express themselves in English through the course. Students also reported developing their skills regarding communication ability, creativity, and collaboration, while none of the students felt they had engaged in critical thinking during the course, despite it being one of the four skills integrated into the curriculum. Regarding character development throughout the course curiosity and courage were the most developed characteristics followed by mindfulness. Students stated that they developed these character traits through giving presentations and participating in group work, namely the tasks and projects used in the course.

The data collected from the student reflection sheets most included references to their emotional reactions about specific class activities and tasks. The mid-term and final projects were the most referenced activities. The students felt that the activities piqued their interest to learn new things and visit new places, provided chances to work with randomly assigned classmates, and engage in teamwork. Engaging in these activities throughout the semester were only possible due to the flipped learning approach used in the class.

Possible replication studies

- Carrying out this study with two separate groups of students, one as a control group receiving regular textbook-based class lessons and the other as a test group could yield different results.
- This study was conducted over one semester, conducting it over the year with the same group of students could produce different results.

PART IV

CONCLUSION

The Golden Pavilion and PETS

In November 2009, when working at a high school in Japan, I accompanied my students on their school trip. We visited Beppu in Oita Prefecture, Hiroshima, Osaka, and Kyoto, before returning to Fukushima. After Tokyo, Kyoto is probably the most globally well-known city in Japan, due to its magnificent history, elegant culture, and amazing architecture. One place that fuses these three points together perfectly is *Kinkakuji*, also known as the "Golden Pavilion." Kinkakuji is such a beautiful place that it is difficult not to take a photo that makes you look like a professional. Or so I had thought before I took the photo below on my trip in 2009.

Figure 4.1 *The blurry Kinkakuji*

It was a wet morning and it had been raining overnight, so our time at Kinkakuji was quite limited. I played around with the zoom and other functions on my digital camera and quickly took the photo before rushing back to the bus. When I had a chance to check my photo (Figure 4.1), I was utterly disappointed because, as you can see, Kinkakuji was out of focus. However, on closer inspection, it became clear that Kinkakuji was there the whole time (Figure 4.2); I just had to flip the photo and look at it more closely to see. Now, the photo has become a valuable memory for me; so much so that I even decided to share it in this book.

I think the same thing could be said about language teaching. It isn't always easy for us to come up with the most effective ways to teach our students, but perhaps we are thinking about it in the wrong way. As I

Figure 4.2 *The flipped clear Kinkakuji*

think has been quite evident throughout this book, by flipping our lessons, we can provide our students with opportunities to learn at the time and place that suits them best. We can use our face-to-face sessions to focus on the students and their ideas. We can help students discover their weaknesses and consider strategies to turn those weaknesses into strengths.

Based on the studies that have been covered in this book, both in-depth and just briefly, I want to suggest a four-step process to consider when flipping your classes. Each step of the flipped learning structure, which I am going to call PETS, is designed to help create a clearer picture for both you, the teacher, and your students to get the most out of the limited class time you have together.

Presentation through pre-class materials

Although there are other possible techniques, using videos to give explanations of class content is the norm in flipped learning. Doing so opens up more time in the face-to-face sessions for students to interact and use the target language effectively. Just about every study covered in this book has shown the benefits of running our classes in this way, but it seems that we can do so much more.

Generally, whether they are made by the teachers themselves or borrowed from video-sharing websites on the Internet, the videos include explicit explanations and examples of the lesson focus (e.g., pronunciation, grammatical structures, essay writing construction), introductions to strategies students might use in their learning, descriptions of background information to the topics to build students' schemata, or clarification of topics for discussion that will be held during the face-to-face session. With improvement in technology, we are now seeing, for example, speech recognition software, gamification, online interaction activities, and students' self-made videos as part of the pre-class materials as well. Just giving a simplified version of what you would typically do in a traditional class still may make the cut, but incorporating other techniques that have been successful in SLA research to the pre-class materials, students are likely to make even further progress in their studies.

Evaluation and encouragement

In the second step of PETS, I want to encourage you to look for ways to evaluate how much students have understood the content of the pre-class materials and get an understanding of whether there are any misunderstandings of what the students did (or were supposed to do) before the class. There are various ways of doing this in the first 5 or 10 minutes of the class, such as through **focused tasks**, short speeches conducted in pairs[43], or fun quizzes using gamification ideas such as the popular Kahoot®.

The encouragement given to students at this stage is based on how well they have understood the content of the pre-class materials. Feedback and praise are often best focused on the efforts the students expended in completing the pre-class tasks rather than their ability (or inability) to get high scores in the quizzes and tasks used to open the face-to-face sessions; focusing on the process of students when praising (or scolding if necessary) is more effective for strengthening students' motivation than simply looking at the final product (Dweck, 2017; Johnston, 2004, 2012; Leis, 2021a, 2021b).

Tasks and teamwork

Third, which should entail the majority of your face-to-face class sessions, students participate in **unfocused tasks**, practice exercises, discussions, debates, writing activities, or teamwork projects that encourage as much language production as possible. Depending on the length of your lesson (e.g., 45 minutes, 75 minutes, 90 minutes), it is possible to conduct just the one task or discussion or whatever production activity you choose, but spending too much time on the one task may result in a decline in students' enthusiasm to actively participate in the lesson.

Our students will usually enjoy the different tasks and activities that we do in class, but if we continue them for too long, students' focus and interest tend to weaken. One approach I like to use to keep students' interest levels high is based on the Japanese term *harahachibu*. *Harahachibu*, literally meaning "my stomach is 80% full," suggests that we should not eat until we are completely full; this will make us feel sick. The same can

---

[43] If you are interested in a short-speech idea for your speaking classes that allows you to check how well students can use the target structure or language function as well as develop students' bottom-up and, if taken to a second stage, top-up listening skills, see my short paper, *Every Minute Counts: A Warm-up Speaking and Listening Activity to Build Fluency* (Leis, 2014).

be said for tasks and teamwork activities conducted in class. Aim to stop the task just before students get bored. It does take time as you get to know your students better, but it is essential "for us to judge how long particular children will stay involved in an activity, and to anticipate any decline in the children's involvement" (Paul, 2002, p. 30).

Strengthening and strategizing

The last step in the PETS process is related to what we have students do after class. Students have had opportunities to listen to the teacher's explanations prior to class and show their understanding and ability to use the language successfully through tasks conducted during the face-to-face sessions. However, the learning should not stop there. Through the different stages of the lesson, both before and during the class, students will have identified points that they have understood confidently and points that they have not. Post-class reflection and review to reinforce their strong points and strengthen their weaknesses can be done through, for example, summary writing, further gamification, and revisiting speech recognition software sites to notice their improvements can lead to heightened motivation to do better.

Post-class activities can also be used to trigger students' metacognition as they reflect on their study habits when preparing for the lesson using the pre-class materials and during the face-to-face session itself. Encourage students to self-reflect on their learning through questions such as:

- Was the place I chose to watch the teacher's video appropriate?
- Could I concentrate enough at the time I was preparing for class, or were there distractions?
- Did I just rely on closed captions during the videos, or did I listen intently to what the teaching was saying?
- Was I active during the tasks conducted during class, or did I just sit back and let others do all of the work?
- Was I too powerful in the discussions held during class, not allowing others to share their opinions to instigate effective communication?
- How can I do better next time?

This final question is crucial as it encourages students to strategize to do better next time, leading to improved performance in future classes and learning. I often have my students respond to reflection questions, such as the ones above, in the final two or three minutes of my face-to-face sessions to spur the reflection processes within them and give them self-created evidence over the period of the course of what works for them and what does not.

So, there you have it: the four steps of PETS. The ideas and suggestions within are all based upon the successes discussed throughout this book. Like any suggestion for teaching, each step can, of course, be adapted to match the way you want to run your flipped classrooms, your style of face-to-face teaching, and to meet the needs of your students. I hope that the PETS model, like all of the ideas and suggestions I have shared within this book, will be helpful for you and your students to have a more fulfilling language learning experience. That's about all I have for now; it's time to call it a day.

Just before we go, though, finally, I would like to recommend some other books for further reading. This list is not complete by any stretch of the imagination, and they may not necessarily be connected directly to using flipped learning in EFL education. However, there are many discussions related to flipped learning which may ignite some ideas of your own. The full references for the books can be found in the reference list at the back of the book.

Best practices for flipping the college classroom
  (Julee B. Waldrop and Melody A. Bowdon)
Flip it! Strategies for the ESL classroom
  (Robyn Brinks Lockwood)
Flip your classroom: reach every student in every class every day
  (Jonathon Bergmann and Aaron Sams)
Flipped learning: A guide for higher education faculty
  (Robert Talbert)
Flipped learning: Gateway to students' engagement
  (Jonathon Bergmann and Aaron Sams)
Flipped mastery learning: An insanely simple guide
  (Cara Johnson with Jon Bergmann)
Flipping the college classroom: Practical advice from faculty
  (Barbi Honeycutt)
In-class flip: A student-centered approach to differentiated learning
  (Martha A. Ramírez and Carolina R. Buitrago)
Innovations in flipping the language classroom
  (Jeffery Mehring and Adrian Leis)
It works for me, flipping the classroom: Shared tips for effective teaching
  (Hal Blyth, Charlie Sweet, and Russell Carpenter)
Promoting active learning through the flipped learning model
  (Jared Keengwe, Grace Onchwari, and James Oigara)

Glossary

Affective filter – The basis of Stephen Krashen's affective filter hypothesis, reflecting the anxiety and lack of self-confidence students feel in language learning. Krashen suggests language students should not be forced to speak until their affective filters have been lowered and they are comfortable using the language.

Agency – Learner agency refers to the mindset that humans have the power to control learning. Much of the early work related to learner agency was centered around the research of Martin Seligman.

ANCOVA – An acronym referring to an Analysis of covariance, a statistical analysis method used when comparing two or more groups whose scores at the pre-test stage of the study are significantly different (i.e., $p < .05$). The ANCOVA adjusts the pre-test scores so each group is identical to give a more reliable indication of differences among the groups at the post-test stage of the analysis and how much each group has actually changed over the course of the study.

ANOVA – An acronym referring to an Analysis of variance, a statistical analysis method used when comparing the data set of three or more groups. The ANOVA will tell you whether or not a statistically significant difference ($p < .05$) occurs among groups. If a significant difference is observed, you can follow up the ANOVA with a post hoc analysis, such as a Tukey test. cf. Independent-samples t-tests, Paired-samples t-tests, Tukey test.

Anxiety – A feeling of nervousness when using or learning a foreign language. High foreign language learning anxiety might be due to concerns about grammatical accuracy or misunderstandings while communicating in the foreign language. High foreign language anxiety usually results in low language performance. Leading researchers in foreign language anxiety include Elaine Horwitz and Peter MacIntyre.

Audiolingual method – A teaching method popular in the 1940s and 1950s that involves extensive use of drills to help students memorize set patterns of language. The Audiolingual method gained a reputation of enabling students to quickly pick up the target language and thus was a popular method of training soldiers preparing for conflict in non-English speaking nations.

Automaticity – is achieved when language students are able to use the target language with grammatical accuracy without thinking carefully about the language structures. Automaticity can be achieved through repeated use of the target language structure though practice conversations and drills. c.f. Fossilization.

Blended learning – Blended learning is a way of teaching that uses both technology, including online materials, and traditional face-to-face education. Flipped learning is a well-known example of blended learning as it provides a hybrid of students tasked to study online in their own time and follow-up discussions held in the face-to-face classes.

Bottom-up process – Bottom-up processing in listening and reading refers to the mechanism of focusing on the smaller parts of language (e.g., sounds, parts of words, meaning, grammatical relationships) to the overall meaning of what one is hearing or reading. cf. Top-down process.

CALL – Computer Assisted Language Learning. Although initially, CALL covered the use of devices requiring electricity (e.g., devices used in language laboratories), in recent years, it usually refers to the use of the Internet in language learning.

Case study – A case study is a detailed description of a situation or case (in education it will often concern a particular class or student) that has been analyzed over a long period of time. Unlike action research, a case study might not actually supply a solution to an identified problem, instead sharing observations that contribute to deeper understanding of the issue at hand.

CBI – Content-based Instruction. See CBLT.

CBLT – Content-Based Language Teaching. Related to immersion education, CBLT is an umbrella term that refers to the teaching of language through studying another subject. Students in Japan studying language pedagogy in English is an example of CBLT. CBLT courses might be content-driven, in which the students are assessed on their understanding of the content, or language-driven, in which the students are assessed on their language skills. CBLT is sometimes referred to as Content-based Instruction (CBI). cf. CLIL.

CEFR – The CEFR (Common European Framework for Reference) scale is one of the most popular ways of describing students' language proficiency. The CEFR scale provides clear concrete descriptions of various language proficiency from A2 (absolute beginner) to C1 (highly proficient). Using the CEFR scale to describe the language proficiency of the participants in your study allows a wider audience to have a clearer understanding of their language ability.

CLIL – Content and Language Integrated Learning. According to most researchers, CLIL is part of the CBLT continuum, with students being assessed both on their understanding of the course content and their language skills. Some researchers make a distinction from CBLT, in that the CLIL teacher is a specialist of the content matter being taught (e.g., a mathematics instructor teaching math in Japan,

Glossary **149**

but using English as the primary language). cf. CBLT.

Cloze test – Cloze tests are often used as part of assessment. Students are presented with a short passage which has some words replaced with blanks. Students are required to fill in the blanks either from a list given to them or writing an appropriate word. Traditionally, cloze tests would have every fifth or seventh word replaced with a blank but selecting which words from the passage that you want to fill in can result in a more valid form of assessment.

CMC – Computer-Mediated Communication. CMC referring to communication, both written and spoken, made possible through the use of computers, especially via the Internet and Intranet systems.

Coding – is a process used when analyzing data for qualitative research. When reading through qualitative data sets (e.g., interview transcripts, essays), the researcher will look for common patterns and themes that appear. When a common theme has been identified, the researcher will label these themes (e.g., positive feedback, lowered anxiety) to make the patterns and relationships among them easier to identify.

Concept mapping – Proposed by Novak (1990), concept mapping is a technique used to organize ideas when brainstorming in preparation for, for example, giving a speech, writing an essay, or running a conference. Concept maps make use of visuals rather than words, starting with main ideas that then link to more detailed concepts.

Correlation – A correlation is used to understand the relationship between two (or more) objects or actions. For example, a researcher might use a correlation analysis to find out the relationship between eating ice cream and happiness (Are we happy when we eat ice cream?) After running the experiment for say a month, the analysis of the data would give the researcher a result (a Pearson correlation coefficient, which is represented as r, is one of the most common ways). The results will always be between -1.00 and $+1.00$. A result of $r = -1.00$ suggests a very strong negative correlation (i.e., if you eat ice cream, it is extremely likely that you will be very sad) and a result of $r = +1.00$ suggests a very strong positive correlation (i.e., if you eat ice cream, it is extremely likely that you will be very happy). A result of $r = 0.00$ means there is no relationship at all.

Cronbach's alpha – Cronbach's alpha, often shown using the Greek letter α, shows the reliability of a data set. It is commonly used to check the reliability of items in questionnaires and the scores given by those rating participants' speaking or writing scores. The maximum score is 1.00 and the minimum score is 0.00. Usually, $\alpha = .80$–.90 is said to be ideal, but $\alpha > .70$ is acceptable. If you use questionnaires in your research, especially if you developed the questionnaires yourself, it is best to use a reliability measure such as Chronbach's alpha (there are other possibilities) to show that your data set can be trusted.

d – Cohen's *d* is used when reporting the effect sizes of t-tests. Generally, *d* = 0.02 is seen as a small effect, *d* = 0.5 is seen as a medium effect, and *d* = 0.8 or higher is considered a large effect size. Cf. η^2, η_p^2.

Deaf and hard-of-hearing students – People who have no sense of hearing from birth are usually described as deaf. Those who have lost their hearing due to various reasons such as illness or accidents but can still hear to some degree are usually describe as hard-of-hearing. The degree of hearing loss can be described in decibels (dB). According to the American Speech-Language-Hearing Association, hearing from -10dB to 15dB is described as normal, hearing loss from 16dB to 25dB as slight, 25dB to 40dB as mild, 41dB to 55dB as moderate, 56dB to 70dB as moderately severe, 71dB to 90dB as severe and more than 91dB as profound (American Speech-Language-Hearing Association, 2014).

Deliberate practice – Deliberate practice refers to the action of exerting extra effort to focus on specific points when repeatedly practicing a skill. For example, rather than just going to the golf range and simply hitting 500 balls, it would be more effective to hit less balls, but focus carefully on each shot, thinking about the position of your hips, elbow, head, etc. Many athletes use video cameras in practice in games to reflect on their weaknesses and focus their practice time on improving their weaknesses as part of their deliberate practice. See the work of K. Anders Ericsson for more on deliberate practice.

Demotivation – refers to a situation in which a student has lost their motivation. Demotivation suggests that the student was at one time motivated (regardless of whether that motivation was implicit or explicit), but due to some experience or circumstance, lost that motivation.

Display questions – Display questions are questions used to check how well the other person has comprehended what they have heard or read. There are usually correct and incorrect answers and the person asking the question can usually predict what the respondee will say. Examples of display questions include, "According to the announcement, what time will the train depart?" and "According to the recipe, how long should we simmer the vegetables?" Although display questions can be used to check comprehension, many educators recommend using more referential questions to increase students' communication skills and initiate communication. c.f. Referential questions.

Dynamics – Improvements in our proficiency (or lack thereof) do not always follow gradual increases or declines. Instead, we often see combinations of spikes and dips in our performances. These spikes and dips describe the dynamics of our performances. For more on dynamics in language learning (from a motivational perspective), see Motivational Dynamics in Language Learning by Zoltán Dörnyei, Peter MacIntyre, and Alastair Henry (2015).

Effect sizes – In modern research, it is expected that the researcher will provide effect sizes as part of their results in quantitative research. Effect sizes give readers an idea of how effective the intervention in a study would be if it were implemented into a different group of the same size or larger. The higher the effect size, the more effective one can predict the intervention will be in that new group. Effect sizes are calculated differently depending on the statistical analysis with which it is used (e.g., paired-samples t-test, ANOVA) and reported accordingly (e.g., η^2, d).

EFL – English as a Foreign Language. EFL refers to studying English in a community where English is generally not used outside of the classroom or in daily communication. Often, these are countries listed in Kachru's (1982, 1985, 1986) expanding circle (e.g., Japan, China, Italy, France). cf. ESL.

ESL – English as a Second Language. ESL refers to studying English in a community where English is the main language used outside of the classroom and in daily communication. Often, these are countries listed in Kachru's (1982, 1985, 1986) inner circle (e.g., Australia, New Zealand, the United States, England). cf. EFL.

ESP – English for Specific Purposes. English language teaching that is focused on the language used in certain careers, such as nursing, business, the airline industry, and hospitality.

η^2 – Eta squared is one method used to report the effect sizes of ANOVA. In some cases, the researcher may be required to use partial eta squared (i.e., η_p^2).

F-ratio – An F-ratio is calculated to understand whether or not statistically significant differences can be observed between two or more groups, especially when analyzing multiple groups such as in ANOVA and ANCOVA. The F-ratio is usually reported with a p-value to indicate if the differences are seen as statistically significant. As the F-ratio score gets larger, the p-value decreases, showing greater statistical difference.

Focused task – A focused task is a task that forces students to use a particular grammatical structure, such as past tense or interrogatives. c.f. Unfocused task.

Fossilization – occurs when a speaker automatically uses a grammatical structure incorrectly. Because the student has created a habit of using the language structure incorrectly, it is often difficult to amend. c.f. Automaticity.

Function – A language function refers to how language is used in authentic situations, such as, greetings, introducing yourself, ordering a pizza, and asking for directions. Most language learning textbooks will use a syllabus focused on language functions or grammatical structures.

Gamification – is the addition of games and the principles of rewards for achieving goals and tasks. For example, many smart watch applications include rewards of badges and points for achieving monthly goals. In language education, students might be awarded with digital trophies for studying a set number of vocabulary items.

Incidental learning – Incidental learning is learning that occurs without intention. Students may pick up new vocabulary items or phrases through, for example, watching movies, talking with friends in the L2, or reading for pleasure.

Independent-samples t-test – In quantitative data analyses, an independent-samples t-test is often used when comparing two groups whose members are different. For example, if a researcher were comparing the English language proficiency scores of students in a flipped classroom and students in a traditional classroom, they would most likely use an independent-samples t-test. cf. Paired-samples t-test.

Inter-rater reliability – When judging students' language proficiency, especially in speaking and writing skills, it is often preferable to use more than one person to make judgements on each student's language ability. To ensure the scores given by the judges are similar, thus a reliable measure of the students' proficiency, it is advisable to conduct an inter-rater reliability test. This is usually measured using either Cronbach's alpha or Cohen's *d*.

Intervention – An intervention usually refers to the main part of a study, or when the experiment is actually being conducted. A research design often follows a structure of pre-test, intervention, and post-test.

Intonation phrases – Chunks of language that appear between our pauses as we speak are known as intonation phrases. Tench (1996) explains that in usual speech, intonation phrases typically last between one and two seconds. For more on intonation phrases, see Wells (2006).

Intrinsic motivation – Intrinsic motivation refers to a part of motivation from the perspective of the self-determination theory. The self-determination theory suggests that humans have three main psychological needs: the need for autonomy, the need for relatedness, and the need for competency. When all three of these psychological needs are met to a high degree, one's motivation can be described as intrinsic. Intrinsically motivated language students find studying foreign languages fun and when they do so, time may seem to go by very quickly.

Item – In academia, questions or statements in assessment that students are required to respond to are usually called items. In casual conversation, it is acceptable to say "questions," of course, but because tests might include short essays, fill in the gap, and other non-question types of problems, "item" is the more accepted terminology to use in academic discussions.

L1 (First Language) – An acronym referring to one's first language, native language, or mother tongue, which usually refers to the language which is your most proficient. There are debates among research of bilingualism regarding whether or not one can be described as having two L1s or not.

LGBTQ – Lesbian, Gay, Bisexual, Transgender, Queer. For more on LGBTQ research in second language acquisition, see the work by John Gray.

Likert scale – A Likert scale is often used in surveys and questionnaires to measure the degree of participants' reactions and opinions to various items. Likert scales usually have strong positive responses (e.g., Strongly Agree) at one end of the scale and strong negative responses at the other end of the scale (e.g., Strongly disagree). Much debate is held among researchers about whether Likert scales should have an odd number of selections (e.g., 5, 7, 9, etc.), which allows neutral or no-opinion responses in the middle, or an even number of selections (e.g., 6, 8), which encourages participants to actively choose one side of the scale.

Lingua Franca – Lingua Franca refers to a language that is used by two non-native speakers to communicate. For example, in the case in which a French speaker and Chinese speaker were using English to communicate, English is the Lingua Franca. Although English is the most popular Lingua Franca, other well-known examples include Afrikaans, French, and Spanish.

LMS – Learner Management System. An LMS is an online hub in which the teacher is able to easily manage and contact students in the class. Teachers can also easily distribute materials and exams as well, using such a system. Examples of popular LMSes include Blackboard, Google Classroom, Microsoft Teams, and Moodle.

Longitudinal study – A longitudinal study refers to a research project which is conducted over an extensive time span. Researchers often gather data at several times throughout the time span to observe changes during the period.

M – is used when reporting statistical results to display the mean or average score of a set of numerical data.

Metacognitive strategies – A controlling function within the mental processes of metacognition (i.e., thinking about how we think). Metacognitive strategies are used when we reflect on our academic performances, for example, and consider ways to achieve better results in the future.

Microteaching – is often used in teacher training to develop teaching skills. It often involves giving practice lessons in front of peers and then holding discussions related to how the lessons were conducted and more effective techniques.

Mixed-design study – A mixed-design study uses both empirical data gathered through questionnaires, surveys, or proficiency tests combined with qualitative data obtained through written journals, interviews or essays for analysis. cf. Qualitative research, Quantitative research

MOOC – Massive Open Online Courses. MOOCs are free courses made available online to which anyone can enroll. The majority of MOOCs are free, so it is easy to join and leave courses. As a result, MOOCs often have very low completion rates.

Mora-timed – A mora-timed rhythm in language is similar to syllable-timed rhythm. A mora is a minimal phonological or metrical unit and often smaller than a single syllable; that is, a heavy syllable (consonant-vowel-consonant rhythm or consonant-vowel-vowel rhythm) consists of two morae/moras while a light syllable (consonant-vowel) consists of a mora. Japanese is well known as a typical example of a mora-timed language. Each kana (hiragana/katakana) in the Japanese alphabet represents a single mora.

n – The letter n refers to the number of students in a study or group within a study. It is usually displayed in italics and in lower case.

Online skill – In this use, the word "online" is completely unrelated to using the Internet. Speaking and listening are often referred to as online skills because learners do not have time to think about the meaning carefully like they do when reading and writing.

p – The p-value is reported when looking at the statistically significance of a data set. Usually, a p-value of less than .05 (usually reported as $p < .05$) is seen as statistically significant. The lower the p-value, the more significant the results are and are often reported as $p < .01$ or $p < .001$. Recently, many scientists report the exact p-value if it is more than .001 (e.g., $p = .018$). Some statistical analysis software reports the p-value as 0.000. This result does not mean that the p-value is zero (that is in fact impossible), but that the p-value is extremely small. If your statistical analysis software gives a p-value of 0.000, I suggest you report it as $p < .001$.

Paired-samples t-test – In quantitative data analyses, a paired-samples t-test is used to compare to sets of data coming from the same subjects. Paired-samples t-tests are commonly used in pre-test-post-test design research. For example, if a researcher were to compare the grammatical accuracy of a group of students at the beginning of a flipped course and then again at the end of the flipped course, they would use a paired-samples t-test. When conducting a paired-samples t-test, it is important to make sure all of the students in the pre-test and all of the students in the post-test are the same. If any

students were absent from either test, their data should be deleted from the set. cf. Independent-samples t-test.
- η_p^2 – Partial eta squared is one method used to report the effect sizes of ANOVA. In some cases, the researcher may be required to use eta squared (i.e., η^2).
- **Pecha Kucha** – Pecha Kucha (meaning "chit chat" in Japanese) is a presentation style in which speakers give short presentations using 20 slides that can be shown for 20 seconds each (i.e., a total of 400 seconds for each presentation).
- **Post Hoc** – A post hoc data analysis is conducted after the initial data set has been observed and analyzed to a certain degree. You might conduct pos hoc analyses to search for answers to questions emerging from the initial data analysis.
- **PPP** – Present Practice Produce. PPP is a traditional teaching structure, which often includes the use of the students' L1 and translations. PPP lessons often begin with an explanation of the grammar structure given by the teacher, followed by repeated drills in which students aim for automaticity, and finally time for language production, in which students are given opportunities to use the language freely based on a topic or theme related to the grammar structure taught in the class.
- **Pre-test-post-test design** – An experiment design that looks at participants' levels before the experiment and then compares those levels after the experiment. What the researcher does during the experiment is often referred to as the intervention. In recent years, many researchers have criticized the pre-test-post-test design as it gives only two measures of students' abilities (or motivation or whatever is being researched). There are calls for more longitudinal studies and qualitative studies that consider the dynamics of students' learning.
- **Project-based learning** – Project-based learning refers to classroom activities in which students use the target language to complete authentic assignments given by the teacher. Examples of projects include giving presentations on global problems, writing articles identifying environmental issues, and suggesting possible solutions to challenges in society. For more on project-based language, see Project-Based Language Learning and CALL: From Virtual Exchange to Social Justice (Thomas & Yamazaki, 2021).
- **Qualitative research** – Qualitative research is research based on non-numerical data. Common ways of obtaining data for qualitative research include through interviews, essays, and open-ended questions in surveys. cf. Mixed-design study, Quantitative research.
- **Quantitative research** – Quantitative research is research based on numerical data (also referred to as empirical data). Common ways of obtaining data for quantitative research include proficiency tests and

questionnaires using numerical scales (also called Likert scales). cf. Mixed-design study, Qualitative research.

Quasi-experimental study – Quasi- is a prefix meaning partly. Therefore, a quasi-experimental study refers to a study in which one or more factors affect the pureness of the experiment. For example, in a true experiment, the subjects are chosen randomly, but in a quasi-experimental study, researchers may choose to use the students in their classes. Other factors that may result in an experiment being described as quasi-experimental include the researcher being the teacher in the classroom where the experiment is being conducted and the non-inclusion of a control group in the study.

Recast – One of the strategies used when giving corrective feedback. When teachers hear students using English with a grammatical inaccuracy (e.g., My birthday is on May), they might use the recast strategy to repeat what the student has said, but with grammatical accuracy (e.g., Oh, your birthday is in May).

Referential questions – Referential questions are questions that do not have a clear correct answer. The person asking referential questions usually does not know how the other person will answer. Example of referential questions in the classroom include, "Why do you think the author says this?" and "What do you predict is going to happen next?" Referential questions often increase opportunities for communication in comparison to display questions, so are recommended by many educators, especially in EFL classrooms. c.f. Display questions.

Reflexive diaries – Reflexive diaries are often kept by researchers as a record of the research processes and decisions conducted throughout the project.

Sample – The participants in a study. The number of participants in a study is often referred to as the sample size.

Scaffolding – Like the scaffolding used when building a house, this refers to the help a teacher gives students in their learning. As students become more able to handle challenges, teachers take a step back to let the students take charge. Scaffolding is not about telling the students the answer to problems; it refers more to giving hints and encouragement to help them find the answers. For an excellent example of scaffolding, check out how Maurice Cheeks assists 13-year-old Natalie Gilbert as she struggles through singing the national anthem in Game 3 of the Mavericks-Trail Blazers playoff series in 2003.

Schema (Schemata) – Schema and its pluralized form schemata refer to one's background knowledge about a certain topic. Even if the vocabulary in conversations or texts is simple, unless one has the background knowledge of the topic, it will be difficult to create an image of what is written or what is being said.

SD – Standard deviation (*SD*) is one of the most common ways of analyzing data by comparing it to the average. The *SD* basically refers to the average distance each piece of numerical data is from the overall average. For example, the data set 2, 4, 6, 8, 10 has an average of 6.00 (30÷5 [pieces of numerical data] =6). To work out the *SD*, we look at the distance of each number from the average. So, we have 4 (the difference between 2 and 6), 2 (the difference between 4 and 6), 0 (the difference between 6 and 6), 2 (the difference between 8 and 6), and 4 (the difference between 10 and 6). Next, we work out the average of these numbers (4, 2, 0, 2, 4), which is 2.4 (12÷5=2.4). The *SD* is important as it gives us an idea of the distribution of the data set. The example above has quite a wide distribution of data (assuming the maximum score was 10), but when we look at the data set 5, 5, 6, 7, 7, which has the same average of 6 but a *SD* of 0.8, we can see that the scores are much more bunched together. When looking at a data set, try to look at the average score, the *SD*, the minimum possible score, and the maximum possible score together to get a better feeling for the scores you are looking at.

Semi-structured Interview – Semi-structured interviews are often used in qualitative research. Although the interviewer has a few questions prepared to ask the participant, further questions may evolve based on the answers that the interviewee gives to other questions. cf. Structured interview, Unstructured interview.

SLA – Second Language Acquisition. This is the study of how second and foreign languages are acquired and learned. This field involves pretty much everything that has anything to do with learning languages other than your mother tongue.

Split-plot ANOVA – A split-plot ANOVA, also known as a Mixed-Design ANOVA, is used in quantitative research when comparing how much multiple groups improve or worsen due to some kind of factor(s) (e.g., teaching technique) over time. Let's assume that a researcher wishes to compare Group A instructed by Technique X and Group B by Technique Y. If Group A's average proficiency score improved from 480 before the instruction to 650 after the instruction and Group B's average score improved from 520 to 730, the researcher could use a split-plot ANOVA to measure whether Group A's improvement (170 points) was significantly greater than Group B's improvement (210 points) in order to prove whether or not technique B is more effective than technique A (or vice-versa).

Stress-timed – A stress-timed rhythm in language refers to a rhythm that follows a consonant-vowel-consonant structure. This allows a great range of syllable structures and reduction in unstressed vowels when compared with vowels in stressed syllables. Stress-timed languages include English, German, and Dutch.

Structured interview – Structured interviews are often used in qualitative research. Interviewers prepare sets of questions, and the interview does not deviate from those questions or topics. Cf. Semi-structured interview, unstructured interview.

Subjects – The individual participants of your study. Some researchers are of the opinion that the term "subjects" has a slightly cold feeling to it. Therefore, the researcher could consider using other descriptions such as participants, students, pupils, learners, or adolescents.

Syllable-timed – A syllable-timed rhythm in language refers to a rhythm that follows a consonant-vowel structure. In Japanese, for example, the word "strike" will be read as *sutoraiku*, as a vowel sound is often inserted between consonant sounds. Spanish and Mandarin Chinese are commonly said to be syllable-time languages. cf. Stress-timed

Target Language (TL) – The target language is the language that is being studied in the classroom. Because I usually teach English, English is the target language. From time to time when I teach a bit of Japanese, Japanese is the target language.

TBLT – Task-Based Language Teaching. TBLT uses tasks to get students using the language in meaningful ways. TBLT is generally not focused on particular grammatical structures, but teachers can use focused tasks that encourage students to repeatedly use a target structure while emphasis is put on the meaning.

TED Talks – TED (Technology, Entertainment, and Design) Talks is a conference format that began in the early 1990s where many short presentations of around 20 minutes are given on a variety of topics. All of the talks given at a TED conference are uploaded to the TED website, where they can be viewed for free.

This – A word used to point to objects, either visible or abstract, which are close to you.

TOEFL – The Test of English as a Foreign Language is a standardized test often used to measure the English proficiency of non-native speakers. It is one of the most highly respected proficiency tests used globally and a large number of universities will require a TOEFL score as proof of a student's language ability when entering as an international student or as someone from a non-English speaking background.

Top-down process – Top-down processing in listening and reading refers to the mechanism of calling upon one's prior knowledge of the topic that is being spoken or written about and using that background knowledge to predict what will appear in the spoken or written discourse.

Tukey test – A Tukey test, also known as Tukey's honest significance test, is similar to a t-test. It is often conducted after an ANOVA and used to check for significant differences between groups when there are three or more groups in the data set. For example, if there are three groups (let's say, Group A, Group B, and Group C), and the ANOVA has reported that a significant difference among the groups exists, the Tukey test will act as a post hoc test and analyze the differences between Group A and Group B, Group A and Group C, and Group B and Group C. It is generally not accepted to do multiple t-tests to conduct the same analyses. When reporting the results of your Tukey test, make sure you don't do what I did and make a spelling mistake, calling it a Turkey test. That was a little embarrassing!

Two-way repeated measures ANOVA – A way of analyzing numerical data. The ANOVA indicates that comparisons are being made between two or more groups. "Two-way" means that two factors have been used in both groups. "Repeated measures" shows that all of the subjects' data have been measured or have been affected by all of the factors.

Unfocused task – An unfocused task is a task that encourages students to communicate without forcing them to use a particular grammatical structure. c.f. Focused task.

Unstructured interview – Unstructured interviews are used in qualitative research. Although there might be a main theme to the interview, there are no set questions, perhaps other than the opening question, and the interview flows like a natural conversation. Some researchers refer to unstructured interviews as being like a "wine and chat" setting. cf. Structured interview, Semi-structured interview.

Validity – is often used in testing and assessment. Usually, educators refer to three varieties of validity: Content Validity (Does the content of this test reflect what we studied in class?), Face Validity (Does this test look familiar to our students?), and Construct Validity (Are we using the same kinds of items that reflect what we did in class? [e.g., input through multiple choice; output through open-ended items].)

Web 2.0 – A terminology used to describe advancements to the World Wide Web that allowed users to create their own materials to put on the Internet. Whereas Web 1.0 was mainly used for searching, members of the general public were unable to create their own materials. Web 2.0 enables users to create and comment on, for example, blogs and web sites, and collaborate with other users.

World Englishes – World Englishes (note that "Englishes" is pluralized) is a terminology referring to varieties of English that have emerged and are generally accepted by linguists, despite often having pronunciation and grammatical structures that had previously been unacceptable by language researchers. Examples of World Englishes include Indian English, Japanese English, and Singapore English.

ZPD – Based on the descriptions provided by Vygotsky (1978), the Zone of Proximal Development (ZPD) refers to an area of human development in which tasks can be achieved with the help (i.e., scaffolding) of a person who is more capable or experienced in that skill. Students' ZPD will change as their skills increase.

References

Abaeian, H., & Samadi, L. (2016). The effect of flipped classroom on Iranian EFL learners' L2 reading comprehension: Focusing on different proficiency levels. *Journal of Applied Linguistics and Language Research*, *3*(6), 295–304. https://www.jallr.com/index.php/JALLR/article/view/442

Abdullah, M. Y., Hussin, S., & Ismail, K. (2019). Implementation of flipped classroom model and its effectiveness on English speaking performance. *International Journal of Emerging Technologies in Learning*, *14*(9), 130–147. http://dx.doi.org/10.3991/ijet.v14i09.10348

Aburezeq, I. M. (2020). The impact of flipped classroom on developing Arabic speaking skills. *The Asia-Pacific Education Researcher*, *29*(4), 295–306. http://dx.doi.org/10.1007/s40299-019-00483-z

Ahmed, S. Z. (2016). The flipped classroom model to develop Egyptian EFL students' listening comprehension. *English Language Teaching*, *9*(9), 166–178. https://doi.org/10.5539/elt.v9n9p166

Al-Hamlan, S., & Baniabdelrahman, A (2015). A needs analysis approach to EFL syllabus development for second grade students in secondary education in Saudi Arabia: A descriptive analytical approach to students' needs. *American International Journal of Contemporary Research*, *5*(1), 118–145. http://www.aijcrnet.com/journals/Vol_5_No_1_February_2015/15.pdf

Al-Harbi, S. S., & Alshumaimeri, Y. A. (2016). The flipped classroom impact in grammar class on EFL Saudi secondary school students' performances and attitudes. *English Language Teaching*, *9*(10), 60–80. http://dx.doi.org/10.5539/elt.v9n10p60

Al-Naabi, I. S. (2020). Is it worth flipping? The impact of flipped classroom on EFL students' grammar. *English Language Teaching*, *13*(6), 64–75. https://doi.org/10.5539/elt.v13n6p64

Alemi, M., & Khatoony, S. (2020). Virtual reality assisted pronunciation training (VRAPT) for young EFL learners. *Teaching English with Technology*, *20*(4), 59–81. https://files.eric.ed.gov/fulltext/EJ1271706.pdf

American Speech-Language-Hearing Association. (2014). *Degree of hearing loss*. https://www.asha.org/public/hearing/degree-of-hearing-loss/

Amiryousefi, M. (2017). The incorporation of flipped learning into conventional classes to enhance EFL learners' L2 speaking, L2 listening, and engagement. *Innovation in Language Learning and Teaching*, *13*(2), 147–161. https://doi.org/10.1080/17501229.2017.1394307

Anderson, L. W., & Krathwohl, D. R. (2001). *A taxonomy for learning, teaching, and assessing: A revision of Bloom's taxonomy of educational objectives*.

Longman.

Anderson, N., & McCutcheon, N. (2019). *Activities for task-based learning: Integrating a fluency first approach into the ELT classroom*. Delta Publishing.

Aoyama, T., & Takahashi, T. (2020). International students' willingness to communicate in English as a second language: The effects of L2 self-confidence, acculturation, and motivational types. *Journal of International Students, 10*(3), 703–723. https://doi.org/10.32674/jis.v10i3.730

Aronson, E. (1978). *The jigsaw classroom*. Sage Publications

Aronson, E. (2002). Building empathy, compassion, and achievement in the jigsaw classroom. In J. Aronson (Ed.), *Improving academic achievement* (pp. 209–225). Academic Press. https://doi.org/10.1016/b978-012064455-1/50013-0

Aronson, E. (2004). Reducing hostility and building compassion: Lessons from the jigsaw classroom. In A. G. Miller (Ed.), *The social psychology of good and evil* (pp. 469–488). The Guilford Press.

Asaka, S., Shinozaki, F., & Yoshida, H. (2018). The effect of a flipped classroom approach on EFL Japanese junior high school students' performances and attitudes. *International Journal of Heritage, Art and Multimedia, 1*(3), 71–87. http://www.ijham.com/PDF/IJHAM-2018-03-12-05.pdf

Ashby, P. (2011). The flipped lecture–A pre-vodcasting trial. *The phonetics teaching and learning conference: Proceedings 2011* (pp. 7–10). https://www.researchgate.net/profile/Patricia-Ashby/publication/267979737_PTLC2011_THE_FLIPPED_LECTURE/links/545e12a00cf27487b44eee36/PTLC2011-THE-FLIPPED-LECTURE.pdf

Ashcroft, R. J., Cvitkovic, R., & Praver, M. (2018). Digital flashcard L2 vocabulary learning out-performs traditional flashcards at lower proficiency levels: A mixed-methods study of 139 Japanese university students. *The EuroCALL Review, 26*(1), 14–28. http://dx.doi.org/10.4995/eurocall.2018.7881

Asher, J. (1977). *Learning another language through actions: The complete teacher's guidebook*. Sky Oaks Productions.

Assalahi, H. M. (2013). Why is the grammar-translation method still alive in the Arab world? *Theory and Practice in Language Studies, 3*(4), 589–599. http://dx.doi.org/10.4304/tpls.3.4.589-599

Azizi, M., Tkácová, H., Pavlíková, M., & Jenisová, Z. (2020). Extensive reading and the writing ability of EFL learners: The effect of group work. *European Journal of Contemporary Education, 9*(4), 726–739. https://doi.org/10.13187/ejced.2020.4.726

Bachman, L. F. (1990). *Fundamental considerations in language testing*. Oxford University Press.

Baker, J. W. (2000). The "classroom flip": Using web course management tools to become the guide by the side. *Selected Papers from the 11th International Conference on College Teaching and Learning*, 9–17. http://

www.classroomflip.com/files/classroom_flip_baker_2000.pdf

Baleghizadeh, S., Timcheh Memar, A., & Timcheh Memar, H. (2011). A sociocultural perspective on second language acquisition: The effect of high-structured scaffolding versus low-structured scaffolding on the writing ability of EFL learners. *Reflections on English Language Teaching, 10*(1), 43–54. https://www.nus.edu.sg/celc/research/books/relt/vol10/43to54-baleghizadeh.pdf

Bamford, J., & Day, R. R. (Eds.). (2004). *Extensive reading activities for teaching language*. Cambridge University Press.

Barrot, J. S. (2020). Integrating technology into ESL/EFL writing through Grammarly. *RELC Journal*. Advance online publication. http://dx.doi.org/10.1177/0033688220966632

Base, G. (2004). *The water hole*. Puffin Books.

BBC News. (2018, April 26). *Iran blocks video and images on Telegram messaging app*. BBC News. https://www.bbc.com/news/technology-43907246

Beckett, G. H., & Slater, T. (2018). Project-based learning and technology. *The TESOL encyclopedia of English language teaching*, 1–7. https://doi.org/10.1002/9781118784235.eelt0427

Bergmann, J. (2018, August 18). *No video, no Internet, no problem: The low-tech flipped class*. Flipped Learning Review. https://flr.flglobal.org/no-video-no-internet-no-problem-the-low-tech-flipped-class/

Bergmann, J., & Sams, A. (2010). *MAST Institute*. http://mast.unco.edu/programs/flipped/

Bergmann, J., & Sams, A. (2012). *Flip your classroom: Reach every student in every class every day*. International Society for Technology in Education.

Bergmann, J., & Sams, A. (2014). *Flipped learning: Gateway to student engagement*. International Society for Technology in Education.

Birdsell, B. J. (2020). A review of the critical literature on CLIL and steps to move Japan CLIL forward. *The Journal of the Japan CLIL Pedagogy Association, 2*, 110–126. https://www.j-clil.com/_files/ugd/d705d2_6a4c8405350f4d2c8a5288695e1f42ef.pdf

Birjandi, P., & Hadidi Tamjid, N. (2012). The role of self-, peer and teacher assessment in promoting Iranian EFL learners' writing performance. *Assessment & Evaluation in Higher Education, 37*(5), 513–533. http://dx.doi.org/10.1080/02602938.2010.549204

Birketveit, A., Rimmereide, H. E., Bader, M., & Fisher, L. (2018). Extensive reading in primary school EFL. *Acta Didactica Norge, 12*(2), 164–186. https://doi.org/10.5617/adno.5643

Bitchener, J. (2008). Evidence in support of written corrective feedback. *Journal of Second Language Writing, 17*(2), 102–118. https://doi.org/10.1016/j.jslw.2007.11.004

Bitchener, J., & Ferris, D. R. (2012). *Written corrective feedback in second language acquisition and writing*. Routledge.

Blau, I., & Shamir-Inbal, T. (2017). Re-designed flipped learning model in an academic course: The role of co-creation and co-regulation. *Computers & Education*, *115*, 69–81. http://dx.doi.org/10.1016/j.compedu.2017.07.014

Bloom, B. S. (1956). *Taxonomy of educational objectives: The classification of educational goals*. David McKay.

Blythe, H., Sweet, C., & Carpenter, R. (2015). *It works for me, flipping the classroom: Shared tips for effective teaching*. New Forums Press.

Brazil, D. (2010). *The communicative value of intonation in English*. Cambridge University Press

Brinks Lockwood, R. (2014). *Flip it! Strategies for the ESL classroom*. University of Michigan Press.

Brown, C. J. (2018). Flipping the ESL/EFL academic reading classroom: A group leader discussion activity. In J. Mehring & A. Leis (Eds.), *Innovations in flipping the language classroom* (pp. 147–168). Springer.

Brown. H. D., & Lee, H. (2015). *Teaching by principles: An interactive approach to language pedagogy* (4th ed.). Pearson.

Bryfonski, L., & McKay, T. H. (2019). TBLT implementation and evaluation: A meta-analysis. *Language Teaching Research*, *23*(5), 603–632. http://dx.doi.org/10.1177/1362168817744389

Buran, A., & Filyukov, A. (2015). Mind mapping technique in language learning. *Procedia-social and Behavioral Sciences*, *206*, 215–218. http://dx.doi.org/10.1016/j.sbspro.2015.10.010

Burri, M. S., Baker, A. A., & Actone, W. (2019). Proposing a haptic approach to facilitating L2 learners' pragmatic competence. *Humanizing Language Teaching*, *21*(3), 1–15. https://ro.uow.edu.au/cgi/viewcontent.cgi?article=5545&context=sspapers

Cameron, L., & McKay, P. (2010). *Brining creative teaching into the young learner classroom*. Oxford University Press.

Capone, R., Del Sorba, M. R., & Fiore, O. (2017). A flipped experience in physics education using CLIL methodology. *EURASIA Journal of Mathematics Science and Technology Education*, *13*(10), 6579–6582. http://dx.doi.org/10.12973/ejmste/77044

Carkin, S. (2005). English for academic purposes. In E. Hinkel (Ed.), *Handbook of research in second language teaching and learning* (pp. 85–98). Lawrence Erlbaum.

Cenoz, J. (2015). Content-based instruction and content and language integrated learning: the same or different? *Language, Culture and Curriculum*, *28*, 8–24. https://doi.org/10.1080/07908318.2014.1000922

Chan, A. Y. (2011). Bilingualised or monolingual dictionaries? Preferences and practices of advanced ESL learners in Hong Kong. *Language and Curriculum*, *24*(1), 1–21. http://dx.doi.org/10.1080/07908318.2010.510196

Chang, K.-E., Sung, Y.-T., Chang, R.-B., & Lin, S.-C. (2005). A new assessment for computer-based concept mapping. *Journal of Educational Technology & Society*, *8*(3),138–148. https://www.researchgate.net/

profile/Kuo-Chang-3/publication/220374894_A_New_Assessment_for_Computer-based_Concept_Mapping/links/02e7e5361c08b14126000000/A-New-Assessment-for-Computer-based-Concept-Mapping.pdf

Chen, C. M., Liu, H., & Huang, H. B. (2019). Effects of a mobile game-based English vocabulary learning app on learners' perceptions and learning performance: A case study of Taiwanese EFL learners. *ReCALL, 31*(2), 170–188. http://dx.doi.org/10.1017/S0958344018000228

Chen, L. (2006). The effect of the use of L1 in a multimedia tutorial on grammar learning: An error analysis of Taiwanese beginning EFL learners' English essays. *The Asian EFL Journal Quarterly, 8*(2), 76–110. http://asian-efl-journal.com/June_2006_EBook_editions.pdf#page=76

Chen, M. A., & Hwang, G. (2020). Effects of a concept mapping-based flipped learning approach on EFL students' English speaking performance, critical thinking awareness and speaking anxiety. *British Journal of Educational Technology, 51*(3), 817–834. https://doi.org/10.1111/bjet.12887

Chen, Y. (2012). Dictionary use and vocabulary learning in the context of reading. *International Journal of Lexicography, 25*(2), 216–247. http://dx.doi.org/10.1093/ijl/ecr031

Cheng, Y. C. (2018). *The effect of using board games in reducing language anxiety and improving oral performance.* [Master's thesis, The University of Mississippi]. Electronic Theses and Dissertations. https://egrove.olemiss.edu/etd/899

Chou, M. (2014). Assessing English vocabulary and enhancing young English as a Foreign Language (EFL) learners' motivation through games, songs, and stories. *Education 3–13, 42*(3), 284–297. https://doi.org/10.1080/03004279.2012.680899

Chou, M. (2017). A task-based language teaching approach to developing metacognitive strategies for listening comprehension. *International Journal of Listening, 31*(1), 51–70. https://doi.org/10.1080/10904018.2015.1098542

Clintondale High School. (2010). *Our story.* Clintondale High School. https://www.flippedhighschool.com/ourstory/

Cockrum, T, (2014). *Flipping your English class to reach all learners.* Routledge.

Cohen, A. D., & Macaro, E. (2007). *Language learner strategies.* Oxford University Press.

Cooke, S., & Leis, A. (2018). Dictogloss: Redefining dictation exercises in the EFL classroom. In *2018 5th International Conference on Business and Industrial Research (ICBIR)* (pp. 526-529). IEEE.

Covington, M. V. (1992). *Making the grade: A self-worth perspective on motivation and school reform.* Cambridge University Press.

Covington, M. V. (1998). *The will to learn: A guide for motivating young people.*

Cambridge University Press.

Coyle, D., Hood, P., & Marsh, D. (2010). *Content and language integrated learning*. Cambridge University Press.

Crouch, C. H., & Mazur, E. (2001). Peer instruction: Ten years of experience and results. *American Journal of Physics, 69*(9), 970–977. https://doi.org/10.1119/1.1374249

Crystal, D. (2008). *A dictionary of linguistics and phonetics* (6th ed.). Wiley-Blackwell. http://dx.doi.org/10.1002/9781444302776

Darnon, C., Buchs, C., & Desbar, D. (2012). The jigsaw technique and self-efficacy of vocational training students: A practice report. *European Journal of Psychology of Education, 27*(3), 439–449. https://doi.org/10.1007/s10212-011-0091-4

Dauer, R. M. (1983). Stress-timing and syllable-timing re-analysed. *Journal of Phonetics, 11*, 51–62. https://doi.org/10.1016/S0095-4470(19)30776-4

Day, R. R., & Bamford, J. (2002). Top ten principles for teaching extensive reading. *Reading in a Foreign Language, 14*(2), 136–141. https://scholarspace.manoa.hawaii.edu/bitstream/10125/66761/1/14_2_10125_66761_day.pdf

de Boer, P. (2015, November 15). *Different types of language learning explained*. https://www.clilmedia.com/different-types-of-language-learning-explained/#:~:text=CBLT%3A%20Content%20through%20language&text=This%20sounds%20a%20lot%20like,In%20other%20words.

DeKeyser, R. M. (2007). *Practice in a second language: Perspectives from applied linguistics and cognitive psychology*. Cambridge University Press.

Deng, L., & Li, X. (2013). Machine learning paradigms for speech recognition: An overview. *IEEE Transactions on Audio, Speech, and Language Processing, 21*(5), 1060–1089. https://doi.org/10.1109/TASL.2013.2244083

Derry, S. J., & Murphy, D. A. (1986). Designing systems that train learning ability: from theory to practice. *Review of Educational Research, 56*(1), 1–39. http://dx.doi.org/10.3102/00346543056001001

Dewaele, J. M., & MacIntyre, P. D. (2014). The two faces of Janus? Anxiety and enjoyment in the foreign language classroom. *Studies in Second Language Learning and Teaching, 4*(2), 237–274. http://dx.doi.org/10.14746/ssllt.2014.4.2.5

Dewaele, J-M., & MacIntyre, P. D. (2019). The predictive power of multicultural personality traits, learner and teacher variables on foreign language enjoyment and anxiety. In M. Sato & S. Loewen (Eds.) *Evidence-based second language pedagogy: A collection of instructed second language acquisition studies* (pp. 263–286). Routledge.

Dillon, T., & Wells, D. (2021). Student perceptions of mobile automated speech recognition for pronunciation study and testing. *English Teaching, 76*(4), 101–122. http://dx.doi.org/10.15858/engtea.76.4.202112.

101
Dirección de Formación Inicial Docente. (2010). *Teaching jazz chants - Carol Graham*. [Video]. YouTube. https://www.youtube.com/watch?v=R_nPUuPryCs

Dixon, S. (2016). *Fifty ways to teach reading: Fifty ways to teach: Tips for ESL/EFL teachers*. Wayzgoose Press.

Donaldson, J., & Scheffler, A. (1999). *The gruffalo*. Macmillan Children's Books.

Donato, R. (1994). Collective scaffolding in second language learning. In J.P. Lantolf & G. Appel (Eds.), *Vygotskian approaches to second language research* (pp. 33-56). Ablex Publishing

Dörnyei, Z., & Skehan, P. (2003). Individual differences in second language learning. In C. J. Doughty & M. H. Long (Eds.), *The Handbook of second language acquisition* (pp. 589–630). Blackwell Publishing.

Dörnyei, Z., MacIntyre, P, & Henry, A. (2015). *Motivational dynamics in language learning*. Multilingual Matters.

Doughty, C., & Williams, J. (1998). Pedagogical choices in focus on form. In C. Doughty & J. Williams (Eds.), *Focus on form in classroom second language acquisition* (pp. 197–261). Cambridge University Press.

Dudeney, G., & Hockly, N. (2007). *How to teach English with technology*. Pearson.

Duman, S. K., Yalçın, Ş., & Erçetin, G. (2021). Working memory and language aptitude in relation to listening strategy instruction in an instructed SLA context. *Annual Review of Applied Linguistics, 41*, 108–117. http://dx.doi.org/10.1017/S0267190521000040

Dweck, C. S. (2017). *Mindset - updated edition: Changing the way you think to fulfil your potential*. Robinson.

Efklides, A. (2006). Metacognition and affect: What can metacognitive experiences tell us about the learning process? *Educational Research Review, 1*(1), 3–14. https://doi.org/10.1016/j.edurev.2005.11.001

Ekmekci, E. (2017). The flipped writing classroom in Turkish EFL context: A comparative study on a new model. *Turkish Online Journal of Distance Education, 18*(2), 151–167. https://doi.org/10.17718/tojde.306566

El-Bassuony, J. M. (2016). The effectiveness of flipped learning in developing English grammatical performance of underachieving language learners at the secondary stage. *International Journal of English Language Teaching, 4*(8), 76–101. https://www.eajournals.org/journals/international-journal-of-english-language-teaching-ijelt/vol-4-issue-8-september-2016/effectiveness-flipped-learning-developing-english-grammatical-performance-underachieving-language-learners-secondary-stage/

Elahifar, M., Ebrahimi, F., & Azizi, Z. (2022). The effect of using dictogloss as a while-listening activity for listening comprehension development of EFL learners. *Education Research International, 2022*, 1–9. http://dx.doi.org/10.1155/2022/3016643

Elgort, I. (2010). Deliberate learning and vocabulary acquisition in a second language. *Language Learning, 61*(2), 367–413. http://dx.doi.org/10.1111/j.1467-9922.2010.00613.x

Ellis, N. C. (1996). Sequencing in SLA: Phonological memory, chunking, and points of order. *Studies in Second Language Acquisition, 18*(1), 91–126. http://dx.doi.org/10.1017/S0272263100014698

Ellis, R. (1990). *Instructed second language acquisition*. Blackwell.

Ellis, R. (2002). Methodological options in grammar teaching materials. In E. Hinkel & S. Fotos (Eds.), *New perspectives on grammar teaching in second language classrooms* (pp. 155–179). Lawrence Erlbaum.

Ellis, R. (2009). Task-based language teaching: Sorting out the misunderstandings. *International Journal of Applied Linguistics, 19*(3), 221–246. https://doi.org/10.1111/j.1473-4192.2009.00231.x

Ellis, R. (2010). Epilogue: A framework for investigating oral and written corrective feedback. *Studies in Second Language Acquisition, 32*(2), 335–349. https://doi.org/10.1017/s0272263109990544

Ellis, R. (2016). Focus on form: A critical review. *Language Teaching Research, 20*(3), 405–428. https://doi.org/10.1177/1362168816628627

Ellis, R., Basturkmen, H., & Loewen, S. (2002). Doing focus-on-form. *System, 30*(4), 419–432. http://dx.doi.org/10.1016/S0346-251X(02)00047-7

Ellis, R., Skehan, P., Li, S., Shintani, N., & Lambert, C. (2019). *Task-based language teaching: Theory and practice*. Cambridge University Press.

Ericsson, K. A., Krampe, R. Th., & Tesch-Römer, C. (1993). The role of deliberate practice in the acquisition of expert performance. *Psychological Review, 100*(3), 363–406. https://doi.org/10.1037/0033-295x.100.3.363

Ersöz, A. (2007). *Teaching English to young learners*. EDM Publishing. https://files.eric.ed.gov/fulltext/EJ997523.pdf

Esnawy, S. (2016). EFL/EAP reading and research essay writing using jigsaw. *Procedia-Social and Behavioral Sciences, 232*(2016), 98–101. https://doi.org/10.1016/j.sbspro.2016.10.033

Estes. M. D., Ingram, R., & Liu, J. C. (2014). A review of flipped classroom research, practice, and technologies. *International HETL Review, 4*(7), 1–8. https://www.hetl.org/a-review-of-flipped-classroom-research-practice-and-technologies/

Evers, K., & Chen, S. (2020). Effects of an automatic speech recognition system with peer feedback on pronunciation instruction for adults. *Computer Assisted Language Learning*, Advance online publication. https://doi.org/10.1080/09588221.2020.1839504

Farrell, T. C. S. (2015). *Promoting teacher reflection in second language education: A framework for TESOL professionals*. Routledge.

Farrell, T. S. C. (2022). *Insights into professional development in language teaching*. Castledown Publishers. https://doi.org/10.29140/9781914291036

Fernandez, E. M., & H. L. Cairns. (2011). *Fundamentals of psycholinguistics*. Wiley-Blackwell.

Ferris, D. R. (2012). Written corrective feedback in second language acquisition and writing studies. *Language Teaching*, *45*(4), 446–459. https://doi.org/10.4324/9780203832400

Fethi, K., & Marshall, H.W. (2018). Flipping movies for dynamic engagement. In J. Mehring & A. Leis (Eds.), *Innovations in flipped learning in the language classroom: Theories and practice*. (pp. 185–202). Springer.

Filatova, O. (2015). Teaching practical grammar in foreign language studies. In H. Blythe, C. Sweet, & R. Carpenter (Eds.), *It works for me, flipping the classroom: Shared tips for effective teaching* (pp. 64–65). New Forums.

Finardi, K. R. (2015). Current trends in ELT and affordances of the inverted CLIL approach. *Studies in English Language Teaching*, *3*(4), 326–338. http://dx.doi.org/10.22158/selt.v3n4p326

Finardi, K. R., Silveira, N., Lima, S., & Mendes, A. R. (2106). MOOC in the inverted CLIL approach: Hybridizing English teaching/learning. *Studies in English Language Teaching*, *4*(4), 473–493. http://dx.doi.org/10.22158/selt.v4n4p473

Flipped Learning Network. (2014a). *The four pillars of F-L-I-P™* https://flippedlearning.org/wp-content/uploads/2016/07/FLIP_handout_FNL_Web.pdf

Flipped Learning Network. (2014b). *Who we are*. https://flippedlearning.org/who-we-are/

Forster, E. (2006). The value of songs and chants for young learners. *Encuentro*, *16*, 63–68. https://ebuah.uah.es/xmlui/bitstream/handle/10017/1201/07-Forster2.pdf?sequence=1&isAllowed=y

Forsythe, E. (2017a). Pedagogical rationale for flipped learning and digital technology in second language acquisition. In J. P. Loucky & J. L. Ware (Eds.), *Flipped instruction: Breakthroughs in research and practice* (pp. 1–20). IGI Global.

Forsythe, E. (2017b). Integrating recent CALL innovations into flipped instruction. In J. P. Loucky & J. L. Ware (Eds.), *Flipped instruction: Breakthroughs in research and practice* (pp. 270–277). IGI Global.

Fotos, S. (1998). Shifting the focus from forms to form in the EFL classroom. *ELT Journal*, *52*(4), 301–307. http://dx.doi.org/10.1093/elt/52.4.301

Franco, H., Bratt, H., Rossier, R., Rao Gadde, V., Shriberg, E., Abrash, V., & Precoda, K. (2010). EduSpeak®: A speech recognition and pronunciation scoring toolkit for computer-aided language learning applications. *Language Testing*, *27*(3), 401–418. https://doi.org/10.1177/0265532210364408

Freed, B. F. (1990). Language learning in a study abroad context: The effects of interactive and non-interactive out-of-class contact on grammatical achievement and oral proficiency. In J. E. Alatis (Ed.), *Linguistics, language teaching and language acquisition: The interdependence of theory, practice and research* (pp. 459–477). Georgetown University Press.

Freeman, S., O'Connor, E., Parks, J. W., Cunningham, M., Hurley, D.,

Haak, D., Dirks, C., & Wenderoth, M. P. (2007). Prescribed active learning increases performance in introductory biology. *CBE—Life Sciences Education*, *6*(2), 132–139. https://doi.org/10.1187/cbe.06-09-0194

Fung, Y. M., & Min, Y. L. (2016). Effects of board game on speaking ability of low-proficiency ESL learners. *International Journal of Applied Linguistics and English Literature*, *5*(3), 261–271. http://www.journals.aiac.org.au/index.php/IJALEL/article/view/2289/2004

Galali, A., & Cinkara, E. (2017). The use of L1 in English as a foreign language classes: Insights from Iraqi tertiary level students. *Advances in Language and Literacy Studies*, *8*(5), 54–64. http://dx.doi.org/10.7575/aiac.alls.v.8n.5p.54

Gallo, G. (2017). Applying innovation to CLIL. *Issues and Ideas in Education*, *5*(2), 155–173. https://doi.org/10.15415/iie.2017.52010

Garrison, D. R. (2016). *Thinking collaboratively: Learning in a community of inquiry*. Routledge.

Garrison, D. R., Anderson, T., & Archer, W. (1999). Critical inquiry in a text-based environment: Computer conferencing in higher education. *The Internet and Higher Education*, *2*(2–3), 87–105. https://doi.org/10.1016/S1096-7516(00)00016-6.

Gaudart, H. (1999). Games as teaching tools for teaching English to speakers of other languages. *Simulation & Gaming*, *30*(3), 283–291. http://www.savie.ca/SAGE/Articles/100017_17_Gaudart_1999.pdf

Gavriilidou, Z., & Mitits, L. (2021). *Situating language learning strategy use: Present issues and future trends*. Multilingual Matters.

Genessee, F., & Lindholm-Leary, K. (2013). Two case studies of content-based language education. *Journal of Immersion and Content-based language Education*, *1*(1), 3–33. http://dx.doi.org/10.1075/jicb.1.1.02gen

Gilakjani, A. P., & Sabouri, N. B. (2016). A study of factors affecting EFL learners' reading comprehension skill and the strategies for improvement. *International Journal of English Linguistics*, *6*(5), 180–187. http://dx.doi.org/10.5539/ijel.v6n5p180

Godwin-Jones, R. (2015). Contributing, creating, curating: Digital literacies for language learners. *Language Learning & Technology*, *19*(3), 8–20. https://scholarspace.manoa.hawaii.edu/bitstream/10125/44427/19_03_emerging.pdf

Godwin-Jones, R. (2017). Smartphones and language learning. *Language Learning & Technology*, *21*(2), 3–17. http://llt.msu.edu/issues/june2017/emerging.pdf

Graham, C. (1978). *Jazz chants*. Oxford University Press.

Graney, J. M. (2018). Flipped learning and formative assessment in an English language class. In J. Mehring & A. Leis (Eds.), *Innovations in flipping the language classroom* (pp. 59–68). Springer.

Grant, C. (2013). First inversion: a rationale for implementing the 'flipped approach' in tertiary music courses. *Australian Journal of Music*

Education, *1*, 3–12. https://files.eric.ed.gov/fulltext/EJ1061810.pdf

Graus, J., & Coppen, P. A. (2016). Student teacher beliefs on grammar instruction. *Language Teaching Research*, *20*(5), 571–599. http://dx.doi.org/10.1177/1362168815603237

Greenland, S., Senn, S. J., Rothman, K. J., Carlin, J. B., Poole, C., Goodman, S. N., & Altman, D. G. (2016). Statistical tests, P values, confidence intervals, and power: A guide to misinterpretations. *European Journal of Epidemiology*, *31*, 337–350. https://www.ncbi.nlm.nih.gov/pubmed/27209009

Gregersen, T. S. (2003). To err is human: A reminder to teachers of language-anxious students. *Foreign Language Annals*, *36*(1), 25–32. https://doi.org/10.1111/j.1944-9720.2003.tb01929.x

Gregersen, T., MacIntyre, P. D., & Meza, M. D. (2014). The motion of emotion: Idiodynamic case studies of learners' foreign language anxiety. *Modern Language Journal*, *98*, 574–588. https://doi.org/10.1111/modl.12084

Hambrick, D. Z., Oswald, F. L., Altmann, E. M., Meinz, E. J., Gobert, F., & Campitelli, G. (2014). Deliberate practice: Is that all it takes to become an expert? *Intelligence*, *45*, 34–45. https://doi.org/10.1016/j.intell.2013.04.001

Harmer, J. (2007). *The practice of English language teaching*. Pearson.

Harris, J., & Leeming, P. (2022). The impact of teaching approach on growth in L2 proficiency and self-efficacy: A longitudinal classroom-based study of TBLT and PPP. *Journal of Second Language Studies*, *5*(1), 114–143. https://doi.org/10.1075/jsls.20014.har

Hasegawa, A. (2021). Recommended resource: Picturebooks in European primary English language teaching (PEPELT) mini e-lessons. *Children's Literature in English Language Education*, *9*(1), 82–86. https://clelejournal.org/recommended-alison-hasegawa/

Hasegawa, A., Yanase, C., Masatsugu, K., & Ito, L. (2020). Using picture books to engage and inspire learners. *The Language Teacher*, *44*(4), 35–38. https://jalt-publications.org/sites/default/files/pdf-article/44.4-tlt-art-1.pdf

Hashemifardnia, A., Namaziandost, E., & Esfahani, F. R. (2018). The effect of teaching picture-books on elementary EFL learners' vocabulary learning. *Journal of English Language Teaching and Linguistics*, *3*(3), 247–258. http://dx.doi.org/10.21462/jeltl.v3i3.151

Hattem, D., & Lomicka, L. (2016). What the Tweets say: A critical analysis of Twitter research in language learning from 2009 to 2016. *E-learning and Digital Media*, *13*(1–2), 5–23. https://doi.org/10.1177/2042753016672350

Hayton, T. (n.d.). Throwing them in at "the deep end". *British Council*. https://www.teachingenglish.org.uk/article/throwing-them-%E2%80%98-deep-end%E2%80%99

Henry, A. (2019). Online media creation and L2 motivation: A socially suited perspective. *TESOL Quarterly, 53*(2), 372–404. https://doi.org/10.1002/tesq.485

Hirata, Y., & Hirata, Y. (2020). Flipped classroom approaches in computer programming courses in Japan. *2020 International Symposium on Educational Technology (ISET) Proceedings* (pp. 109–113). IEEE. http://dx.doi.org/10.1109/ISET49818.2020.00032

Honeycutt, B. (Ed.). (2016). *Flipping the college classroom: Practical advice from faculty.* Magna.

Horwitz, E. K. (2020). *Becoming a language teacher: A practical guide to second language learning and teaching* (2nd ed.). Castledown Publishers.

Horwitz, E. K., Horwitz, M. B., & Cope, J. (1986). Foreign language classroom anxiety. *The Modern Language Journal, 70*(2), 125–132. https://doi.org/10.1111/j.1540-4781.1986.tb05256.x

Hsu, L. (2016). An empirical examination of EFL learners' perceptual learning styles and acceptance of ASR-based computer-assisted pronunciation training. *Computer Assisted Language Learning, 29*(5), 881–990. https://doi.org/10.1080/09588221.2015.1069747

Hsu, T. C. (2019). Using a concept mapping strategy to improve the motivation of EFL students in Google Hangouts Peer-Tutoring Sessions with native speakers. *Interactive Learning Environments, 27*(2), 272–285. http://dx.doi.org/10.1080/10494820.2018.1463268

Hu, M., & Nation, I. S. P. (2000). Unknown vocabulary density and reading comprehension. *Reading in a Foreign Language, 13*(1), 403–430. https://www.researchgate.net/publication/234651421_Unknown_Vocabulary_Density_and_Reading_Comprehension

Hudson, T. (2007). *Teaching second language reading.* Oxford University Press.

Hughes, A., & Hughes, J. (2020). *Testing for language teachers* (3rd Ed.). Cambridge University Press

Hung, H.-T. (2018). Gamifying the flipped classroom using game-based learning materials. *ELT Journal, 72*(3), 296–308. http://dx.doi.org/10.1093/elt/ccx055

Hwang, G. J., Chen, M. R. A., Sung, H. Y., & Lin, M. H. (2019). Effects of integrating a concept mapping-based summarization strategy into flipped learning on students' reading performances and perceptions in Chinese courses. *British Journal of Educational Technology, 50*(5), 2703–2719. http://dx.doi.org/10.1111/bjet.12708

Hyland, K. (2008). Disciplinary voices: Interactions in research writing. *English Text Construction, 1*(1), 5–22. https://doi.org/10.1075/etc.1.1.03hyl

Imperio, A. (2018). Flipped classroom, C.L.I.L. and classroom setting: Innovative learning experiences in an Italian primary school class. In M. Carmo (Ed.), *Education and new developments 2018* (pp. 346–350). InScience Press. http://end-educationconference.org/wp-content/uploads/2020/02/Education-and-New-Developments_2018.pdf

Jenkins, J. (2000). *The phonology of English as an international language.* Oxford University Press.

Jenkins, J. (2006). Current perspectives on teaching world Englishes and English as a lingua franca. *TESOL Quarterly, 40*(1), 157–181. http://dx.doi.org/10.2307/40264515

Jeong, H. (2021). Effects of jigsaw strategy into flipped learning on EFL pre-serviced kindergarten teachers' English attitude and motivation with online-based classroom. *International Journal of Information and Education Technology, 11*(11), 510–516. http://dx.doi.org/10.18178/ijiet.2021.11.11.1558

Jiang, M. Y.-C., Jong, M. S.-Y., Lau, W. W.-F., Chai, C.-S., & Wu, N. (2021). Using automatic speech recognition technology to enhance EFL learners' oral language complexity in a flipped classroom. *Australasian Journal of Educational Technology, 37*(2), 110–131. https://doi.org/10.14742/ajet.6798

Jingxia, L. (2010). Teachers' code-switching to the L1 in EFL classroom. *The Open Applied Linguistics Journal, 3*(1), 10–23. http://dx.doi.org/10.2174/1874913501003010010

Johnson, C. (2018). *Flipped mastery learning: An insanely simple guide.* Fl Global Publishing.

Johnson, G. B. (2013). *Student perceptions of the flipped classroom* [Master's thesis, The University of British Columbia]. Open Collections UBC Theses and Dissertations. https://open.library.ubc.ca/media/stream/pdf/24/1.0073641/1

Johnson, L., & Renner, J. (2012). *Effect of the flipped classroom model on secondary computer applications course: Student and teacher perceptions, questions and student achievement.* [Doctoral dissertation, University of Louisville]. The Flipped Classroom Files. https://theflippedclassroom.files.wordpress.com/2012/04/johnson-renner-2012.pdf

Johnson, L., Adams Becker, S., Estrada, V., & Freeman, A. (2014). *NMC Horizon report: 2014 K–12 Edition.* The New Media Consortium. https://cdc.qc.ca/pdf/2014-Horizon-Report-creative-commons-copy.pdf

Johnston, P. H. (2004). *Choice words: How our language affects children's learning.* Stenhouse Publishers.

Johnston, P. H. (2012). *Opening minds: Using language to change lives.* Stenhouse Publishers.

Jones, A., Kukulska-Hulme, A., Norris, L., Gaved, M., Scanlon, E., Jones, J., & Brasher, A. (2017). Supporting immigrant language learning on smartphones: A field trial. *Studies in the Education of Adults, 49*(2), 228–252. https://doi.org/10.1080/02660830.2018.1463655

Jonsson, A., & Svingby, G. (2007). The use of scoring rubrics: Reliability, validity and educational consequences. *Educational Research Review, 2*(2), 130–144. http://dx.doi.org/10.1016/j.edurev.2007.05.002

Joyce, M. F. (2011). *Vocabulary acquisition with kindergarten children using song picture books*. [Doctoral dissertation, Northern University]. Northern University Library. https://repository.library.northeastern.edu/files/neu:1137/fulltext.pdf

Kachru, B. B. (1982). *The other tongue. English across cultures*. University of Illinois Press.

Kachru, B. B. (1985). Standards, codification, and sociolinguistic realism: The English language in the outer circle. In R. Quirk & H. Widdowson (Eds.) *English in the world: Teaching and learning the language and the literature*. Cambridge University Press.

Kachru, B. B. (1986). *The alchemy of English: The spread, function, and models in nonnative English*. Oxford University Press.

Kalantari, F., & Hashemian, M. (2016). A story-telling approach to teaching English to young EFL Iranian learners. *English Language Teaching, 9*(1), 221–234. http://dx.doi.org/10.5539/elt.v9n1p221

Kalra, R., & Siribud, S. (2020). Public speaking anxiety in the Thai EFL context. *LEARN Journal: Language Education and Acquisition Research Network, 13*(1), 195–209. https://files.eric.ed.gov/fulltext/EJ1242957.pdf

Kanaoka, M., Ushioda, E., Watanabe, A., & Kato, C. (2017, August 30). *Integration of person in context theory (PICT) and spirituality: Aimed at establishing tangible self-awareness of L2 motivation toward self-and-language maturity* [Conference session]. JACET 56th International Convention, Tokyo, Japan. http://www.jacet.org/wp-content/uploads/56_Program_DATE.pdf

Karimi, M., & Hamzavi, R. (2017). The effect of flipped model of instruction on EFL learners' reading comprehension: Learners' attitudes in focus. *Advances in Language and Literary Studies, 8*(1), 95–103. http://dx.doi.org/10.7575/aiac.alls.v.8n.1p.95

Keefe, J. (2007). What is personalization? *Phi Delta Kappan, 83*(6), 440–448. https://doi.org/10.1177/003172170708900312

Keengwe, J., Onchwari, G., & Oigara, J. (2014). *Promoting active learning through the flipped learning model*. IGI Global.

Keller, J. M. 2010. *Motivational design for learning and performance: The ARCS model approach*. Springer.

Khan, S. (2012). *The one world schoolhouse: Education reimagined*. Twelve.

Khezrlou, S. (2022). *Insights into task-based language teaching*. Castledown Publishers.

Kikuchi, K., & Sakai, H. (2009). Japanese learners' demotivation to study English: A survey study. *JALT Journal, 31*(2), 183–204. https://jalt-publications.org/recentpdf/jj/2009b/art3.pdf

Kirkpatrick, A. (2007). *World Englishes*. Cambridge University Press.

Kırmızı, Ö., & Kömeç, F. (2019). The impact of the flipped classroom on receptive and productive vocabulary learning. *Journal of Language and Linguistic Studies, 15*(2), 437–449. http://dx.doi.org/10.17263/jlls.586096

Knežević, L., Županec, V., & Radulović, B. (2020). Flipping the classroom to enhance academic vocabulary learning in an English for academic purposes (EAP) course. *SAGE Open, 10*(3), 1–15. http://dx.doi.org/10.1177/2158244020957052

Knowles, S., & Clement, R. (1996). *Edwina the emu*. Angus & Robertson.

Köroglu, Z. Ç., & Çakir, A. (2017). Implementation of flipped instruction in language classrooms: An alternative way to develop speaking skills of pre-service English language teachers. *International Journal of Education and Development using Information and Communication Technology, 13*(2), 42–55. https://files.eric.ed.gov/fulltext/EJ1153321.pdf

Koyama, T., & Takeuchi, O. (2004). How look up frequency affects EFL learning: An empirical study on the use of handheld-electronic dictionaries. In W. Meng Chan, K. Nyet Chin, P. Martin-Lau, & T. Suthiwan (Eds). *Proceedings of the CLaSIC 2004 conference: Current perspectives and future directions in foreign language teaching and learning* (pp. 1018–1024). Centre for Language Studies, National University of Singapore.

Krashen, S. (1982). *Principles and practice in second language acquisition*. Prentice-Hall International.

Krashen, S. (1985). *The input hypothesis: Issues and implications*. Longman.

Krashen, S., & Terrell, T. (1983). *The natural approach*. Alemany Press.

Krathwohl, D. R. (2002). A revision of Bloom's taxonomy: An overview. *Theory Into Practice, 41*(4), 212–218. http://dx.doi.org/10.1207/s15430421tip4104_2

Kurek, M., & Hauck, M. (2014). Closing the "digital divide"–a framework for multiliteracy training. In J. P. Guikema & L. Williams (Eds.). *Digital literacies in foreign and second language education* (pp. 119–140). CALICO.

Ladefoged, P. (1982). *A course in phonetics*. Harcourt Brace Jovanovich.

Ladefoged, P., & Johnson, K. (2015). *A course in phonetics* (7th ed). Cengage Learning.

Lage, M. J., Platt, G. J., & Treglia, M. (2000). Inverting the classroom: A gateway to creating an inclusive learning environment. *The Journal of Economic Education, 31*(1), 30–43. https://doi.org/10.2307/1183338

Lamb. M. (2012). A self system perspective on young adolescents' motivation to learn English in urban and rural settings. *Language Learning, 64*(4), 997–1023. http://dx.doi.org/10.1111/j.1467-9922.2012.00719.x

Lambert, C., & Oliver, R. (Eds.) (2020). *Using tasks in second language teaching: Practice in diverse contexts*. Multilingual Matters.

Lapkin, S., & Swain, M. (2001). Focus on form through collaborative dialogue: Exploring task effects. In M. Bygate, P. Skehan, & M. Swain (Eds.), *Researching pedagogic tasks: Second language learning, teaching, and testing* (pp. 109–128). Routledge.

Larsen-Freeman, D., & Anderson, M. (2011). *Techniques and principles in language teaching* (3rd ed.). Oxford University Press.

Lasagabaster, D. (2011). English achievement and student motivation in CLIL and EFL settings. *Innovation in Language Learning and Teaching, 5*(1),

3–18. http://dx.doi.org/10.1080/17501229.2010.519030

Laufer, B. (1989). What percentage of text-lexis is essential for comprehension? In C. Lauren & M. Nordman (Eds.), *Special language: From humans to thinking machines* (pp. 316–323). Multilingual Matters.

Laufer, B. (1992). How much lexis is necessary for reading comprehension? In P. J. L. Arnaud & H. Béjoint (Eds.), *Vocabulary and applied linguistics* (pp. 126–132). Palgrave Macmillan. http://dx.doi.org/10.1007/978-1-349-12396-4_12

Learning Network (FLN). (2014a). *Who are we?* https://flippedlearning.org/who-we-are/

Learning Network (FLN). (2014b). *The four pillars of F-L-I-P™.* www.flippedlearning.org/definition.

Lee, G., & Wallace, A. (2018). Flipped learning in the English as a foreign language classroom: Outcomes and perceptions. *TESOL Quarterly, 52*(1), 62–84. https://doi.org/10.1002/tesq.372

Lee, J., Schallert, D. L., & Kim, E. (2019). Effects of extensive reading and translation activities on grammar knowledge and attitudes for EFL adolescents. *System, 52,* 38–50. https://doi.org/10.1016/j.system.2015.04.016

Lee, S. P., Lee, S. D., Liao, Y. L., & Wang, A. C. (2015). Effects of audio-visual aids on foreign language test anxiety, reading and listening comprehension, and retention in EFL learners. *Perceptual and Motor Skills: Perception, 120*(2), 576–590. https://doi.org/10.2466/24.pms.120v14x2

Leis, A. (2014). Every minute counts: A warm-up speaking and listening activity to build fluency. *The Language Teacher, 38*(2), 20–21. https://jalt-publications.org/tlt/issues/2014-03_38.2

Leis, A. (2015). Dynamics of effort in flipped classrooms in an EFL environment. *Educational Informatics Research, 14.* 15–26. file:///Users/adrian/Downloads/1348-1983-2015-14-15%20(2).pdf

Leis, A. (2016). Intonation phrases in the use of closed-captions for deaf and hard-of-hearing Students in EFL classes. *Tohoku TEFL, 6,* 23–37. https://sites.google.com/view/jacettohoku/%E6%94%AF%E9%83%A8%E7%B4%80%E8%A6%81journal?authuser=0

Leis, A. (2018a). Maintaining student effort through flipped learning. *The European Journal of Applied Linguistics and TEFL, 7*(2), 121–136. https://www.proquest.com/docview/2342473867?pq-origsite=gscholar&fromopenview=true

Leis, A. (2018b). Content-based language teaching and the flipped classroom: A case study in the Japanese EFL environment. In J. Mehring, & A. Leis (Eds.), *Innovations in Flipping the Language Classroom* (pp. 221–230). Springer.

Leis, A. (2021a). The effects of praise on the mindsets of university students in an EFL environment. *Theory and Practice of Second Language Acquisition, 7*(2), 37–59. https://doi.org/10.31261/TAPSLA.9098

Leis, A. (2021b). Mindsets of Japanese EFL students. *Tohoku TEFL, 9,*

15–27. https://sites.google.com/view/jacettohoku/

Leis, A. (2022a). Flipped learning and linguistic self-confidence. *International Journal of Computer-Assisted Language Learning and Teaching, 12*(1), 1–14. http://dx.doi.org/10.4018/IJCALLT.291107

Leis, A. (2022b). A self-worth perspective of Japanese first-year junior high school students' attitudes towards studying English. *JACET International Convention Selected Papers, 8*, 55–83. https://www.jacet.org/SelectedPapers/JACET60_2021_SP_8_2

Leis, A., & Brown, K. (2018). Flipped learning in an EFL environment: Does the teacher's experience affect learning outcomes? *The EUROCALL Review, 3*(1), 3–13. https://doi.org/10.4995/eurocall.2018.8597

Leis, A., & Cooke, S. (2019a). *Ultimate listening: Advanced.* Kaitakusha.

Leis, A., & Cooke, S. (2019b). *Ultimate listening: Intermediate.* Kaitakusha.

Leis, A., Cooke, S., & Tohei, A. (2015). The Effects of flipped classrooms on English composition writing in an EFL environment. *International Journal of Computer-Assisted Language Learning and Teaching, 5*(4), 37–51. https://doi.org/10.4018/ijcallt.2015100103

Leis, A., Takemori, T., Abe, K., Himori, E., Suenaga, R, & Umino, K. (2022). Japanese adolescents' attitudes towards learning English: A perspective from the self-worth theory. *Language Teaching Research*, Advance online publication, 1–30. https://doi.org/10.1177/13621688211068368

Leis, A., Tohei, A., & Cooke, S. D. (2015). Smartphone assisted language learning and autonomy. *International Journal of Computer-Assisted Language Learning and Teaching, 5*(3), 75–88. https://doi.org/10.4018/ijcallt.2015070105

Levis, J., & Pickering, L. (2004). Teaching intonation in discourse using speech visualization technology. *System, 32*(4), 505–524. https://doi.org/10.1016/j.system.2004.09.009

Levy, M. (2009). Technologies in use for second language learning. *The Modern Language Journal, 93*(1), 769–782. https://doi.org/10.1111/j.1540-4781.2009.00972.x

Li, S. (2010). The effectiveness of corrective feedback in SLA: A meta-analysis. *Language Learning, 60*(2), 309–365. https://doi.org/10.1111/j.1467-9922.2010.00561.x

Li, S. (2016). The construct validity of language aptitude. *Studies in Second Language Acquisition, 38*, 801–842. http://dx.doi.org/10.1017/S027226311500042X

Li, S. (2019). Six decades of language aptitude research: A comprehensive and critical review. In Z. E. Wen, P. Skehan, A. Biedroń, S. Li, & R. L. Sparks (Eds.), *Language aptitude: Advancing theory, testing, research, and practice* (pp. 78–96). Routledge.

Li, S., & Suwanthep, K. (2017). Integration of flipped classroom model for EFL speaking. *International Journal of Learning and Teaching, 3*(2), 118–123. http://dx.doi.org/10.18178/ijlt.3.2.118-123

Li, Y., Gao, Y., & Zhang, D. (2016). To speak like a TED speaker—A case study of TED motivated English public speaking study in EFL teaching. *Higher Education Studies*, *6*(1), 53–59. http://dx.doi.org/10.5539/hes.v6n1p53

Lightbrown, P. M., & Spada, N. (2013). *How languages are learned*. Oxford.

Lin, C.-J. (2019). An online peer assessment approach to supporting mind-mapping flipped learning activities for college English writing courses. *Journal of Computers in Education*, *6*, 385–415. https://doi.org/10.1007/s40692-019-00144-6

Little, D., Dam, L., & Legenhausen, L. (2017). *Language learner autonomy: Theory, practice and research*. Multilingual Matters.

Littlewood, W. (2010). *Communicative language teaching: An introduction*. Cambridge.

Liu, P.-L. (2014). Using eye tracking to understand learners' reading process through the concept-mapping learning strategy. *Computers & Education*, *78*, 237–249. http://dx.doi.org/10.1016/j.compedu.2014.05.011

Long, M. (1991). Focus on form: A design feature in language teaching methodology. In K. De Bot, R. Ginsberg, & C. Kramsch (Eds.), *Foreign language research in cross-cultural perspectives* (pp. 39–52). John Benjamins.

Long, M. H. (1988). Instructed interlanguage development. In L.M. Beebe (Ed.) *Issues in second language acquisition: Multiple perspectives* (pp. 115–141). Newbury House Publishers.

Lopera Medina, S. (2012). Effects of strategy instruction in an EFL reading comprehension course: A case study. *Profile Issues in Teachers' Professional Development*, *14*(1), 79–89. http://www.scielo.org.co/scielo.php?pid=S1657-07902012000100006&script=sci_arttext&tlng=en

Lubis, A. H., & Rahmawati, E. (2022). Incorporating flipped learning in teaching English grammar for EFL students across proficiency levels. *Advances in Social Science, Education and Humanities Research*, *624*, 68–73. http://dx.doi.org/10.2991/assehr.k.220201.012

Luo, Z., O'Steen, B., & Brown, C. (2020). Flipped learning wheel (FLW): A framework and process design for flipped L2 writing classes. *Smart Learning Environments*, *7*(10), 1–21. https://doi.org/10.1186/s40561-020-00121-y

Lyster, R., & Ballinger, S. (2011). Content-based language teaching: Convergent concerns across divergent contexts. *Language Teaching Research*, *15*(3), 279–288. http://dx.doi.org/10.1177/1362168811401150

Lyster, R., Collins, L., & Ballinger, S. (2009). Linking languages through a bilingual read-aloud project. *Language Awareness*, *18*(3–4), 366–383. http://dx.doi.org/10.1080/09658410903197322

Lyster, R., Quiroga, J., & Ballinger, S. (2013). The effects of biliteracy instruction on morphological awareness. *Journal of Immersion and Content-Based Language Education*, *1*(2), 169–197. http://dx.doi.org/10.1075/jicb.1.2.02lys

Mabrey III, P. E., & Liu, J. (2013). Social media and public speaking: student-produced multimedia informative presentations. In S. Ferris & H. Wilder (Eds.) *The plugged-in professor: Tips and techniques for teaching with social media* (pp. 121–149). Chandos Publishing.

Mabuan, R. A. (2017). Developing ESL/EFL learners' public speaking skills through Pecha kucha presentations. *English Review: Journal of English Education*, 6(1), 1–10.

MacIntyre, P. D. (2007). Willingness to communicate in the second language: Understanding the decision to speak as a volitional process. *The Modern Language Journal*, 91(4), 564–576. http://dx.doi.org/10.1111/j.1540-4781.2007.00623.x

MacIntyre, P. D. (2017). An overview of language anxiety research and trends in its development. In C. Gkonou, M. Daubney, & J-M. Dewaele (Eds.), *New insights into language anxiety* (pp. 11–30). Multilingual Matters.

MacIntyre, P. D., & Serroul, A. (2015). Motivation on a per-second timescale: Examining approach-avoidance motivation during L2 task performance. In Z. Dörnyei, P. MacIntyre, & A. Henry. *Motivational dynamics in language learning* (pp. 109–138). Multilingual Matters.

MacIntyre, P. D., Dörnyei, Z., Clément, R., & Noels, K. A. (1998). Conceptualizing willingness to communicate in a L2: A situational model of L2 confidence and affiliation. *The Modern Language Journal*, 82(4), 545–562. https://doi.org/10.1111/j.1540-4781.1998.tb05543.x

MacIntyre, P., & Gregersen, T. (2012). Affect: The role of language anxiety and other emotions in language learning. In S. Mercer, S., Ryan & M. Williams (Eds.), *Psychology for language learning* (pp. 103–118). Palgrave Macmillan. http://dx.doi.org/10.1057/9781137032829_8

Macwan, H. J. (2015). Using visual aids as authentic material in ESL classrooms. *Research Journal of English Language and Literature*, 3(1), 91–96. http://rjelal.com/3.1.15/HIRAL%20JOSEPH%20MACWAN%2091-96.pdf

Malik, A., Heyman-Schrum, C., & Johri, A. (2019). Use of Twitter across educational settings: a review of the literature. *International Journal of Educational Technology in Higher Education*, 16(1), 1–22. https://doi.org/10.1186/s41239-019-0166-x

Marshall, H. W. (2017). The synchronous online flipped learning approach. *FLGI Community Blog.* https://community.flglobal.org/the-synchronous-online-flipped-learning-approach/

Marshall, H. W., & Kostka, I. (2020). Fostering teaching presence through the Synchronous Online Flipped Learning Approach. *TESL-EJ*, 24(2), 1–14. http://tesl-ej.org/pdf/ej94/int.pdf

Marshall, H. W., & Wallestad, C. K. (n.d.) The synchronous online flipped learning approach (SOFLA®) in a literacy methods course for teachers. *Edzil Session.* https://edzil.la/sessions/3rRkPKMfSMulWW2ijR1rZ9wVtCDvltj Gn0YrF9kX.pdf

Martin, B., & Carle, E. (1967). *Brown bear, brown bear, what do you see?* Doubleday & Company.

Mathew, N. G., & Alidmat, A. O. H. (2013). A study on the usefulness of audio-visual aids in EFL classroom: Implications for effective instruction. *International Journal of Higher Education*, *2*(2), 86–92. https://doi.org/10.5430/ijhe.v2n2p86

Matsuda, P. K. (1997). Contrastive rhetoric in context: A dynamic model of L2 writing. *Journal of Second Language Writing*, *6*(1), 45–60. https://doi.org/10.1016/s1060-3743(97)90005-9

Matsuda, P. K. (2001). Voice in Japanese written discourse: Implications for second language writing. *Journal of Second language Writing*, *10*(1–2), 35–53. https://doi.org/10.1016/s1060-3743(00)00036-9

Matsuda, P. K. (2014). The lure of translingual writing. *PMLA/Publications of the Modern Language Association of America*, *129*(3), 478–483. https://doi.org/10.1632/pmla.2014.129.3.478

Matsuda, P. K. (2015). Identity in written discourse. *Annual Review of Applied Linguistics*, *35*, 140–159. https://doi.org/10.1017/s0267190514000178

Matsuda, P. K., & Silva, T. (Eds.). (2014). *Second language writing research: Perspectives on the process of knowledge construction*. Routledge.

Matsuda, P. K., & Tardy, C. M. (2007). Voice in academic writing: The rhetorical construction of author identity in blind manuscript review. *English for Specific Purposes*, *26*(2), 235–249. https://doi.org/10.1016/j.esp.2006.10.001

Matsumoto, J., Aoki, S., & Watanabe, M. (2012). Positive psychological and interpersonal effects by karaoke. In E. Cambouropolous, C. Tsougras, P. Mavromatis, & K. Pastiadis (Eds.), *Proceedings of the 12th international conference on music perception and cognition and the 8th triennial conference of the European society for the cognitive sciences of music, July 23–28, 2012* (pp. 666–669). http://icmpc-escom2012.web.auth.gr/files/papers/666_Proc.pdf

Mazur, E. (1997). Peer instruction: Getting students to think in class. *AIP Conference Proceedings*, 981–988. https://doi.org/10.1063/1.53199

McKay, P. (2006). *Assessing young language learners*. Cambridge University Press.

McLaughlin, B. (1987). *Theories of second language learning*. Arnold.

Mehring, J. (2015). Examining learner motivation during new teaching practices: An action-based research study. *Perspectives*, *23*(2), 5–11. https://issuu.com/tesolarabia-perspectives/docs/perspectives_june_2015

Mehring, J. (2016). Present research on the flipped classroom and potential tools for the EFL classroom. *Computers in the Schools*, *33*(1), 1–10. http://dx.doi.org/10.1080/07380569.2016.1139912

Mehring, J., & Leis, A. (Eds.) (2018). *Innovations in flipping the language classroom*. Springer.

Mercer, S. (2012). The complexity of learner agency. *Apples-Journal of Ap-*

plied Language Studies, *6*(2), 41–50. https://jyx.jyu.fi/bitstream/handle/123456789/ 40858/Final_Mercer.pdf?sequence=1

Mermelstein, A. D. (2015). Improving EFL learners' writing through enhanced extensive reading. *Reading in a Foreign Language*, *27*(2), 182–198. https://files.eric.ed.gov/fulltext/EJ1078420.pdf

Merrill, M. D. (2002). First principles of instruction. *Educational Technology Research and Development*, *50*(3), 43–59. https://doi.org/10.1007/BF02505024.

Met, M. (1998). Curriculum decision-making in content-based language teaching. In J. Cenoz & F. Genesee (Eds.), *Beyond bilingualism: Multilingualism and multilingual education* (pp. 35–63). Multilingual Matters.

Millington, N. T. (2011). Using songs effectively to teach English to young learners. *Language Education in Asia*, *2*(1), 134–141. http://dx.doi.org/10.5746/LEiA/11/V2/I1/A11/Millington

Miner, A. S., Haque, A., Fries, J. A., Fleming, J. A., Wilfey, D. E., Wilson, G. T., Milstein, A., Jurafsky, D., Arnow, B., A., Agras, W. S., Fei-Fei, L. & Shah, N. H. (2020). Assessing the accuracy of automatic speech recognition for psychotherapy. *npj Digit. Med.*, *3*(82), 1–8. https://doi.org/10.1038/s41746-020-0285-8

Mohebbi, H. (2023). *Insights into teaching and learning writing: A practical guide for early-career teachers*. Castledown Publishers.

Moraros, J., Islam, A., Yu, S., Banow, R., & Schindelka, B. (2015). Flipping for success: evaluating the effectiveness of a novel teaching approach in a graduate level setting. *BMC Medical Education*, *15*(1), 1–10. https://doi.org/10.1186/s12909-015-0317-2

Moravec, M., Williams, A., Aguilar-Roca, N., & O'Dowd, D. K. (2010). Learn before lecture: A strategy that improves learning outcomes in a large introductory biology class. *CBE—Life Sciences Education*, *9*(4), 473–481. https://doi.org/10.1187/cbe.10-04-0063

Moreira, M., & Moreira, S. (2011). Meaningful learning: Use of concept maps in foreign language education. *Aprendizagem Significativa em Revista/Meaningful Learning Review*, *1*(2), 64–75.

Morgana, V., & Kukulska-Hulme, A. (Eds.) (2021). *Mobile assisted language learning across educational contexts*. Routledge.

Mourão, S. (2016). Picturebooks in the primary EFL classroom: Authentic literature for an authentic response. *CLELE Journal*, *4*(1), 25–43. https://run.unl.pt/bitstream/10362/70030/1/Picturebooks_Authentic_literature_for_an_authentic_response_ CLELEjournal_4.1.pdf

Movahed, R. (2014). The effect of metacognitive strategy instruction on listening performance, metacognitive awareness and listening anxiety of beginner Iranian EFL students. *International Journal of English Linguistics*, *4*(2), 88–99. https://doi.org/10.5539/ijel.v4n2p88

Murphey, J. M. (2014). Intelligible, comprehensible, non-native models in ESL/EFL pronunciation teaching. *System*, *42*, 258–269. https://doi.org/10.1016/j.system.2013.12.007

Namaziandost, E., Gilakjani, A. P., & Hidayatullah. (2020). Enhancing pre-intermediate EFL learners' reading comprehension through the use of Jigsaw technique. *Cogent Arts & Humanities*, *7*(1), 1–15. https://doi.org/10.1080/23311983.2020.1738833

Nassaji, H., & Cumming, A. (2000). What's in a ZPD? A case study of a young ESL student and teacher interacting through dialogue journals. *Language Teaching Research*, *4*(2), 95–121. http://dx.doi.org/10.1177/136216880000400202

Nassaji, H., & Swain, M. (2000). A Vygotskian perspective on corrective feedback in L2: The effect of random versus negotiated help on the learning of English articles. *Language Awareness*, *9*(1), 34–41. http://dx.doi.org/10.1080/09658410008667135

Nation, I. S. P. (2006). How large a vocabulary is needed for reading and listening? *Canadian Modern Language Review*, *63*(1), 59–82. http://dx.doi.org/10.3138/cmlr.63.1.59

Nation, I. S. P., & Waring, R. (2019). *Teaching extensive reading in another language*. Routledge. https://doi.org/10.4324/9780367809256

Nation, I. S., & Webb, S. A. (2011). *Researching and analyzing vocabulary*. Heinle, Cengage Learning.

Nederveld, A., & Berge, Z. L. (2014). Flipped learning in the workplace. *Journal of Workplace Learning*, *27*(2), 162–172. http://dx.doi.org/10.1108/JWL-06-2014-0044

Nishihara, T., & Leis, A. (2014). Rhythm in English: The intelligibility of Japanese English. *Journal of the Tohoku English Language Education Society*, *34*, 65–74.

Noels, K. (2013), Learning Japanese; Learning English: Promoting motivation through autonomy, competence and relatedness. In M. T. Apple, D. Da Silva, & T. Fellner (Eds.), *Language learning motivation in Japan* (pp. 15–34). Multilingual Matters.

Norris, J. M., & Ortega, L. (2000). Effectiveness of L2 instruction: A research synthesis and quantitative meta-analysis. *Language Learning*, *50*(3), 417–528. http://dx.doi.org/10.1111/0023-8333.00136

Novak, J. D. (1990). Concept mapping: A useful tool for science education. *Journal of Research in Science Teaching*, *27*(10), 937–949. http://dx.doi.org/10.1002/tea.3660271003

Novak, J. D. (2002). Meaningful learning: The essential factor for conceptual change in limited or inappropriate propositional hierarchies leading to empowerment of learners. *Science Education*, *86*(4), 548–571. http://dx.doi.org/10.1002/sce.10032

Nunan, D. (1999). *Second language teaching & learning*. Heinle & Heinle.

Nunan, D. (2004). *Task-based language teaching*. Cambridge University Press.

Nunan, D. (2015). *Teaching English to speakers of other languages: An introduction*. Taylor & Francis.

O'Malley, J. M., & Chamot, A. U. (1990). *Learning strategies in second lan-

guage acquisition. Cambridge University Press.

Obari, H., & Lambacher, S. (2015). Successful EFL teaching using mobile technologies in a flipped classroom. In F. Helm, L, Bradley, M. Guarda, & S. Thouesny (Eds.) *Critical CALL–Proceedings of the 2015 EUROCALL Conference, Padova, Italy* (pp. 433–438). Research-publishing.net. http://dx.doi.org/10.14705/rpnet.2015.000371

Oh, E. Y., & Song, D. (2021). Developmental research on an interactive application for language speaking practice using speech recognition technology. *Educational Technology Research and Development, 69*(2), 861–884. https://doi.org/10.1007/s11423-020-09910-1

Oliver, J. (2016, May 8). Scientific Studies: Last Week Tonight with John Oliver (HBO) [Video File]. YouTube. https://www.youtube.com/watch?v=0Rnq1NpHdmw

Østerlie, O. (2018) Can flipped learning enhance adolescents' motivation in physical education? An intervention study. *Journal for Research in Arts and Sports Education, 2*(1), 1–15. https://doi.org/10.23865/jased.v2.916

Oxford, R. (2006). Task-based language teaching and learning: An overview. *Asian EFL Journal, 8*(3), 94–121. https://www.researchgate.net/publication/237259483_Task-Based_Language_Teaching_and_Learning_An_Overview

Papi, M., Bondarenko, A. V., Wawire, B., Jiang, C., & Zhou, S. (2019). Feedback-seeking behavior in second language writing: Motivational mechanisms. *Reading and Writing, 33*(2), 485–505. https://doi.org/10.1007/s11145-019-09971-6

Paul, D. (2002). *Teaching English to children in Asia*. Longman Group.

Peck, S. (2001). Developing children's listening and speaking in ESL. In M. Celce-Murcia (Ed.) *Teaching English as a second or foreign language* (3rd Ed.) (pp. 139–149). Heinle & Heinle.

Pedersen, M. (2015, July 14). Best practices: What is the optimal length for video content? *Ad Age*. https://adage.com/article/digitalnext/optimal-length-video-content/299386

Perl, S. (1980). A look at basic writers in the process of composing. In L. N. Kasden & D. R. Hoeber (Eds.), *Basic writing* (pp. 13–32). National Council of Teachers of English.

Philippines, E. C., & Tan, M. J. (2020). Effectiveness of using a flipped classroom in improving English grammar proficiency. *International Journal of Sciences: Basic and Applied Research (IJSBAR), 51*(2), 45–57. https://www.researchgate.net/profile/Esperval-Cezhar-Cadiao/publication/344378748_Effectiveness_of_Using_a_Flipped_Classroom_in_Improving_ English_Grammar_Proficiency/links/5f6e03d192851c14bc94f513/Effectiveness-of-Using-a-Flipped-Classroom-in-Improving-English-Grammar-Proficiency.pdf

Pickering, L. (2017). Pronunciation in discourse contexts. In O. Kang, R. I. Thomson, & J. M. Murphey (Eds.) *The Routledge handbook of contemporary English pronunciation* (pp. 432–436). Routledge.

Poonpon, K. (2017). Enhancing English skills through project-based learning. *The English Teacher, 40,* 1–10. https://melta.org.my/journals/TET/downloads/tet40_01_01.pdf

Prabhu, N. S. (1987). *Second language pedagogy.* Oxford University Press.

Practor, C., & Celce-Murcia, M. (1979). An outline of language teaching approaches. In M. Celce-Murcia & L. McIntosh (Eds.), *Teaching English as a second or foreign language* (pp. 3–5). Newbury House.

Praveen, S. D., & Rajan, P. (2013). Using graphic organizers to improve reading comprehension skills for the middle school ESL students. *English Language Teaching, 6*(2), 155–170. http://dx.doi.org/10.5539/elt.v6n2p155

Quyen, T.T.T., & Loi, N.V. (2018). Flipped model for improving students' English-speaking performance. *Can Tho University Journal of Science, 54*(2), 90–97. https://doi.org/10.22144/ctu.jen.2018.012

Rachayon, S. (2018). *The effects of task-based instruction using a digital game in a flipped learning environment (TGF) on English oral communication ability of Thai undergraduate nursing students.* [Doctoral dissertation, Thammasat University]. Language Institute Thammasat University. http://grad.litu.tu.ac.th/assets/public/kcfinder/upload_grad_web/public/20_2018_SUPHATHA%20RACHAYON_2019-07-30.pdf

Rachayon, S., & Soontornwipast, K. (2019). The effects of task-based instruction using a digital game in a flipped learning environment on English oral communication ability of Thai undergraduate nursing students. *English Language Teaching, 12*(7), 12–32. https://doi.org/10.5539/elt.v12n7p12

Rachmat, M., Muliastuti, L., & Iskandar, I. (2021). The effectiveness of flipped classroom learning model for increasing students' reading comprehension in Covid-19 Pandemic. *Basic and Applied Education Research Journal, 2*(2), 66–77. http://dx.doi.org/10.11594/baerj.02.02.02

Ramírez, M. (2018). Flipping a pronunciation lesson for a teacher training course. In J. Mehring & A. Leis (Eds.), *Innovations in flipping the language classroom* (pp. 45–57). Springer.

Ramírez, M. A. (2015). *A teacher training blended course in communicative pronunciation pedagogy for in service English teachers in Colombia - a situated approach.* Uniandes. https://repositorio.uniandes.edu.co/handle/1992/12878

Ramirez, M. A., & Buitrago, C. A. (2022). *In-class flip: A student-centered approach to differentiated learning.* International Society for Technology in Education.

Ranta, L. (2002). The role of learners' language analytic ability in the communicative classroom. In P. Robinson (Ed.), *Individual differences and instructed language learning* (pp. 159–180). John Benjamins.

Raschka, C. (2007). *Yo! Yes?* Scholastic Inc.

Renandya, W. A., Hidayati, M., & Ivone, F. M. (2021). Extensive reading: Top ten implementation issues. *JACET Journal, 65,* 11–21. https://

doi.org/10.32234/jacetjournal.65.0_11

Reynolds, G. (2011). *PresentationZen: Simple ideas on presentation design and delivery*. New Riders.

Rezaei, M., & Davoudi, M. (2016). The influence of electronic dictionaries on vocabulary knowledge extension. *Journal of Education and Learning*, *5*(3), 139–148. http://dx.doi.org/10.5539/jel.v5n3p139

Roach, P. (1982). On the distinction between 'stress-timed' and 'syllable-timed' languages. In D. Crystal (Ed.) *Linguistic controversies* (pp. 73–79). Arnold.

Roach, T. (2014). Student perceptions toward flipped learning: New methods to increase interaction and active learning in economics. *International Review of Economics Education*, *17*, 74–84. https://doi.org/10.1016/j.iree.2014.08.003

Robinson, K. (2006, February). *Do schools kill creativity?* [Video]. TED Talks. https://www.ted.com/talks/sir_ken_robinson_do_schools_kill_creativity?language=en

Rokhaniyah, H. (2019). Exploring PechaKucha in EFL learners' speaking fluency. *Journal on English as a Foreign Language*, *9*(29), 146–162. http://dx.doi.org/10.23971/jefl.v9i2.1326

Roth, C., & Suppasetseree, S. (2016). Flipped classroom: Can it enhance English listening comprehension for pre-university students in Cambodia? *Proceedings of CLaSIC 2016*, 255–264.

Rubin, H. (2021, February 6). *SOFLA® holistic rubric*. Presented in an online workshop in the 2021 EVO SOFLA session.

Rubin, J., Chamot, A. U., Harris, V., & Anderson, N. J. (2007). Intervening in the use of strategies. In A. Cohen & E. Macaro (Eds.), *Language learner strategies: Thirty years of research and practice* (pp. 141–160). Oxford University Press.

Sáfár, A., & Kormos, J. (2008). Revisiting problems with foreign language aptitude. *International Review of Applied Linguistics in Language Teaching*, *46*(2), 113–136. http://dx.doi.org/10.1515/iral.2008.005

Saito, K. (2007). The influence of explicit phonetic instruction on pronunciation in EFL settings: The case of English vowels and Japanese learners of English. *Linguistics Journal*, *3*(3), 16–40.

Saito, K. (2011a). Identifying problematic segmental features to acquire comprehensible pronunciation in EFL settings: The case of Japanese learners of English. *RELC Journal*, *42*(3), 363–378. http://dx.doi.org/10.1177/ 0033688211420275

Saito, K. (2011b). Examining the role of explicit phonetic instruction in native-like and comprehensible pronunciation development: An instructed SLA approach to L2 phonology. *Language Awareness*, *20*(1), 45–59. http://dx.doi.org/10.1080/09658416.2010.540326

Sasaki, M. (2011). Effects of varying lengths of study abroad experiences on Japanese EFL students' L2 writing ability and motivation: A longitudinal study. *TESOL Quarterly*, *45*(1), 81–105. http://

dx.doi.org/10.5054/tq.2011.240861

Sato, R. (2009). Suggestions for creating teaching approaches suitable to the Japanese EFL environment. *The Language Teacher, 33*(9), 11–14. Retrieved from http://jalt-publications.org/tlt/issues/2009-09_33.9

Sato R. (2010). Reconsideration for the effectiveness and suitability of PPP and TBLT in the Japanese EFL classroom. *JALT Journal, 32*(2), 189–200. http://jalt-publications.org/jj/issues/2010-11_32.2

Schindelka, B., Moraros, J., Banow, R. & Yu, S. (2013). Flipping for Success: Application of the Flipped Classroom Model in a Graduate Level Setting. In J. Herrington, A. Couros, & V. Irvine (Eds.), *Proceedings of EdMedia 2013—World conference on educational media and technology* (p. 664). Association for the Advancement of Computing in Education (AACE). https://www.learntechlib.org/primary/p/112027/.

Schmitt, N., Jiang, X., & Grabe, W. (2011). The percentage of words known in a text and reading comprehension. *Modern Language Journal, 95*(1), 26–43. http://dx.doi.org/10.1111/j.1540-4781.2011.01146.x

Schuetze, U., & Weimer-Stuckmann, G. (2011). Retention in SLA lexical processing. *Calico Journal, 28*(2), 460–472. http://dx.doi.org/10.11139/cj.28.2.460-472

Schumm, J.S. (Ed.). (2006). *Reading assessment and instruction for all learners.* Guilford Press.

SEE Team. (2019, January 8). Flipped classroom – How this model can enhance the educational procedure "Flip your classroom". *SoFIA Education Experts.* https://www.sofiaeducationexperts.com/post/flipped-classroom-how-this-model-can-enhance-the-educational-procedure-flip-your-classroom

Seery, M. K. (2013). Harnessing technology in chemistry education. *New Directions, 9*(1), 77–86. http://dx.doi.org/10.11120/ndir.2013.00002

Seligman, Martin, & Seligman, Mandy. (2019, July 18–21). *Marty, Mandy, & living positive psychology* [Plenary speech]. 6th World Congress on Positive Psychology, Melbourne.

Serri, F., Boroujeni, A. J., & Hesabi, A. (2012). Cognitive, metacognitive, and social/affective strategies in listening comprehension and their relationships with individual differences. *Theory and Practice in Language Studies, 2*(4), 843–849. http://dx.doi.org/10.4304/tpls.2.4.843-849

Şevik, M. (2012). Teaching listening skills to young learners through "listen and do" songs. *English Teaching Forum, 50*(3), 10–17.

Şevik, M. (2014). Young EFL learner beliefs about classroom songs. *International Journal of English and Education, 3*(1), 50–59. http://ijee.org/yahoo_site_admin/assets/docs/5.0143704.pdf

Sheen, R. (2002). 'Focus on form' and 'focus on forms'. *ELT Journal, 56*(3), 303–305. http://dx.doi.org/10.1093/elt/56.3.303

Sheen, R. (2005). Focus on forms as a means of improving accurate oral production. In A. Housen & M. Pierrard (Eds.) *Investigations in instructed second language acquisition* (pp. 271–310). Mouton de Gruyter.

Sheen, Y. (2007). The effect of focused written corrective feedback and language aptitude on ESL learners' acquisition of articles. *TESOL Quarterly*, *41*, 255–283. http://dx.doi.org/10.1002/j.1545-7249.2007.tb00059.x

Sheen, Y. (2010). Introduction: The role of oral and written corrective feedback in SLA. *Studies in Second Language Acquisition*, *32*(2), 169–179. https://doi.org/10.1017/s0272263109990489

Shintani, N. (2015). The incidental grammar acquisition in focus on form and focus on forms instruction for young beginner learners. *TESOL Quarterly*, *49*(1), 115–140. http://dx.doi.org/10.1002/tesq.166

Shintani, N. (2016). The effects of computer-mediated synchronous and asynchronous direct corrective feedback on writing: A case study. *Computer Assisted Language Learning*, *29*(3), 1–22. https://doi.org/10.1080/09588221.2014.993400

Shintani, N., Ellis, R., & Suzuki, W. (2014). Effects of written feedback and revision on learners' accuracy in using two English grammatical structures. *Language Learning*, *64*(1), 103–131. http://dx.doi.org/10.1111/lang.12029

Shulevitz, U. (1985). *Writing with pictures: How to write and illustrate children's books*. Watson-Guptill Publications

Singh, C. K. S., Singh, H. S. S. J., Singh, T. S. M., Ja'afar, H., Abdullah, M. S., Mostafa, N. A., & Zamri, M. L. (2018). Flipped classroom approach for improving speaking skills of TVET trainees. *International Journal of Applied Linguistics and English Literature*, *7*(7), 27–39. http://dx.doi.org/10.7575/aiac.ijalel.v.7n.7p.27

Slattery, M., & Willis, J. (2001). *English for primary teachers: A handbook of activities & classroom language*. Oxford University Press.

Song, M. J. (1998). Teaching reading strategies in an ongoing EFL university reading classroom. *Asian Journal of English Language Teaching*, *8*(1), 41–54. https://www.cuhk.edu.hk/ajelt/vol8/art3.htm

Stockwell, G. (2012). *Computer-assisted language learning: Diversity in research and practice*. Cambridge University Press.

Stockwell, G. (2013). Technology and motivation in English-language teaching and learning. In E. Ushioda (Ed.), *International perspectives on motivation* (pp. 156–175). Palgrave Macmillan. https://doi.org/10.1057/9781137000873_9

Stockwell, G. (2016). Mobile language learning. In F. Farr & L. Murray (Eds.), *The Routledge handbook of language learning and technology* (pp. 322-333). Routledge.

Stockwell, G. (2022). *Mobile assisted language learning: Concepts, contexts and challenges*. Cambridge University Press.

Strayer, J. F. (2007). *The effects of the classroom flip on the learning environment: A comparison of learning activity in a traditional classroom and a flip classroom that used an intelligent tutoring system* [Doctoral dissertation, The Ohio State University]. Ohio Link. https://etd.ohiolink.edu/apexprod/

rws_etd/send_file/send?accession=osu1189523914&disposition=inline

Strayer, J. F. (2012). How learning in an inverted classroom influences cooperation, innovation and task orientation. *Learning Environments Research*, *15*(2), 171–193. https://doi.org/10.1007/s10984-012-9108-4

Strayer, J. F., Hart, J. B., & Bleiler, S. K. (2015). Fostering instructor knowledge of student thinking using the flipped classroom. *Primus*, *25*(8), 724–735. http://dx.doi.org/10.1080/10511970.2015.1031306

Su Ping, R. L., Verezub, E., Adi Badiozaman, I. F. B., & Chen, W. S. (2020). Tracing EFL students' flipped classroom journey in a writing class: Lessons from Malaysia. *Innovations in Education and Teaching International*, *57*(3), 305–316. https://doi.org/10.1080/14703297.2019.1574597

Sugito, M. (1999). Kotoba no supiidokan towa nanika? [What is the speed of words?]. *Gengo*, *28*(9), 30–34.

Sun, Y. C. (2010). Extensive writing in foreign-language classrooms: A blogging approach. *Innovations in Education and Teaching International*, *47*(3), 327–339. https://doi.org/10.1080/14703297.2010.498184

Sun, Z., & Xie, K. (2020). How do students prepare in the pre-class setting of a flipped undergraduate math course? A latent profile analysis of learning behavior and the impact of achievement goals. *The Internet and Higher Education*, *46*, 1–13. http://dx.doi.org/10.1016/j.iheduc.2020.100731

Suzuki, W., Nassaji, H., & Sato, K. (2019). The effects of feedback explicitness and type of target structure on accuracy in revision and new pieces of writing. *System*, *81*, 135–145. https://doi.org/10.1016/j.system.2018.12.017

Swain, M. (1985). Communicative competence: Some roles of comprehensible input and comprehensible output in its development. In S. Gass & C. Madden (Eds.), *Input in second language acquisition* (pp. 165–179). Newbury House.

Swan, M., & Walter, C. (2011). *Oxford English grammar course: Intermediate*. Oxford University Press.

Sylvén, L. K., & Ohlander, S. (2015). The CLISS project: Receptive vocabulary in CLIL versus non-CLIL groups. *Moderna Språk*, *108*(2), 80–114. https://ojs.ub.gu.se/index.php/modernasprak/article/view/2789

Talbert, R. (2015). Inverting the transition-to-proof classroom. *PRIMUS*, *25*(8), 614–626. http://dx.doi.org/10.1080/10511970.2015.1050616

Talbert, R. (2016). Three critical conversations started and sustained by flipped learning. In B. Honeycutt (Ed.), *Flipping the college classroom: Practical advice from faculty* (pp. 32–34). Magna.

Talbert, R. (2017). *Flipped learning: A guide for higher education faculty*. Stylus.

Talking Tree Creative. (2020, January 10). How long should videos be? The ideal length for marketing. *Talking Tree Creative*. https://www.talkingtreecreative.com/blog/video-marketing-2/the-impact-of-video-length-on-engagement/

Teigen, K. H. (1994). Yerkes-Dodson: A law for all seasons. *Theory & Psychology*, *4*(4), 525–547. http://dx.doi.org/10.1177/0959354394044004

Tench, P. (1996). *The intonation systems of English*. Cassell.

Teng, F. (2017). Flipping the classroom and tertiary level EFL students' academic performance and satisfaction. *The Journal of Asia TEFL*, *14*(4), 605–620. http://dx.doi.org/10.18823/asiatefl.2017.14.4.2.605

Teng, M. (2019). *Autonomy, agency, and identity in teaching and learning English as a foreign language*. Springer.

Thomas, M., & Yamazaki, K. (Eds.) (2021). *Project-based language learning and CALL: From virtual exchange to social justice*. Equinox Publishing Limited.

Thornbury, S. (2017). *The new A–Z of ELT: A dictionary of terms and concepts*. Macmillan.

Tsui, A. B., & Fullilove, J. (1998). Bottom-up or top-down processing as a discriminator of L2 listening performance. *Applied Linguistics*, *19*(4), 432–451. https://doi.org/10.1093/applin/19.4.432

Uchida, A. V. (2020). Integrating the four-dimensional education framework into an EFL course curriculum. *Relay Journal*, *3*(1), 25–47. https://doi.org/10.37237/relay/030103

Ulloa Salazar, G., & Díaz Larenas, C. (2018). Using an audiovisual materials-based teaching strategy to improve EFL young learners' understanding of instructions. *How*, *25*(2), 91–112. https://doi.org/10.19183/how.25.2.419

Ur, P. (2012). *A course in English language teaching* (2nd ed.). Cambridge University Press.

Ur, P. (2013, October). *A voyage of discovery*. Plenary presented at JALT2013: Learning is a Lifelong Voyage, Kobe.

Ushiro, Y., Hamada, A., Mori, Y., Hosoda, M., Tada, G., Kamimura, K., & Okawara, N. (2018). Goal-oriented L2 reading processes in maintaining the coherence of narrative comprehension. *JACET Journal*, *62*, 109–128. https://www.jstage.jst.go.jp/article/jacetjournal/62/0/62_109/_pdf

Ushiro, Y., Ogiso, T., Hosoda, M., Nahatame, S., Kamimura, K., Sasaki, Y., Kessoku, M., & Sekine, T. (2019). How EFL readers understand the protagonist, causal, and intentional links of narratives: An eye-tracking study. *ARELE: Annual Review of English Language Education in Japan*, *30*, 161–176. https://www.jstage.jst.go.jp/article/arele/30/0/30_161/_pdf

Vale, D., & Feunteun, A. (1995). *Teaching children English: A training course for teachers of English to children*. Cambridge University Press.

Van Lommel, S., Laenen, A., & d'Ydewalle, G. (2006). Foreign-grammar acquisition while watching subtitled television programmes. *British Journal of Educational Psychology*, *76*(2), 243–258. http://

dx.doi.org/10.1348/000709905X38946

Vandergrift, L. (2003). Orchestrating strategy use: Toward a model of the skilled second language listener. *Language Learning, 53*(3), 463–496. http://dx.doi.org/10.1111/1467-9922.00232

Vanderplank, R. (2016). "Effects of" and "effects with" captions: How exactly does watching a TV programme with same-language subtitles make a difference to language learners? *Language Teaching, 49*(2), 235–250. http://dx.doi.org/10.1017/S0261444813000207

Verity, D. (2005). Vygotskyan concepts for teacher education. In P. Ross, T. Newfields, Y. Ishida, M. Chapman, & M. Kawate-Mierzejewska (Eds.), *Proceedings of the May 14–15 2005 Pan-SIG conference lifelong learning* (pp. 1–9). http://jalt.org/pansig/2005/HTML/Verity.htm

Vitta, J. P., & Al-Hoorie, A. H. (2020). The flipped classroom in second language learning: A meta-analysis. *Language Teaching Research* Advance online publication. http://dx.doi.org/10.1177/1362168820981403

Vygotsky, L. S. (1962). Thought and word. In L. Vygotsky, E. Hanfmann, & G. Vakar (Eds.), *Thought and language* (pp. 119–153). MIT Press. https://doi.org/10.1037/11193-007

Vygotsky, L. S. (1987). Thinking and speech. In L. S. Vygotsky, R. W. Rieber (Series Eds.), & A. S. Carton (Vol. Ed.), *The collected works of L. S. Vygotsky. Vol. 1: Problems in general psychology* (N. Minick, Trans.). Plenum.

Vygotsky, L. S., & Cole, M. (1978). *Mind in society: Development of higher psychological processes*. Harvard University Press.

Wajnryb, R. (1990). *Grammar dictation*. Oxford University Press.

Waldrop, J. B., & Bowdon, M. A. (Eds.) (2016). *Best practices for flipping the college classroom*. Routledge.

Walker, A., & White, G. (2013). *Technology enhances language learning: Connecting theory and practice*. Oxford.

Waller, L., & Papi, M. (2017). Motivation and feedback: How implicit theories of intelligence predict L2 writers' motivation and feedback orientation. *Journal of Second Language Writing, 35*, 54–65. https://doi.org/10.1016/j.jslw.2017.01.004

Waluyo, B., & Bucol, J. L. (2021). The impact of gamified vocabulary learning using Quizlet on low-proficiency students. *Computer Assisted Language Learning Electronic Journal, 22*(1), 164–185. http://callej.org/journal/22-1/Waluyo-Bucol2021.pdf

Wang, J., An, N., & Wright, C. (2018). Enhancing beginner learners' oral proficiency in a flipped Chinese foreign language classroom. *Computer Assisted Language Learning, 31*(5-6), 490–521. http://dx.doi.org/10.1080/09588221.2017.1417872

Wang, L., & MacIntyre, P. D. (2021). Second language listening comprehension: The role of anxiety and enjoyment in listening metacognitive awareness. *Studies in Second Language Learning and Teaching, 11*(4), 491–515. https://doi.org/10.14746/ssllt.2021.11.4.2

Warschauer, M., & Grimes, D. (2007). Audience, authorship, and artifact: The emergent semiotics of Web 2.0. *Annual Review of Applied Linguistics, 27*, 1–23. https://doi.org/10.1017/s0267190508070013

Watkins, P. (2017). *Teaching and developing reading skills.* Cambridge.

Webb, M., & Doman, E. (2016). Does the flipped classroom lead to increased gains on learning outcomes in ESL/EFL contexts? *CATESOL Journal, 28*(1), 39–67. https://files.eric.ed.gov/fulltext/EJ1111606.pdf

Weir, C. J. (1990). *Communicative language testing.* New York.

Wells, J. C. (2006). *English intonation: An introduction.* Cambridge University Press.

Willis, J. (1996). *A framework for task-based learning.* Longman Limited.

Willis, J., & Varley, S. (1963). *The monster bed.* Andersen Press.

Winke, P., & Brunfaut, T. (2020). *The Routledge handbook of second language acquisition and language testing.* Routledge.

Wright, A. (2008). *Storytelling with children.* Oxford University Press.

Wu, W. C. V., Hsieh, J. S. C., & Yang, J. C. (2017). Creating an online learning community in a flipped classroom to enhance EFL learners' oral proficiency. *Journal of Educational Technology & Society, 20*(2), 142–157. https://www.j-ets.net/collection/published-issues/20_2

Yaikhong, K., & Usaha, S. (2012). A measure of EFL public speaking class anxiety: Scale development and preliminary validation and reliability. *English Language Teaching, 5*(12), 23–35. http://dx.doi.org/10.5539/elt.v5n12p23

Yang, W., (2014). Content and language integrated learning next in Asia: evidence of learners' achievement in CLIL education from a Taiwan tertiary degree programme. *International Journal of Bilingual Education and Bilingualism, 18*(4), 361–382. https://doi.org/10.1080/13670050.2014.904840

Yashima, T. (2009). International posture and the ideal L2 self in the Japanese EFL context. In E. Ushioda & Z. Dörnyei (Eds.), *Motivation, language identity and the L2 self* (pp. 144–163). Multilingual Matters.

Yashima, T., Zenuk-Nishide, L., & Shimizu, K. (2004). The influence of attitudes and affect on willingness to communicate and second language communication. *Language Learning, 50*(1), 119–152. https://doi.org/10.1111/j.1467-9922.2004.00250.x

Yavas, M. (1998). *Phonology development and disorders.* Singular Publishing Group.

Yerkes, R. M., & Dodson, J. D., (1908). The relation of strength of stimulus to rapidity of habit-formation. *Journal of Comparative Neurology and Psychology, 18*, 459–482. https://www.ida.liu.se/~769A09/Literature/Stress/Yerkes,%20Dodson_1908.pdf

Yeşilçınar, S. (2019). Using the flipped classroom to enhance adult EFL learners' speaking skills. *PASAA: Journal of Language Teaching and Learning in Thailand, 58*, 206–234. https://files.eric.ed.gov/fulltext/EJ1227386.pdf

Yu-Chih, S. (2008). The Toastmasters approach: An innovative way to teach public speaking to EFL learners in Taiwan. *RELC Journal, 39*(1), 113–130. http://dx.doi.org/10.1177/0033688208091143

Yuvita, Y., Sulistyaningsih, E., & Dhiya'Ulhaq, N. (2022). The effect of flipped classroom model towards students' reading comprehension. *Advances in Social Science, Education and Humanities Research, 629,* 165–172. https://www.atlantis-press.com/proceedings/icons-21

Zahra, R. O. (2014). The use of jigsaw technique in improving students' ability in writing a descriptive text. *Journal of English and Education, 2*(1), 64–75. https://ejournal.upi.edu/index.php/L-E/article/view/748/544

Zamel, V. (1976). Teaching composition in the ESL classroom: What we can learn from research in the teaching of English. *TESOL Quarterly,* 67–76. https://doi.org/10.2307/3585940

Zamel, V. (1982). Writing: The process of discovering meaning. *TESOL Quarterly, 16*(2), 195–209. https://doi.org/10.2307/3586792

Zamel, V. (1985). Responding to student writing. *TESOL Quarterly, 19*(1), 79–101. https://doi.org/10.2307/3586773

Zamel, V. (1992). Writing one's way into reading. *TESOL Quarterly, 26*(3), 463–485. https://doi.org/10.2307/3587174

Zhan, X. (2019). Research on the English reading teaching based on flipped classroom. *Advances in Social Science, Education and Humanities Research, 371,* 51–54. https://www.atlantis-press.com/proceedings/erss-19

Zhang, R., & Yuan, Z. M. (2020). Examining the effects of explicit pronunciation instruction on the development of L2 pronunciation. *Studies in Second Language Acquisition, 42*(4), 905–918. http://dx.doi.org/10.1017/S0272263120000121

Zhang, S. (2009). The role of input, interaction and output in the development of oral fluency. *English Language Teaching, 2*(4), 91–100. http://dx.doi.org/10.5539/elt.v2n4p91

Zheng, B., & Warschauer, M. (2017). Epilogue: Second language writing in the age of computer-mediated communication. *Journal of Second Language Writing, 36,* 61–67. https://doi.org/10.1016/j.jslw.2017.05.014

Zou, D. (2016). Comparing dictionary-induced vocabulary learning and inferencing in the context of reading. *Lexikos, 26,* 372–390. http://dx.doi.org/10.5788/26-1-1345

Index

affect, 40, 63, 64
affective filter, 25, 27, 147
agency, 14, 15, 16, 23, 37, 56, 61, 65, 130, 136, 147
anxiety, 14, 15, 21, 25, 27, 38, 39, 40, 44, 45, 46, 53, 55, 64, 85, 86, 87, 98, 99, 112, 113, 114, 136, 147
ASR. *See* automatic speech recognition
assessment, 10, 54, 86, 87, 95–99
audiolingual method, 37, 44, 147
automatic speech recognition, 40, 41, 42, 43, 45, 118
automaticity, 82, 147
blended learning, 4, 128, 134, 148
Bloom's taxonomy, 8, 9, 10, 11
bottom-up process, 58, 63, 66, 148
CBLT. *See* content-based learning
CLIL. *See* content and language integrated learning
closed captions, 15, 16, 18, 22–26, 64, 65, 89, 90
CMC. *See* computer-mediated communication
computer-mediated communication, 47, 48, 149
concept mapping, 38, 40, 44, 112–114, 149
confidence, 5, 14, 15, 16, 28, 33, 41, 43, 44, 45, 51, 52, 60, 78, 132
content and language integrated learning, 87, 88, 89, 90, 91, 93, 94, 115, 116, 117, 148
content-based language teaching, 87, 88, 89, 90, 148
deaf and hard-of-hearing students, 22, 23, 24, 25, 150

demotivation. *See* motivation
display questions, 94, 150
dynamics, 53, 106, 150
English for specific purposes, 85, 126, 128, 151
ESP. *See* English for specific purposes
extensive reading, 66, 67, 69, 70, 71
FLCAS. *See* foreign language classroom anxiety scale
focus on form, 66, 67, 69, 70
focus on forms, 66, 67, 69, 70
focused task. *See* task
foreign language classroom anxiety scale, 39
fossilization, 82, 151
gamification, 39, 40, 42, 44, 45, 72, 74, 78, 85, 86, 126, 127, 143, 144, 152
grammar instruction, 41, 48, 53, 66, 75–83, 86, 132, 135, 136
incidental learning, 64, 76, 80, 152
intensive reading, 66, 69
intonation phrases, 24, 25, 36, 152
intrinsic motivation. *See* motivation
learning management system, 10, 29, 46, 71, 72, 85, 93, 97, 116, 153
lingua franca, 36, 153
listening, 10, 24, 39, 57–65, 86, 91, 92, 109, 110, 111, 112, 113, 114, 127, 128
LMS. *See* learning management system
massive open online course, 89, 154
metacognitive strategies, 11, 63, 64, 107, 153
MOOC. *See* massive open online

193

course
mora-timed rhythm. *See* rhythm
motivation
  de-, 75, 81, 150
  intrinsic, 19, 73, 116, 134, 152
PPP. *See* present practice produce
present practice produce, 79, 82, 84, 155
project-based learning, 22, 135, 136, 137, 143, 153
qualitative research, 41, 51, 129, 131, 134, 155
quantitative research, 41, 51, 129, 134, 155
reading, 43, 62, 65–74, 88, 95,
reflexive diary, 129, 156
rhythm
  mora-timed, 36, 154
  stress-timed, 36, 129, 157
  syllable-timed, 36, 129, 158
scaffolding, 6, 7, 8, 19, 90, 94, 95, 156
speaking, 10, 21, 24, 25, 26, 34–47, 58, 75, 78, 82, 85, 86, 91, 93, 96, 109, 110, 111, 112, 113, 114, 119, 125, 128, 129
stress-timed rhythm. *See* rhythm
syllable-timed rhythm. *See* rhythm
task
  focused, 76, 79, 82, 83, 84, 143, 151
  unfocused, 76, 82, 83, 86, 143, 159
task-based language teaching, 76, 80, 82, 84, 85, 86, 87, 125, 126, 128, 158
TBLT. *See* task-based language teaching
TED Talks, 38, 39, 113, 158
top-down process, 58, 63, 64, 66, 158
unfocused task. *See* task
vocabulary acquisition, 42, 61, 66, 67, 69, 71, 72, 73, 74, 85, 86, 89, 90, 92, 93, 124, 126, 127
Web 2.0, 4, 12, 13, 159
world Englishes, 36, 159
writing, 21, 23, 33, 38, 46–57, 58, 67, 69, 70, 74, 75, 78, 81, 82, 83, 89, 90, 96, 97, 111, 120, 121, 130, 131, 132, 136, 142, 143, 144
young learners, 90–95, 115–117
ZPD. *See* Zone of Proximal Development
Zone of Proximal Development, 7, 8, 159, 160

www.ingramcontent.com/pod-product-compliance
Lightning Source LLC
Chambersburg PA
CBHW072051110526
44590CB00018B/3123